Williston:

Winter
The Man Camp

Bill Harvey

Printed in the United States of America

Isbn 979-8-9888182-3-6

Library of Congress Number 2017918959

Available at BillHarveyBooks.com

Sunset Boulevard Press
775 Post St #210
San Francisco, CA 95409

Cover Photography with the kind permission of...

Travis Liviei
Prairie Wildlife Research
tliveri@prairiewildlife.org

Oil is said to be fungible. 'Fungible' is a rather ridiculous word meaning –more or less- that something is the same here as it is over there. The Arab's oil burns just as hot as the oil coming out of Canada –where America gets much of its oil.

Of course this is something as an oversimplification. Oil from the north shore of Alaska needs to be heated and pumped about two thousand miles through a big pipe to a port on the southern coast of Alaska, and then it takes another even longer trip in a tanker to get to a refinery in California. Compare this to oil from a Texas field that is piped to a refinery in Louisiana and sold in a gas station in Georgia. By the same token, sweet crude is easy to get out of the ground and easy to transport, while oil from the tar sands of Calgary is a bitch to get out of the ground and takes all manner of heating and pre-refining to get it to the point it can then be pumped to another finer refinery for more refining. But having been refined into any of the dozens of petroleum products that make our world go around, these products are essentially the same.

The 'fungible-ness' of oil is now clear. There is no way to tell where the particular squirt of *refined* oil you put into your car's gas tank came from. The guy who sells it to you does not know or much care. Nor –in all likelihood- does the guy who sold it to him. Somewhere up the line, someone somewhere knows if the oil came from Saudi Arabia or North Dakota, but he or she has only a remote idea of where it will end up. None of these people anywhere along the line have more than a microscopic amount of control of the price. Well, in all fairness, the House of Saud, (the guys w/ Oxford degrees who wear table-cloths on their heads), have more than a microscopic influence, but Standard, Exxon, British Petroleum and all the big evil oil companies pretty much have to dance to the tune set by the faceless market for a fungible commodity.

Money is also fungible, but it's much easier to get money from one place to another than it is to move oil around. Money pipelines are so very slippery that money is said to be 'liquid', and essential for this business of getting oil from underground to your gas tank. No small amount of money must also be spent in filing out various forms for the government. All this extracting, heating, pumping, transporting, refining, report filing, and ultimately selling oil in one form or another takes money –rather a lot of money. Money for the on-going costs of paying various guys in hardhats, truck drivers, ship captains, as well as people in offices who keep track of paychecks and the oil itself. Add to these day-to-day costs of fiddling about with oil, the initial cost –the capitol cost of drilling rigs, all manner of pipes & pumps, trucks & tankers and we see what makes capitalism…well… capitalism. It's also expensive as all hell and this brings up one very important difference between fungible oil and liquid money. Whereas oil is pretty much owned and controlled by only one person at a time –and it may be many people from the farmer who owns the land and mineral rights, all the way up to he point you own it in your gas tank- money is so slippery that it is often controlled by one guy who acts on behalf of the guy who actually owns the money.

Chapter 1

For a wonder, she actually got to class a little early despite working to 2:AM the night before. Despite being so tired she forgot to plug in the engine-block heater, her car started. Not willingly, but it started. Finally, the oil truck drivers, the water truck drivers, sand-truck, pipe-truck, frack-tuck, and the utterly ubiquitous pick-up truck drivers were evidently largely at breakfast so she got thru the intersection of Highways 2 & 85 after only two red lights.

Janet spent the few minutes before 9:AM largely ignoring the sleepy dull faces of the other GED students and considered the only new thing in the room; an older gentleman in a tie for heaven's sake and tweed jacket. So-help-me-God she thought to herself, his jacket even has leather patches on the elbows. Something different from the parkas over hoodies over baseball caps. Made it hard to determine even the gender of the average Williston citizen till you got close –at least in winter.

Might this be the new math teacher they and been promising? He was sitting casually at a table toward the front of the classroom shuffling thru a short stack of papers. Too old to be interesting to her in a personal manner and he didn't look prosperous enough to be valuable in any kind of monetary way. The black bag by his side caught her eye. She had one just like it. She got it when she joined a book cub a year or so back. One of those deals where you get three books free if you agree to by three more. She ordered <u>What Everyone Has to Know About American History</u>, <u>Casual Poetry</u>, and <u>Math Made Easy</u>. What a joke. She made an effort with the math book anyway. Got out a calculator, paper & pencil, and sat down at the kitchen table in the crappy little apartment she shared with her current looser boyfriend. She started to work thru some problems at the beginning of the book. Then he came home and had himself a good laugh at her attempt to learn something. He was unquestionably drunk, probably stoned, and possibly on crack. No way she was calling him on this last one. He had promised to stay off the hard stuff but when she had accused Jack (the Jerk), of breaking his promise, all she had gotten out of it was a black eye and she missed two nights of work. The tips were poor the third night when she had finally went back to work.

The math book went back into the black bag with the poetry book –which she had never even bothered to open, and she threw it all into the back of the closet. The history book was at least was useful on one occasion. She watched Mel Gibson in ***The Patriot*** when babysitting her nieces one evening. Then she looked up the *French and Indian War* and the *American Revolution*. Learned some good stuff and watched the movie again by herself in the middle of the night. She enjoyed it even more with a little historic perspective.

But as to self improvement and getting a diploma and all, she was honest enough with herself to realize she wasn't going to do it her own. One of the girls she worked with had told her about the adult education thing at the local junior college at the east end of town. One Monday before work she drove out to see where it was and how far out of her way it might have been. It was a warm day –for November- and so she took a walk thru the campus. It didn't take long. She had heard of ivy towers, or was it ivory towers? She didn't see any towers. What she did see was a few squat buildings that looked more industrial than academic. Turned out these buildings were where they taught things like diesel mechanics, welding, and petroleum operations. There were a couple of other buildings that looked a little bit like the buildings of the University of Topeka back home, but they still didn't fit her notion of what a college should look like.

There were a few students walking around and she asked a couple of guys playing with a Frisbee if they knew where Career & Technology Center was. Neither of them seemed to know, but as they started walking toward her, her radar went off. Nothing threatening, they were just a couple of nice college boys from North Dakota being friendly and helpful. She wasn't in the mood for a chat, so she turned around and went back the way she came. The students looked to her to be only eighteen years old or so -a little younger than the oil-field workers she was used to. It made her feel her that her twenty seven years made her old -or too old to be a student. For a moment she wondered if maybe the students might have seen her at work. She realized she had been rude, but how in heaven's name was she going to pull off being a student –let alone a GED student- at a place where there were real students studying real college stuff and they were all younger and smarter than she was? She got back in her car and drove downtown to work.

It was another week before she was able to convince herself to return. She figured out where the building was, and found she was able to park close to the front door, walk into the building, down a hall with classrooms on either side, and into the GED classroom. The dumpy middle age woman who greeted her turned out to be a sweetheart. Answered a few questions and got her all signed up. The woman seemed to know how awkward Janet felt and stressed that everyone was here for the same thing and everyone was pulling for her. How did she put it? "Most of our students have been out in the real world for a while. They have careers and are here just to fill a hole in their lives."

By the end of the first week of morning class, she was comfortable with the routine and at the end of the first month had passed her first GED exam. In January she passed the second one. Then she hit a serious snag with the math test. It just wasn't happening. She enjoyed class a little, but not as much as an admittedly silly fantasy she kept all to herself: walking to class she began to imagined herself a real college girl. She had left black fake-leather book-bag that she got with the books from the book-of-the-month-club back in Topeka with Jack-the-Jerk. (Let him sort out what to do when "This Month's Special Selection Arrives in Your Mailbox.") She bought a backpack like she saw the other students carrying –the students that went to classes in Stevens Hall for real college classes. She even got a pair of Clark-Kent-glasses. Contacts and make-up for work, but scruffy clothes, hair in a ponytail, face scrubbed virginally clean, all made her a college girl. But it really was a shame she didn't have the black book bag anymore. It would have been even more fun to have one like a teacher carried.

At the crack of nine the old guy set aside the papers he was reading and stood up with a quiet groan. "Good morning ladies and gentleman, my name is Mike Williams and we are all adults here, so just call me Mike. I will be helping out mornings with the GED classes here at Williston State -mostly helping you with your math. My boss is your regular teacher, Linda, who says she's happy to admit that math is not here strongest area. I have to tell you that I was a terrible math student when I was in high school and so have a very good idea what you are going thru. The good news is that I also remember all the little tricks I used to get myself thru it. As a consequence, I am the best damn math teacher you have ever had and you WILL pass the GED math test." He paused and smeared a great silly grin across his face.

"The problem someone in my place faces is a wide disparity of skill levels in a given class, so I have been looking over the test scores you have gotten on the various practice tests you have been given. Each of you have some strengths and some weaknesses –no big surprise. I gather some of you have already passed the math portion of the test?" A couple off hands went up. He continued, "Congrats. And so I'm guessing you are here to work on your writing?" The was a murmur of agreement, and he continued, "In my experience, it's either math or writing that give people difficulty. Seems that those who do well in math struggle with writing. And vice-versa. But we have to start somewhere, and it's going to be math this morning. I propose to start with functions. Anyone think they have a handle on functions?"

Janice didn't even bother to look around to see if anyone had raised their hands, and the teacher nodded before he went on. "Thought not. But no worries, this subject kind of stands alone –it doesn't need a lot of other background stuff.   Let's get started. How many fingers are there?"
Without thinking, Janet heard the words "That's dumb. It depends on how many hands there are." come out of her own mouth and a half-second later remembered how she was always getting herself so completely and regretfully cross-threaded with the high-school teachers back in Topeka. It was also part of the reason she hadn't graduated from high school about eight or ten years back. Well, part of the reason anyway.

But instead of getting snotty like her high-school teachers did, Mike widened his eyes in mock surprise and smiled. "What did you say?"

"Doesn't it kind of depend on how many hands there are? Or people. Or something?" She hated it when she heard the hesitation in her own voice.

He turned to the white board and wrote in big letters "IT DEPENDS ON…" and then wrote "IT'S A FUNCTION OF…" directly below. He turned back to the class and continued. " 'It depends on…' and 'It's a function of…' mean almost exactly the same thing. But math -being math- has to add some little rules and restrictions, but don't worry about that for the moment. Let's see if we can draw a graph of the number of fingers given some number of hands."

The next three hours went quickly for Janet. She understood everything the teacher said about lines and graphs and slopes and even those effing imponderable negative numbers. They devised little number rules that allowed them to predict where one thing on the graph would come out when another thing -the 'depends on thing'- went in. She was pleased to learn that she was actually doing algebra and she actually understood it. Perhaps she was moving toward her goal. Taking her clothes off at work tonight was going to be… a little less sucky.

Chapter 2

At noon Mike Williams wound up the class and the students filed out with varying degrees of animation, guarded enthusiasm, and sullenness. One of the things he liked about teaching GED to adults was his student's realization that there was no point in sucking up to the teacher. Some of his students tried this during his brief stint as a high school teacher. In this classroom, the students were all there to get thru some tests and the teacher had no part in grading those tests.

All in all, they didn't look much different from the students he had in the Bay Area. He would have to wait to see about the night-school students. In California anyway, such students usually had jobs and were a little more motivated to get it done. The daytime ones didn't have jobs –or day jobs anyway. They were often there because someone was making them show up –parents, employers, spouses, or sometimes the courts & probation officers. But they were adults -or most of them were very like adults. The tall pretty girl in front –for example- was a delight. A little lacking in tact –mouthy even, but she certainly had brightened his morning.

He was contemplating looking over the placement pop-quiz he had given the class, when his new boss came bustling out of her cubical at the end of the long room. She was the very picture of a middle age lit-major who became a reading teacher who left an elementary school somewhere and found herself in charge of a GED program. Nice, enthusiastic, concerned, skillfully in bureaucratic matters, but largely ineffective outside academia. "Well, how was your first day? About what you expected?"

"Pretty much par for the course. I have some concerns about one woman who might be…. at least… well, a little mentally disabled. Or what they call 'learning challenged' in California. Perhaps we use different words here in North Dakota?"

Linda nodded. "We just say 'challenged' But I know who you mean. She has been coming here for more then a year. " She shrugged. "Sally tries and doesn't bother anyone. In fact, sometimes the other students work with her. Seems a nice thing for both."

Mike nodded in kind. "They look pretty much like my students did in California. I'm anxious to see what the night class looks like. We still on track to start one up in a couple of weeks?"

"No –hit a snag in that direction. Budget things from the higher-ups."

He felt like he had been slugged in the gut. "Linda, I understand about budget issues and bureaucracies, but you need to understand that what I earn teaching GED math for 3 hours every morning doesn't even pay my rent at the man camp."

"Couldn't you find some work in the afternoon to sort of tide you over till we sort it out?"

"Well, yes, but from what I understand about the situation here in Williston, are you sure you want me to go out and see what other work there is out there? Anything pays better than teaching, especially in the oil patch. If I could hack the cold, I could be a

10

highway flag-man and make more money. Are you sure there is a demand for two or three sections of GED classes? From what I saw today the certainly is the need."

"Oh dear me yes, there is plenty of demand –particularly for the night class. Lots of people from the in oilfield never finished high school and made –*are making*- very good money- and want to move up in their jobs, but they can't without a diploma."

"Ok for the demand, what about the funding?"

"That's the problem." she sighed.

He sighed. "See you tomorrow." He threw the pop-quizzes in his bag and walked out.

It took him a minute to find his little Japanese pick-up. It was hidden forlornly between a big mud covered 4x4 and an even bigger crew-cab with 'Slumberton' on the side. It started, but not enthusiastically. He murmured a "Thank you Jesus." to himself. Then he wondered if this was blasphemy –for about the hundredth time. And what if it was? It was not like God paid him the least little bit of attention –other than to fuck with him. This was just the latest in a long line of cosmic "Here it it. Ha Ha. No it isn't." God, karma, Buddah, or someone / something seemed to delight in leading him around like a stupid little puppy running back and forth in an unending game of keep-away with a job as the red ball.

He caught himself. He had been down this road way too often. There was a bottle of Prozac somewhere in his luggage –hopefully. Clearly time to dig it out and start taking the little green & white pills again.

He had gotten just a taste of truck traffic when he drove into town late the night before. It was worse during the day. Trucks going every which-a-way, but even so, it was a small town and took only about 10 minutes to get thru a few stop-lights and out of town and then another 10 minutes at more or less freeway speeds to get back to the man-camp north of town. All and all, a much nicer commute than he was used to in Silicone Valley.

His assigned trailer –forth one down in the second row back from the lumpy dirt road and even lumpier parking lot- was empty when he got back and let himself in. The night before, the little Kiwi chap who checked him told him there were three other people living in his trailer, but it was almost 11:PM the night before when he stumbled up the five wooden steps in the dark, muttered to himself as he fiddled with the keys, and finally got in. His room was the one just to the left of the kitchen and it mercifully was unlocked. He was too tired from the drive to do more then glance down the hall to the living room, check out his bathroom, and fall into bed.

That morning he had hurried off to work, but this afternoon he was able to look around a little more carefully. His first impression was that it was inspired by the same designer who laid out German POW camp from the movie 'Stallag13', only with neither kaki laundry flapping in the wind, nor barbwire fences. It was four rows of double wide trailers –each row of 12 trailers down a gentle slope. He walked to the next row between the third and forth row and found it to be absolutely identical to the frozen alley between his own row –the second row- and third row of trailers. At the uphill end was the trailer with the sign where he checked in and a butler building across a dirt parking lot and a ways up the road. There were surprisingly few cars parked, indeed, there were no cars parked anywhere. The few vehicles parked around the perimeter were all pickups and a couple of bigger trucks with tool boxes and mysterious machinery on the back. The horizon was way the hell out there under a whole lot of cold blue sky. Not a tree in sight –just pale beige grass: sparse, brittle, and no more then knee high.

It took about three minutes to suss out the outside and about the same amount of time to check out the interior of the trailers. There was a living room of sorts in the middle of the trailer with a couch, a small dining-room table directly under a big-screen TV mounted on the wall. There was a pretty standard kitchen but with two refrigerators. He noticed the water running in the kitchen sink and was about to turn it off when he noticed a Xeroxed sign stuck in the window above the sink. "Please leave the water running at a trickle or it will freeze." There was a Mr. Coffee on the counter and dishes in the cupboard. One cupboard held what he took to be someone's stash of dry cereal, crackers, and energy / granola bars. The fridges held some small amount of condiments, left-overs, a couple of fast-food bags and a pizza box. Behind the kitchen –dining area and facing the hallway were a stacked washer-dryer on one side of the kitchen and the trailer's furnace on the other side. There were four bedroom doors opening into the hall: two at each end. No doubt all the bedrooms were pretty much identical. A double bed with a small nightstand and lamp, desk, another big screen TV above the desk, and smallish closet with a few particle board cubes on the floor to serve as a dresser. Finally, there was a private bathroom with all the necessaries. Small, but not bad -all things considered. Expensive as all shit, but not bad.

He got a glass, found one of the freezers with some few ice cubes, and schlepped to his bedroom to pour himself a glass of cheap port, with just splash of bourbon. He loosened his tie and stretched out on the couch to continue looking over his student's practice test scores. He lost interest quickly enough. No surprises from his first glance that morning. His students were all over the map. Some barely knew the multiplication tables and one –maybe two- were ready to start on algebra and had a reasonable chance at passing the math portion of the GED exam. He made a mental note to ask his boss if she was OK with having the students work together. He found that with some care –and attentive eyes-in-the-back-of-his-head teaching, it worked pretty well for both sides.

He stuffed the tests back in his black bag and poured another drink. He puzzled out how long he might be able to survive in the Williston oil patch teaching 3 hours a day. It was a simple answer. Not very damn long at all. Time to hit Craigslist.com and do the job-search. Everything he heard about Williston should make it much easier to find work here than in was in recession California. Once again, fate had other plans. The internet was down. He called the man-camp office to ask when it might be up again. A woman answered the phone and told him 'Soon'. As to how soon, the longer answer was, 'Any day now.'

If it wasn't one damn thing, it was six fucking other things. What had he done to piss God off so thoroughly. If he could get a buzz going, -and he damn sure could get a buzz going- he could avoid going back into another 'God-hates-me' spiral like that afternoon.

But first he got up and went back into his room to unpack some more of the banana boxes he used a luggage and was relieved to find he had indeed remembered to pack the bottle of little green and white Prozac pills.

Chapter 3

OPEC fell apart in May of 1980 and crude oil at the well-head dropped from roughly $75 a barrel in 1979 to $24 in '84. It would not turn up in any kind of definitive manner till 1998 after it had briefly bottomed out around $15.

Up until about 1982, Denver touted itself as the New Energy Capitol and was enjoying a hot real estate market compliments of both easy Savings & Loan money and lots of well paid geologists, land men, finance people and of course realtors, developers, & builders. Denver real estate followed oil prices up as well as down, but they dropped by only about half as much as oil.   Still and all, there were a lot of people whose homes were worth a lot less then the mortgages and as the S & L crisis unfolded, more mortgages went into default & were foreclosed upon, and houses put on the market. This caused prices to drop even further which led to more people walking away from their commitments which caused yet lower prices. There was a morbid joke that went around Colorado at the time: "QUESTION: AIDS, gonorrhea, herpes, and condominium. Which does not belong?" ANSWER: Gonorrhea –it's the only one you can get rid of."

Kevin Amundsen was going to school at the University of Denver on a hockey scholarship and lived with four other guys in a small house on the wrong side of University Boulevard. Oil & gas prices –no less real estate prices hardly mattered to him, but he was certainly aware of them.

He graduated with a degree in accounting in '87 to a job market where geologists and engineers with master's degrees were glad to get jobs as waiters. He had no more eligibility to play hockey, so he went home to Williston to have a heart to heart with his dad. Kevin's grades were good enough for law school, and his Dad figured he had just enough money saved up from oil royalties from his small winter-wheat farm to pay for about half the load. The other half would come from his childhood sweetheart if *and once* they were married. Both Dad and Jane insisted that Kevin agree to return to Williston and practice law and start a family in his hometown.

It was not quite a shotgun wedding –Jane was not pregnant- but it was a hurried affair. There was a simple ceremony in the town's biggest Lutheran church where her dad was an elder. The reception was in the church basement. Her mom had died when Jane was 12 –well before she and Kevin got to know each other- and so no one had a big urge to plan –or pay for- a big wedding, not Jane or Kevin, and certainly not her dad. Jane's dad had never quite warmed up to Kevin, despite Kevin and his daughter having dated pretty much thru high-school, and a suitably chaste dating it was –at least thru high school.

Jane had gone off to Bismarck to study literature while Kevin went to Denver to study accounting and finance. They agreed to date other people and both did, but Jane evidently dated more than Kevin. Jane had a boyfriend by the end of the first semester of her freshman year, and that summer tactfully let Kevin know that even though her college fling was over, she had changed. He thought about being jealous, but mostly felt he was behind Jane in matters of sex. It was more embarrassing than anything else. It took him till early in his sophomore year to have his own first sexual experience with a grad student who assisted in his macro-economics class. She was smart, and kind, but not very attractive and suffered in comparison to Jane. Back in Williston during the summer between their sophomore and junior years they fell into a comfortable –if chaste- companionship. His parents liked Jane, but it seemed to Kevin that her dad looked at him like he was some slick fraternity guy in Bismarck rather than the home-town boy. Jane's dad's attitude, Kevin's sexual tension, and finally Jane's enthusiasm about getting back to Bismarck and all that it had to offer, all combined to make both of them relieved to leave Williston and go back to school late in August.

Kevin never quite got a grip on what changed by the next summer –the one before their senior year –it might have been Jane having spent the spring semester in Rome- she never said- but that summer they fucked like rabbits. He kept a foam mattress, blankets and pillows in the trunk of his old Buick and they would drive down a two-rut dirt road to a cottonwood grove in the middle of nowhere and go at it under the stars. Years later, he could vividly bring to his mind's eye the pale glow of Jane's un-suntanned breasts by the light of the Milky Way. They both began to consider marriage, but their discussions were carefully academic, but even so, by the end of that summer, marriage after they graduated had somehow become a for-gone conclusion. Kevin proposed under a full moon in their cottonwood grove the first week after they both got back to Williston after the cap and gown thing. And he did it down on one knee and before they pulled out the mattress and blankets.

Their honeymoon was spent on the way back to Denver in a quaint old hotel in Deadwood South Dakota about a block from the town's old red-light district. Not all that old. Kevin was tickled to learn that the feds had swept in a closed it down only a few years previously -against the wishes of both the girls and many of the townspeople for that matter. They moved into the same house he had lived as an undergrad, but husband and wife now had the bedroom with a bath. Jane got a job as a teacher's assistant at South High across the freeway from DU and they settled into what he would remember fondly as a happy time -aside from the rigors of law school. Jane kept him sane in the matters of competition among the other law-students. She also reminded him that while they had degrees in political-science or history, he had a far more useful undergraduate degree in accounting –he was a double threat. He finished in the top half of his class, and got a couple of plaques from the accountancy side of the things, particularly the people from various associations who handed out certificates and plaques as an entrée to recruiting.

Kevin aced his natural resources law class and got a plaque from the Earth Justice League. They also wanted him to come work for them in D.C. They wouldn't pay him, but he was entitled to 50% of any funds he was able to raise. That was to be the extent of his job. He was conservative both by nature and as a child of a North Dakota farmer, but when he put on his accounting hat and looked at the League's annual report, he quickly realized the cause had far more to do with raising money to pay administrators than it had to do with actually cleaning up the environment. He got curious and sat down with the financial reports of a half dozen other worthy causes and found pretty much the same pattern. Volunteers doing some real work, middle people raising money -as volunteers or on a perverse commission system, and the guys at the top pulling down huge salaries. His disgust pushed him firmly in the direction of the big oil and mining. They were honest about things anyway.

Their first child was born almost to the day nine months after he passed the North Dakota bar and started his practice as a single lawyer. His dad was his first client regarding a matter of a minor oil spill from the single tank that received oil from the single well that the family's single cow –raised simply to fill the family freezer come autumn- had scratched herself against some part of the plumbing to the tank and started a leak. It was off to the races. On his dad's behalf, Kevin claimed damage to his pasture. The oil company claimed his cow had cost them a little over 100 barrels of crude. The counter claim was that the valve was not secured, fenced, or otherwise correctly protected from cattle and it was the oil companies fault. The counter-counter claim was that it wasn't a valve, but rather a pipe that was damaged by a marauding cow and therefore the liability lie with the cow's owner. Finally, some part of the spill made its way to a dry creek bed that led to a larger not quite so dry creek that led –eventually- to the Missouri River and the EPA got involved. It all came to called the *Itchy Cow Case*, got a fair amount of local press, and earned Kevin some valuable –if whimsical- exposure. It settled with more of a whimper than a bang and everyone lost. Except the lawyers. And except that he decided the courtroom was not his milieu and he began studying for the CPA exam.

Over the next few years, he built a clientele of farmers like his dad who had farm income as well as more and more oil royalty income as OPEC drove up the price of crude oil back up. Most of them had more oil income than his dad, but all of them were some pretty smart old boys and very cagey about hedging wheat futures and other commodities like the diesel fuel needed during harvest time, but they were not comfortable negotiating with oil companies. Kevin did a brief study of commodity hedging and concluded it made perfect sense if a business bought a lot of flour to make bread sold under contract to grocery store chains, or plywood to build houses per huge loan contracts, but otherwise, it was simply speculating -a gamble -knowledgeable gambling or otherwise.

Quite early on he learned that 'oil companies' were not monolithic. They were lease holders –farmers usually –both living farmers and their estates, there were operators –both those with actual money involved and those who were 'carried.' There were drillers who were hired by the operators / lease holders. Finally, there were service companies who were hired by the drillers to do various specialized operations. And of course, the State of North Dakota, the federal Departments of the Interior and Energy, and last but not least, the EPA. All of the players had their own often conflicting agendas: making money was the most obvious and the most compelling agenda. It was also the easiest to navigate, but the government players –the regulators- had conflicting goals and no burning desire to resolve or compromise. In fact, their budgets were extended the more they stalled. OSHA said one thing must always be done and the EPA said that that was the very thing must never be done. The state of North Dakota didn't much care one way or the other as long as it was documented and taxes got paid. More then one witty observer posited that there was no compelling need to actually extract oil from the ground, the world's energy needs would be served just as well by burning all the paper the industry generated. Kevin became a trusted advocate for these good old boys and worked to keep them *and himself* out of the courtroom. Some small number of them also needed help keeping their money from the tax man and it was here that he did some of his best work: nearly all of it at his desk.

By 2000 the price of oil had climbed –or recovered- to $35.00 a barrel, and Kevin found himself smack in the middle of it all. He was an in-demand lawyer / accountant with rich clients who were getting richer all the time with his help. He was a respected local businessman in a place that was increasingly important and –while still a small town- it was becoming an internationally important town. It was also a boom town that was filling with people and money far beyond the towns infrastructure of roads, police, beds, gas stations, doctors & hospitals, stores, schools, water and sewer systems. In short, all the things that make life livable but are only ever considered when they break-down

It all started when some good old boys down in Texas figured out how to fracture stubborn 'tight' formations and free up oil. At about the same time, directional drilling became practical and the men and machinery that could steer a drill bit up, down, and sideways two miles underground came to be available: not cheap by any means, but available. Oil prices continued a long and lofty price climb. Deals became more and more complicated and lawyers were needed to sort them out. Finally and most importantly, Kevin's clients were increasingly wealthy.

He knew he didn't know enough about geology to do figure out where to drill for oil, but he was good at advocating on behalf of his farmer clients who would then lease mineral rights to the people who *did* know where to drill for oil and had very deep pockets. Besides which, it was increasingly clear the Bakken shale formation went pretty much everywhere and directional drilling could reach out a mile or more in all directions from the original hole anyway.

He was also equally sure he didn't know enough about the stock market to play in that particular arena. After the meltdown of '08, he was proven very right –or lucky if he were to be honest with himself. So as he was casting around for a means of diversifying his clients, (and making himself a little money), he naturally considered real estate. But the accountant in him simply could not fathom the prices houses were fetching –not in North Dakota and certainly not in the hot real estate markets like Las Vegas, and coastal California. Commercial property on the other hand, where there was no federal Gennies, Freddys, or Fannies to muddy the water, the values *and returns* made good sense. So he bought himself a Butler Building Dealership, put together partnerships to buy land along Highway 85 west of town and talked to his Good-Old-Boy client Vern who had the earth moving company and who could do the site-prep. He found himself a couple of other contractor and tenant-improvement guys who could just barely find the time to slap up the buildings and who were willing to work for participation rather than

actual money. They had more than enough income.   What they needed and what Kevin
was doing for the farmers: finding then ways to keep a little of it out of the hands of the
IRS -in an almost assuredly legal manner. Butler buildings were depreciable / deductible
assets and once up and occupied, were easy to go to a banker, borrow money, and do it
some more. And the interest that was also deductible.

Over a period of four years, he leased one, then another, and finally two more
adjacent buildings to a big oil companies and another three to oil-field service companies
–all of whose stock traded on one exchange or another and all of whose rent checks came
in as regular as clock-work. Boring, conservative, predictable, but with a very adequate
return and admirable tax advantages.

2008 was an altogether pivotal year. The collapse of the housing market and
mortgage implosion wiped out billions of dollars of paper wealth. The rest of the county
was in the shitter, but not Williston, and not his clients, or not as far as the investments
they made in his Butler building limited partnerships anyway. 2008 was also the year he
began to consider something with a little more bang for investment buck than the safe
long-term leases of buildings to oil companies. The notion of doing a man-`camp crossed
his radar. It was also the year he began to consider himself an important financial light
and as such, the notion of a little extra-marital whoopee crossed his mind. Both notions
were fulfilled, but neither worked out as he expected.

Chapter 4

Janet got a few hours of sleep after class before she went into work for the
afternoon shift starting at 4:PM. The short hall from the back door of WILLY'S PLACE
to the dancer's dressing room always smelled of Pine-Sol. She wasn't sure if the smell of
the cleaner was better or worse than what ever it was that it was supposed to be cleaning
up –what ever that might have been –best not to think of it at all. The dressing room
was comparatively empty and she was able to get a space by the big mirror. Why the
putz who ran Willy's couldn't spring for another mirror or two was a mystery. The room
had cheap Formica tables along three walls, and on the forth wall, there were metal
lockers where the girls could lock up their purses etc., and short length of closet rod.
There were some skimpy costumes that once belonged to girls who had moved on, but
mostly the rod held bulky winter coats. Sad flickering worn-out greenish fluorescent
lights that made everyone look a little sick without make-up and made them look
demonic with their faces painted for the customers. Some of the girls schlepped in little
toy make-up mirrors that let her select a colored plastic sleeve to put over the little bulbs
to make the light more natural: office, daylight, or evening. Janet had made the mistake
of putting on her make-up at home only once. She had to stop for gas on the way to work
and was propositioned by the guy filling his monster pick-up next to her car and she had
a hard time getting rid of the ass. When she went in to get a cup of coffee, it started all
over again –this time with the ass behind the counter. It was then that she realized why
otherwise pretty women seemed so absolutely drab & plain when out and about in
Williston –they hid their lights under a bushel for good reason. It was a very lopsided
demographic of single men for single woman. She had heard somewhere that it was

about 20 to 1.

She was about done with her make-up when Tonia bounced in. Tonia always seemed to bounce –even when she was sitting still and most particularly when she was nude. Tonia was a little Asian –many generations in America but her ancestry evidently included some Viking. She had great boobs, almost as good as Janet's, but on her tiny frame, they took on a bouncy life of their own. Sometimes Janet envied Tonia's cute cuddliness, -but only sometimes.

"Hi Tonia, how were the boys for the lunch crowd?"

Tonia plopped down in the chair by Janet and considered her friend's make-up. "A little thin, but tips are good. For the afternoon anyway. You need more eye-shadow."

"No I don't."

"Thanks for filling in for me. If I don't get back on the evening shift soon, I may have to go next door to the Bottoms-Up Club. Ick ! Maybe you could talk to Mel for me? You seem to be his favorite. You know… about better hours."

"I'll try, but the guy creeps me out.

"How did you get to be so… so popular with Mel? You didn't have to…." Tonia finished her sentence by rhythmically moving her small fist up and down over her lap.

"Oh God no. Mel… he…"

As Janet tried to figure out how to answer her friend's question when Tonia interrupted. "This afternoon I have a date with a… friend. And another one later on up in that man camp."

"Friend or a FRIEND?"

"A rich FRIEND, thank you very much. That old wheat farmer widow –or is it widower?, I always get those messed up, anyway, the one with oil money. He is talking about taking me on a vacation with him. What's better, Paris or Rome?"

"Tonia, you aren't going to get the old guy to take you to Europe no matter how much you fuck him. Bismark or maybe Denver for the stock-show. That's about all."

"He's sweet and gives me gifts. He gave me a check, like from Exxon –a royalty check or something. It was for about nine hundred dollars and he signed it right over to me and the bank accepted it, but it was kind of a hassle. That little bitch I told you about where I bank?" Janet nodded.

"Check it out. She got all up in my face about the endorsement or some fucking thing and so I made her go get the manager and I made like I had oil money coming in all the time and if they didn't want my money, I'd go find a bank that would, and the guy got all like 'So very sorry' and 'We value all our customers' and shit. The little bitch makes minimum wage and lives with her parents and wears old-lady clothes and she thinks she's hot 'cause she works in a bank? It was really kind'a fun."

"But don't you make more money here than driving out to the country to see him?"

"It's like I make more money per hour out there, but I work more hours here. Or I would if I can get back on Mel's good side and work a better shift. Kind'a comes out even but with less wear and tear on the va-jay-jay here. The old farmer is sweet. We

don't fuck. Mostly I sit in his lap naked and we talk. Or we pray. Naked praying.
Fucking weird, but he always has a neat little pile of bills all fanned out on the counter
when I get there and sometimes he gives me things like that check."

Most of the money the women made was paper money. Tips from stripping and
private lap-dances, and –for Tonia- wads of twenties and fifties from turning tricks.
Willy's Place night-club issued small paychecks with withholding. It had something to
do with the IRS and reporting income, so all of he girls had checking accounts with
modest sums of money. But they also had piles of cash –or did till they found places to
spend it. Janet nodded. The whole thing was confusing to her. It involved math. She
was always interested in how to get more money and keep what she got.   "Better than
tips I suppose. What's Tom up to? Has he found a job?"

Tonia was working her girls into a bra –somewhat to Janet's relief. "No. that
DUI really messed him up. He's not even sure he wants to drive trucks anymore anyway.
He is doing stuff on line and stuff. He re-did my web-site again."

Janet had seen the web-page Tom made for Tonia to get johns. It was indeed
beautiful – far nicer than most of the other out-call girls posted on TheBackPage.com.
Most of the out-call women would be laughed off the stage and either of Williston's
'gentlemen's clubs', so they posted suggestive language about relaxing massages and
poorly exposed fuzzy pictures on one of two or three websites. The convention on these
sites was not to show faces and Tonia had a hot little body from the neck down in her tiny
gold bikini. Tom had taken picture of her with an expensive camera that she bought for
him. Then she had to buy him expensive photography software. The picture was
undoubtedly hot, but Janet wondered if it all really took two weeks of work that Tom
spent sprawled out on the couch while Tonia was stripping and turning tricks. She kept
her thoughts to herself.

"When are you going to turn a few dates Janet?"

"Oh, I do alright here. I'm sending money home every week and have a lot
stashed. The lawyer guy I'm seeing says he can set me up as a corporation and save me a
lot on taxes and even get me in on some killer investments. He says the only way to get
rich is to own stuff –stocks and real-estate and things. The only things is that I have to
declare all my tips. I don't understand why I can't just pay cash for stuff."

"Is this guy like those lawyer guys on TV or something?"

Janet shook her head. "No. I don't think he goes into court very much. Mostly
works in his office. He took me there once because he said he had to drop off
something. I think he might have been just trying to impress me: all dark paneling and
deep carpets and lots of books. He explained all it to me... kind'a. He collects up groups
of people with… wha'd he call it, mineral rights, -maybe old guys like your rich farmer-
packages them –what ever that means-- and then sells them to oil companies. THEN he
takes THAT money and invests it so they don't have to pay taxes.

"Sounds like a scam. And the IRS is all up in our faces about our tips?"

That's kind'a the thing I don't understand. I've got money, but I can't invest.
WTF? You do too don't you?

"Ya, except what Tom spends it on toys and shit. How did you meet this lawyer guy anyway? Does he have a brother?"

Janet laughed. "Don't know about a brother. But he has an ex-wife. Says she is a bitch. You knew how we met? Our illustrious boss introduced us. Good old Mel said he was a rich guy and really going places.

Tonia interrupted. "You met him here?"

"Ya –in Mel's office even. He thought we might hit it off. Kevin is Mel's accountant or lawyer of something. Mel said he was considering investing some money with him. Said he would be interested in what I thought of the lawyer..,. accountant… something… maybe both. Like I know dick about money –other than earning it ten and twenty dollars at a time. "

"So you are supposed to… like, spy for Mel or something?"

"For sure! What am I gon'na do? Investigate him? You ever heard of the word 'audit'?

"Ya, it's like when they check on the money, like for taxes and things."

"He told me he has to work to make sure that shit doesn't hit… what did he say- 'survives an audit' and then he tried to explain it to me. Way too many numbers. It just doesn't add up that Mel wants my input on investing and it's really unlike Mel –kind'a creepy even

"I would be really scared of anyone Mel introduced me to."

"Me too, but Kevin was like a real gentleman and all. He drives a Mercedes. Our first date he took me out to dinner at The Williston –you know that fancy place that looks like an English manner? Expensive as shit. And then asked me if I would like to go to Aspen or Vail for skiing."

"Did he try to do you after dinner?"

"No, like I say, a gentleman –about as far as you can get from the oil workers that come here. I thought he might be blowing smoke, but he took me to Vail for three days last month. I tired skiing, hated it, but the shopping was wonderful. The weird thing? Mel gave me the time off with out a word."

"Did you fuck him?"

Janet shrugged. "Ya. Seemed like the thing to do. I mean he paid for it the trip and the shopping. But now he's really busy. Taxes and all for his rich old guys. You know that man camp north of town?" Tonia nodded. "That's his. But anyway, he wants to take me to Hawaii or Vegas or somewhere soon, after taxes and all."

"Honey –you are just like me –your lawyer is just like my farmer. Maybe someday and maybe not. But I have to admire you for going it alone. Tom spends my money on computer shit and a lot of it is for games and toys. He thinks I don't know the difference." Tonia pulled on her parka, kissed Janet on the forehead and bounced out the door.

Chapter 5

Mike was nodding off with his computer in his lap when the door opened and three guys stomped in. They were wearing stiff canvas jackets over filthy coveralls: identical and each with a last name on the right breast and "Slumberburton Services" on the left. Two stopped in the hall long enough to take off muddy boots and leave them by the door.   The youngest one didn't bother with his boots and noticed Mike sitting on the couch.

"Who is the pussy in the tie? We have a new room-mate. Smith must have finally gotten the ax."

Mike had no idea how to respond and simply looked at the young guy with his well-practiced displeased-teacher's face. He folded up his lap-top as one of the other guys came into the trailer's common living room. "Shut up Johnson." He held out his hand to shake Mike's. "Pay no mind to this ass –it's our first day off in two weeks. I'm Kermit." Kermit was the oldest of the three –almost Mike's age, black and fiendly looking.

"I'm Mike. I just got in last night."

"Are you a geologist or an engineer of some sort, Mike?

"Nope, I'm a teacher. I just started teaching GED math this morning at Williston State College."

The older guy nodded, "Oh. We don't get a lot of suits here."

Johnson snorted a simple "Oh fuck -a teacher." and he stomped down the hall.

The third guy reappeared from his room down the hall with a bottle of beer in hand. His coveralls were unzipped to the waist with the arms tied around his hips. "I'm Rob. Is there good money in teaching math?"

"Nope again. In fact, I just found out this morning that I don't have as much work as I had hoped. What do you guys do?"

Kermit gestured to the company name on his over-alls, "We all work on a frack crew. There were five of us, but one guy pissed a dirty cup and got canned. The last guy has a family and lives in an apartment down the road a bit."

"Pissed a dirty cup?"

Kermit and Rob exchanged a look. Rob answered the question, "He failed a random drug test. Got himself fired."

"Oh." He nodded. Pause. "Is there good money in fracking?"

Kermit answered. "Yep. If you don't mind working 14 days straight, long hours, getting real dirty and being cold all the damn time. Except when it's hot."

"And when it's hot, you have to wear your fucking FR's." Rob added.

Mike shrugged, "F R's?"

"Means 'Fire Resistant'. You have to wear head-to-toe coveralls all summer long."

"And they test for drugs and alcohol?"

"Nope, just drugs, unless you get a DUI –then you just get fired"

The young guy –Johnson- came back wearing a bathrobe carrying a bottle of Southern Comfort as Mike asked, "Um –any chance they are looking for help?"

"You are too old." Johnson put ice in a glass and poured it half full of whisky.

Kermit and Rob looked at each other again. "Kenny is our derrick hand and a good one. They are the ones you see 100 feet up in the rig in the fingers. Otherwise we would have drowned him in a salt-water tank by now. Good derrick hands are hard to find. And they are usually young and stupid."

Mike had no idea what 'the fingers' were, but he had seen noticed oil rigs with a platform like thing near the top of the rigs he had seen on the outskirts of town. Kenny Johnson seemed not to mind the crack about his stupidity and let it go, but when Mike confirmed his name was 'Kenny', the young guy stepped over the couch and leaned down over Mike. "You got a problem with my name, teacher?"

For the second time in a few minutes, Mike used his displeased teacher face because he didn't know what else to do.

Rob diffused the situation. "Calm down Kenny –he was just trying to know your name."

The kid muttered "Pussy teacher" and stomped back to his room.

Mike gestured confusion and asked. "What the fuck?"

Kermit explained that they all had had a long and difficult week. But mostly he stressed that Kenny was an ass. He also warned that he was even nastier when he was drinking. Mike guessed that the young guy probably was not a good student and had a problem with teachers in high school. He was also getting the notion the kid probably was earning more than his high school teacher.

It was evidently a good night to drink –almost all around. Mike refilled his glass and Rob was on his third beer when he went to his room to shower –leaving Kermit and Mike to talk. Mike offered to share his port and bourbon with Kermit, but he said "No Thanks," and got himself a beer.

Mike asked about fracking. He had certainly heard the controversy about how it was supposed to mess up ground water, but didn't know else much about it. Kermit sat down and took a long pull. "I honestly don't know what the deal is. We do our fracking about a mile or two down –WAY below the water tables. First thing we do is set off shape charges…"

Mike interrupted "Shape charges?"

"Little explosives that…." Kermit gestured with his forefingers pointing at each other and then shooting out towards Mike. "… well, they kind'a explode in on themselves and squirt out in a narrow jet. Really drills into the rock that way. Then we pump this mixture of sand and water down under real high pressure. You could drink the stuff if you didn't mind plugging up your plumbing with sand. Anyway, people have been exploding stuff underground almost as long as they have been drilling for oil. It's all about opening up cracks underground so the oil can ooze out."

Mike tired to find a tactful way to ask about how much money these guys made. He didn't entirely succeed but Kermit caught on. It turned out it was less per hour than he expected, but with lots of overtime –LOTS of overtime. He did a quick mental calculation and realized it was a lot more than he had guessed in his research about Williston before he took the teaching job and drove north.

He asked what sort of education or training was needed to get a job on a frack crew. Not much more then a high school diploma and a commercial driver's license, but the oil field service companies did everything they could do to hire experienced workers. Only when there were no other choices did they hire and train entry level workers, and even then they hired experienced truck drivers to train for the oilfield before they hired anyone else.

Mike sighed. "I guess I'll stay in the teaching business for the time being."

The other guys came back showered and dressed. Rob asked "You guys coming to dinner?"

Kermit patted his ample belly, "I have me some salad and tuna fish in the fridge. I'm not going to spend $16 for sorry-ass spaghetti, wilted salad, and garlic bread."

Mike explained, "I've been eating peanuts with my port and I'm good to go."

Kenny was busy on his little iPad thing and mercifully quiet. Rob moved toward the door, "C'mon Johnson. Let's go."

After the two younger guys left, Kermit asked, "Ya know what Kenny was doing just now? I think he was ordering a hooker. I mean he is an ignorant little fucker, but he does go after what he wants. At any given moment anyway. He don't look real far down the road."

Chapter 6

It hadn't been a bad day. No one quit. The EPA / OSHA / IRS hadn't stopped by. There was one small bit of excitement. One of his guys was airing up a four foot tall tire for one of the loaders. It took as much as fifteen minutes for the small shop compressor to get the job done so the guy hooked it up, turned it on, and went off to do something else. The compressor may have been small, but it was powerful. Vern came into the shop on some minor errand and noticed the tire was dangerously over-inflated. He knew of people getting killed when one of these loader tires blew, so he shut off the compressor, got everyone out of the shop, and pulled out the little twenty two target pistol he got in the Navy. He peaked around a corner and put a shot thru the sidewall. After the pop of the small automatic, the tire blew will less of a bang than a hissing whimper. Seemed to him to take along time to run down. Unless the side wall would hold a patch, a thousand dollar tire was now worthless. Maybe his wife could do something clever with it in the garden.

Then he got a summons from his accountant / lawyer Kevin Amundsen. There was a time when such a summons would have had him on the proverbial pins and needles. Had to be bad news. Was he being audited? Was he loosing money? Was the bank calling in the loans on all his equipment? After a while he came to realize Kevin simply enjoyed the melodrama of summoning Vern to meetings for some important matter that he couldn't be disclosed over the phone. What the hell, he was a good accountant –or so Vern guessed. If melodrama was part of the package, so be it.

Kevin's secretary / administrative aid / para-legal / whatever –Vern never quite got a good grip on the middle aged woman's role, greeted him with a warm "Howdy do. He's on the phone, but y'all go ahead on in." Vern thought she was a nice lady, but she was clearly not from North Dakota.

The office was the very picture of what a lawyer's office ought to be. Vern knew this because a few years back his wife Sherrie and Kevin's wife Jane were friends and Sherrie helped Jane pick out much of the décor. High ceilings, fancy wood paneling about a third of the way up the walls –*coffered wainscoting* Sherrie called it, -a solid bookcase on the wall to one side of the door and pictures of English guys on horses to the other side, -deep maroon carpet, Queen Anne chairs for the clients –Vern thought they were a bit sissy, but kept this view to himself, a big window behind the desk.. Before the women re-did things, the chairs were wood, Kevin's desk was metal, the ceiling was dropped plastic panels over fluorescent lights, and the only decoration was a glass case holding a moth-eaten stuffed jack-alope sitting on a coffee table off to the side. The jack-a-lope was a flea market find Kevin had picked up somewhere. It was really a large stuffed jackrabbit with antelope antlers glued on it's head. Such was the humor of folks who lived on the prairie and who delighted in seeing how many big city folks could be convinced a jack-alope was a real animal. Vern liked the jack-alope better than the English guys on horses.

They knew each other in high school, but didn't really mix. Vern was a couple of years older and played football while Kevin played hockey. Both of their dads were farmers, and both had oil income, but Vern's dad had a lot more. Despite this, Vern's upbringing was the more circumspect and religious of the two. Kevin lived in town and ran with a different crowd than Vern who didn't really run with any particular crowd, but spent most of his time 'out on the farm'. Kevin was the better student –in fact the class valedictorian who would go off the big city on a scholarship and do great things. Vern joined the Navy.

Vern made himself comfortable in one of two girly chairs in front of the guys guy's desk. At least the bug sissy chairs were more comfortable than the old ones. The desk was impressive and the deep red of its mahogany went nicely with the polished brass library lamp with its deep green glass shade. *Sweet Jesus'* he thought to himself, *What is Sherrie turning me into? How do I even know what a library lamp is, let alone care how colors work together.* He decided to distract himself by listening to Kevin side of the conversation while trying not to look like he was eves-dropping. It appeared to be with a banker who was loaning someone money, but only after he approved the loan documents for his and the banks mutual client. It impressed Vern that here was someone who did not just sign what the bank put in front of him, but rather had a lawyer look it over. Maybe someday he would be that guy. He thought he got along well enough with his banker, but maybe in the future, he could take the loan papers to Kevin for a once-over before meekly signing them -just to keep the banker on his toes and all. He had been Kevin s client long enough and besides, their backgrounds had enough in common, and their wives had even more that that in common –at least till the lawyer's divorce anyway.

Both men were just a little above average in height, but the similarities ended there. Vern looked like a heavy equipment operator. Built not for speed as they say, but strength. He had been the starting right tackle in high school. It was a small school back then and Williston High didn't' have enough players for both offensive and defensive teams so he stayed pretty lean and his time in the Navy didn't change him much. But now his wife Sheri's cooking and too many hours at his desk were just starting put a little around Vern's middle. But it was winter and he figured everyone tended to add little insulation for the cold months. Come summer, he made a point of getting away from the desk and spending as much time as possible with his big hands wrapped around the controls of one of his big yellow machines. Showed his men that the boss could still cut a grade in as few passes as possible, and he loved it. His forearms and the back of his neck would turn first red and then by July it would be as brown as the hair hanging out from under his Caterpillar cap or the damn hardhat OSHA said must be worn on the job – even if there was nothing overhead except miles and miles of blue sky.

Used to be that he would sun-burn his nose at the beginning of every summer, but less and less now. His face would darken up a little, but seemed to stay pretty brown year round now. It was a good face as faces went. Open, honest, clean shaved. He tried a moustache once when the kids were little. It came in light and against his sun tanned face it tended to disappear, so Sherrie had him shave it off. She once said that his face looked just intelligence enough to make people comfortable signing multiple thousand dollar contracts for earth moving, but no so much as do doubt the guy's willingness to climb up into a machine and do the work. Vern didn't much care, but if Sherri liked his face, he figured he's stick with it.

On the other hand, Kevin was built for speed. He played hockey in high school as a lightening-quick center, but otherwise moved with slow dignity. He was still lean and wiry, more so now then as a young man. His face was thin with large heavily lidded eyes over high cheekbones that gave him a scholarly look. His large Adams apple, high forehead and vaguely noble profile all stirred together in Vern's mind and reminded him of nothing so much as Disney's Incabod Crane, but with smaller ears and more hair. He was the only man Vern knew who had more than one suit and could be seen wearing one outside of church. Sherrie once told him there were women who thought Kevin was vary attractive –sexy even. Vern nodded and said nothing. He tucked the information away in his brain in about the same mental file drawer where he kept all the information Sherrie gave him about matching colors and textures in decoration: stuff he didn't understand, but wanted to keep at hand just to make his wife happy.

Kevin finished his phone call promising someone the contract would be ready to be picked up the next morning and hung up. "Howdy Vern. Want a beer?"

If it were summertime and Vern had just finished-up a day out in the field, he might have been happy to have a bottle from the little refrigerator he knew he kept well stocked and hidden in his administrative assistant's office cum reception area. "No thanks, not to day." Nor did Kevin want one either. Come to think of it, Vern had never actually seen him ever drink a beer –Vern figured he kept them on hand for his farmer clients.

They did a little of the   'How's business?'   'Cold enough for you?' ' How are the wife and kids?'   'How about 'em Vikings?' small talk. Vern was careful not to ask about the his wife though. Kevin's kids were a little older than Vern's and they were doing fine –the younger one off to college in Bismark, and the older in Minneapolis working in big-box-store last he heard.

Vern broke the ice. "So what's on your mind?"

"Well, a couple of things. I've gotten started on your taxes and you have been with-holding just barley enough. I don't think you will need to come up with a big payment come April 15, but you have used up all the depreciation you have on your equipment *this* year, and *next* years is s gon'na be a different story. Be ready for it."

"What if I was going to buy me another piece of equipment? Say another big Caterpillar.?"

"That would help. Also would help if you were to borrow heavily to do so and deduct the interest payments. But I know you don't like to do the leverage thing."

"I am my father's son –despite our differences. And if I have to pay some income taxes, I guess that's better'n not having income."

The lawyer leaned back in his big judge's chair. "There is another possibility. There is my man camp. I know you decided against investing a while back, and I'm happy you were able to get a piece of it by dong the grading and trenching and so forth for me. I am confident it will pay you a nice little wind-fall down the road, and for that matter, I might buy your little participation back from you at a nice profit, but not now. I'll be honest with you, I'm feeling a little pinch my self –cash wise."

Vern thought he could see it coming and tried not to show his discomfort. Kevin went on. "Frankly, the divorce nearly wiped me out." He paused. "I imagine my Jane… well, I imagine she told your wife all about it. She told a lot of people about it and a lot of the good old boy farmers –like your dad- whom I did investments with, they found other places to put their money. Frustrating as all heck for me because they had done well with my Butler building partnerships and continue to do so now. I still do taxes for a lot of them and many of them lost money in the stock market –but –dang it- not with the partnerships I put together." He paused again and took a deep breath, "But it's water under the bridge. I decided I could just barely do it on my own –with what money Jane hadn't taken anyway"

"To continue, when we started, the city had committed to run water and sewer a little further up Highway 85 to the man camp and *then* they decided to back out about the same time you had finished the earth work and fifty-two double-wide trailers had been paid for and were on their way to town. I had to bite the bullet, drill a well, and install my own damn water treatment plant. Vern, I had to borrow about two hundred thousand dollars under less then favorable terms to get 'er done. The place isn't quite full now, but getting more so every day and when it's at full occupancy, it'll be a license to print money."

Vern nodded. It seemed to him that the other guy was being more open and honest than usual. Talking to him as an equal rather than like a lawyer would ordinarily talk to a client. Still, he was getting –if not more enthused, at least less un-enthused about it now. "But I don't have two hundred grand sitting around."

Just a little of the imperious accountant talking to his innocent client surfaced. "I know you don't. But you have excellent credit, and some money. Listen closely now." Vern kept quiet. Sherri would have been proud. "We can arrange a good loan for you to buy the water treatment plant with a modest down. You can take an investment tax credit on the whole two hundred –should work out to about $12,000 right off your taxes. This does not mean $12,000 off your income and you pay taxes on what's left, it means you figure out what your taxes are, *then* subtract the twelve grand. *Plus* you take

depreciation on the equipment and the building it sits in. There is even some silly environmental tax benefit somewhere along the line. Not worth much -money wise- but give you bragging rights if you find yourself among a bunch of environments."
Both men chuckled. Environmental enlightenment had not made much progress in North Dakota..

 "But anyway, the man camp would buy water from you. At whatever price it took to pay off the loan and give you a little sheltered income on the side -without having to push dirt around. Do something nice for Sherrie."

 Vern had bid on the excavation for the town's new wastewater treatment facility but didn't win the contract. He would later hear that the company that got the job lost money on it. But and over the years he had dug miles of trench for water supply pipes, but had never given any thought to how water came to be in those pipes. Or what happened to it when it had been used. He doubted anyone else had for that matter. Now it occurred to him it might involve equipment not unlike the big yellow machines he used to make his living. Now *this* he understood.

 "What is the depreciation period on the equipment?"

 "Ten years on the tanks and pipes. This is about 30% of the cost. Five years on the treatment equipment and instrumentation, another 50% of the overall cost. The building –one of my Butler buildings- takes up the rest and depreciates over the usual 20 years but you can accelerate it if you need to."

 "Warranties?"

 "The manufacture warranties the equipment for well past the depreciation periods. Certain of the equipment has defined TBO's -Time Before Overhaul. These are mostly pumps. I notice you have similar –or what I take to be similar- maintenance schedules and costs on your equipment."

 "Sure do –follow them religiously. Operating costs?"

 "Electricity for the pumps and some chemicals. Chlorine I gather, but the salesman who sold it to me said you can buy gallon jugs of Clorox laundry stuff in a pinch. I am still using a 55 gallon drum of these big tablet things that came with it. I don't know what another batch of chlorine tablets would cost. Probably not much."

 "Maintenance?"

 "The thing is pretty well automated. I've been out there once about half a dozen times in the last six months to shovel white chlorine pellets into a hopper. They look like white hockey pucks. We have a pretty good maintenance guy out there now and I leave it up to him now."

 "Resale?"

 "No idea. Truth of the matter is that if you sell it all for scrap after the warranties expire and depreciation is used up, we –you- would still be money ahead. Furthermore, it's reasonably portable so if -heaven forbid- the mancamp goes away, you can haul it all away to another job -all except the Butler building."

 Vern was impressed. Obviously Kevin had done his homework and was able to speak to Vern in the language of someone who lived or died with expensive machinery and equipment. He was sincerely interested but needed time to think and of course talk it

over with his wife. "I'll give it some serious thought and have a chat with my banker."
He didn't mention his wife, but was thinking hard about how to broach the subject with
Sherrie.

As he was getting up to leave, Kevin remembered, "Oh, wait, I forgot. I have
the owner's manual. I tried to read it but didn't get very far. You might do better, but
maybe you should go get a degree in chemistry first." They both chuckled and he handed
Vern about an inch thick loose leaf notebook. They finished with a little more small-talk
–most of it was about Kevin's hot new girlfriend.

They finished in time for Vern to make it home for dinner and this didn't happen
always happen. Dark comes early in Williston in February and when fronts come thru,
there are some beautiful sunsets. Effing cold too. Vern pulled into his driveway and took
a moment to enjoy the late sunset: warm reds fading to cool purples and indigoes. Indigo
was a word Sherrie taught him. For that matter, the notion of *warm* and *cool* colors was
her doing too. The dining room drapes are open and he could see into the kitchen's
warm golden light as she bustled from the kitchen to the dinning table "I'm a lucky
man." he said aloud to himself as he climbed out of his pickup and walked to the front
door. For a moment, he wondered if it was not time to get in the habit of locking the
front door to the house. Crime was supposed to be way up since the oil boom started.
They had never worried about locking the door before –other then when they took a
family vacation for a week or so. For that matter, he wasn't even sure his kids even had
keys to the place. He was pretty sure he had some spare keys somewhere his desk in his
home office, but he wasn't sure about that either. He would have to give some thought to
finding the key, getting copies made, and instituting a new family policy -with keys- for
everyone.

Sherrie was at the stove and the kids were in the living room arguing about
something, so he stepped behind her, nuzzled her neck, and gave her bottom a friendly
rub.

"What's for dinner?"

"Hi honey. Tuna fish. Stop it. What does your accountant want?"
Vern noticed that it was now "your accountant". It had been 'our accountant' or even
'Kevin' in years past. "He wants me to invest in that man-camp. Apparently we need
some tax shelter."

Sherrie shook her head. "We will talk about it later. Call the kids for dinner."

"Oh. And he has a new girlfriend –but other than 'She's 'HOT' I don't know
much about her."

"Well, That IS good news." Sherrie could be sarcastic –particularly about
things and people of whom she disapproved.

Beth and Robby's argument came to the table with them. It appeared to be
about the relative merits of a popular singer vs. a soccer player.

"Enough kids. Robby, will you say the blessing tonight?"

The Lutheran grace was supposed to be "Come, Lord Jesus, be our Guest, and
let Thy gifts to us be blessed. Amen. " but the thirteen year old's version came out,
"C'mord-Jus, barst, an'leather-gifs toast bles-a-men." 'Close enough' thought Vern, not

quite the way his own father would have approved of the prayer, but close enough. They made it thru 'How was school?' 'Fine' 'What did you learn?' 'Nothing' from his daughter, and 'Some cool stuff about rocks.' from his son. Ordinarily his daughter would do a monologue about boys and who said something to some girl about some who went something back.   They usually seemed to involve 3 boys and anywhere from 3 to 5 girls. 'She was like, and so he was like, but she was like f'rsure, but he told him that she was….' Vern had long ago given up trying to follow these stories. As near as he could tell, Beth thought most of the boys at her high-school were beneath her. This was not a bad thing. If and when she brought home a story about an older boy –perhaps one going to Williston State College- that's when he would have to pay very close attention. In the mean time, Shirley assured him that mother and daughter had a pretty good communication thing going and he need not worry. Yet.

But this evening, Beth was curiously quiet.   Finally she said, "The Westergards are going to Tahiti for spring break."

Aaaaand here it is. thought Vern. A glance at his wife was all it took for him to understand that mother and daughter had taken this particular conversational issue as far as maternal patience allowed. It was now Vern's turn to deal with it.
Vern knew the Westergards were spending oil royalty money and strongly suspected that they were spending it faster than it came in. "I'm thinking we will take a week or two this summer to visit your cousins in Minnesota."

"Ya, but we go there very year. Can't we go somewhere different?"

"Beth, I can't afford to take the time off. And it would cost a fortune to fly half way around the world." He knew his argument was perfectly valid and he knew further that it held no water in his daughter's eyes. Beth had a brand-new, young, and very liberal social studies teacher the year before. The guy got his daughter in a frightful twist about the rich vs. the poor and the evils of capitalism. Vern made the mistake of sitting her down and trying to teach her about how his business worked and how he was able to support the family with an expensive pile of equipment. An expensive pile of moderately mortgaged equipment. Unfortunately, all Beth heard was that the value of the equipment would more than pay for a wonderful life in California or Hawaii or anyplace besides North Dakota. All he had to was sell it. That wasn't happening.

"But Dad, we are rich."

Vern should have seen it coming and sighed. Once again, he tried to get his daughter to understand. "First, we are not rich. I use a lot of equipment to make a living for our family. Second, if we were, it's your Mom and my money. Ain't no 'we' here." The lower lip came out, and the likelihood of a major melodrama increased by about 200%. Good day for melodrama evidently. First the accountant and now his daughter. There was little hope of heading it off, but he had to try. "Maybe you could go visit Uncle Harry in Minneapolis for spring break. You could take the train all by yourself. Visit your cousins and all." *And give the rest of the family a break from you for a week.* His son Robby might have had the same thought and started to say something but Vern shot him the *shut-up* look. The boy went back to studying his tuna-fish.

It was a close thing, but not quite enough to head off his daughter's tantrum.

She pushed her chair back and stomped off. "I never get to do anything I want to do. Shelly's family always does the cool things. I have to stay here in dumb old Williston all the time." Her bedroom door slammed and the rest of the family continued their meal.

"Robby, you like visiting your cousins in Minneapolis don't' you?"

"Ya dad, I like them and we do cool stuff. I like camping and fishing and stuff. Beth just wants to do stuff with boys and girls her own age. Ned it too old to be any fun for her and Sally is too young, and 'sides, they are cousins."

Vern nodded and glanced at Sherrie. He loved both kids, but Robby was so very much his son and from time to time the kid nailed it. Reminded him of himself. Now if he would just learn to spell and pay a little more attention in English class. Can't have everything.

When the three of them finished dinner and it seemed that Beth had had enough pouting time, he sent Robby to get Beth to come back to the table for the after dinner prayer. Vern expected that there would come a time that the child would rebel against the Lutheran ritual as a matter off course, but not tonight. She sat back at the table and did the prayer –with each word pronounced clearly -if sullenly. *O give thanks unto the Lord, for He is good, for His mercy endureth forever. Amen.*

Chapter 7

Mike and Kermit had reached the point of companionable silence when Rob & Kenny got back from the dining trailer. "How was dinner?"

The young ass answered Kermit, "So so –tacos, but they had strawberry shortcake for desert."

"Frozen strawberry goo, but not bad." Rob answered. "Kermit, are you working in the shop tomorrow?"

"Ya, they have a mess of gauges they want me to calibrate. Planning to sleep late though. You want a ride to the airport?"

"Yep –my plane leaves at noon."

"No worries. Let's leave at nine or ten or so."

Mike considered another drink, but decided against it. "Where you headed Rob?"

"Cheyenne. I'm going to spend the week with my wife and kids. Haven't seen them in a while. Might go skiing. The in-laws have a place up in mountains. Got a little sleep to catch up on too."

"Cool –I used to ski a lot. Lake Tahoe back in the day, but it got too expensive."

Mike and Rob start to compare notes about skiing when Kenny interrupted, "Why you leave there Teach?"

"Leave California? In a nut shell, no work."

"So teaching don't pay the bills, eh? All that fancy education and you have to come to the oil-patch to find work."

Just what was with this little prick? "I thought we had established that."

Kermit saw it coming and interrupted. "You going to Deadwood, right Kenny?"

The kid was drunk enough to be easily distracted. "Damn straight. Gon'a get some sleep and head out tomorrow. Gon'na do a little gambling and fuck me some bitches."

Mike bit his tongue and glanced at Kermit for possible explanation. "Deadwood South Dakota is about a six hour drive south of here. You might have missed if you came up the interstate. But it's a nice little town –lots of history from gold mining back about the turn of the century. And casinos. And evidently…" he looked at Kenny "… local escort talent. Johnson, be sure to fill your gas tank before you start having fun. I am NOT wiring money to you again so you can buy gas to get back up here to work."

Mike glanced at Kermit, but it didn't escape Kenny who snapped, "I make more money that you do teach. How I spend it is my own business. I work hard and I play hard."

"Fine –I don't care."

There is a knock at the door and Kenny jumped up and shortly came back down the hall grinning like an idiot and leading a young woman by the hand. She was short, but once she took off her parka, the three older guys tried not to stare -with varying degrees of success. She wore tight blue jeans –black actually with fancy embroidery and an even tighter lavender sweater that hugged her boobs. She seemed aware of their attention and was not at all uncomfortable. She had long black hair and a pleasant –if lopsided and slightly over-bitten smile. Her eyes, were vaguely Asian -erotic and elfin. She was cute, but figure was undoubtedly her best feature. Her face was not unattractive, but exotic more than appealing. "This is Tonia." He is trying to lead her down the hall to his bedroom but she resisted.

"Sweetie, we have to do the money thing first." As Kenny pulled out his wallet and counted out bills, she smiled at the three older guys in the trailer's common area. "Good evening gentlemen." and without waiting for a response, followed the young guy down the hall.

Kermit shook his head and sighed, "So help me God, that kids spends it faster than he earns it.

Rob agrees, "Ya, but that ain't unique in the oil patch. I suspect he just spent $200 or $300, but give him credit, at least he ain't spending it in the strip-club.

Kermit interrupted, "The only reason he isn't, is because he rides in the crew-truck with us –to the rig and straight back here."

Rob nodded agreement and added, "I've heard of guys that cash a two week paycheck after getting off work and spend it all at Willy's Place by midnight."

Kermit laughs, "And not get anything but blue balls out of it. Kenny is at least… well… you know. There was the time he lost his hardhat somehow and needed to buy another one to get back to work. This was after only a few days after payday and he needed to borrow $20 from me. Thank God for him that the company gives us a meal ticket for the diner. He'da starved otherwise. There was another time he went as far as Portland –I think he used to live there and had a girlfriend. He had to call the foreman to get an advance to get back here."

There is as rhythmic thumping coming from down the hall. Rob and Kermit shrugged. Mike giggled and then –as much to cover his embarrassment as anything-asked, "How can that be? Didn't you say the company provided two way air-line tickets?

"Ya, sometimes they do. Sometimes it's like a reward for no one on the crew getting hurt for a month or something. The whole crew gets a round trip to Denver or somewhere. In Kenny's case, I heard the higher-ups wanted to fire him. The foreman changed their minds –'sides it was the only way they were getting the advance back. "

Mike was confused, "Let me see if I understand this. You guys earn a good wage with lots of overtime. The company pays you for rent and food and even airfare back home. And… and.."

"And lots of guys don't have a pot to piss in." Rob shrugged, "Other than a nice pick-up truck. And by the time they get it's paid off, the dirt roads around here have beaten it to death."

"Ya, that and the way they drive." Kermit added.

A door down the hall opened and all three guys looked up to watch Tonia bouncing into the living room. "That was fun." She pulled business cards out of her jeans pocket and handed one to each of the three guys still in the living room. "Think of me when you are in the mood guys." She put on her coat, turned to the guys, smiled, and pulls up her sweater to show off her girls. "And remember these." She giggled & bounced out the door.

Mike smiles and looks at Kermit and Rob. They look pretty happy too. "That *was* fun. But tell me, how does a good husband explain that sort of thing to his wife?"

"Don't suspect it will come up. Kermit observed, "My wife and I hardly ever discuss other women's naked breast-uses."

Chapter 8

After the kids had gone off to do their homework and then on to bed, Vern and Shirley had themselves a little quiet time in the living room. His own small rebellion from his Lutheran upbringing was a cocktail and Shirley had a glass of white wine. She broke the ice. "Tell me about this thing Amundsen wants us to invest in."

"It's that man camp up north of town. The one I did the grading and site prep for."

"But you did that work without getting paid."

"Ya, but we got a piece of the –what did Kevin call it? 'Partnership equity' or something? I'm a limited partner a or general partner. I forget which." It had been a simple job. Vern's guys smoothed out a few acres of prairie, dug four long trenches for plumbing, and came back after the plumbers were done with their piping and filed in the trenches back up again.

"I don't understand Vern, why is he looking for money if it's all done and such a good investment? I just don't trust Ahmundson. His wife told me some pretty weird stuff during their divorce. Not for me to gossip, but…"

"I think he got himself overextended. He hinted that he divorce really hurt him. I went down to the bank to make a deposit the other day and the loan officer & I got to talking. He said that I could borrow more money with a minimum of fuss. I've kind of got my eye on that big grader for sale down in Denver. Grading drilling pads keeps us nice and busy, but with bigger a grader I could do a lot more business for the department of transportation. The bank seems to like them state boys as customers better than drilling companies –at least as far as collateral for more equipment loans."

"Vern, sweetheart, you work so hard as it is. Maybe it's time to start taking some money out of the business and maybe… well, maybe a nice family vacation to Hawaii wouldn't be such a bad idea. Or maybe you could patch things up with your dad. Help out on the farm a little. God knows, he needs it. Your sister has a young family of her own and I think she and Mark are regretting having built their house so close to the family farm. Ever since your mom died, your dad is asking… well… demanding that she take up the slack from your Mom. Don't get mad honey, but your dad has more money that he will ever spend from the oil. You don't need to prove that you can make it on your own without his help anymore. You have proved it. Maybe it's time to reconcile with him –just a little."

"Oh –that reminds me –Ahmudsen asked about my asking dad to invest. I told him that was NOT going to happen –if I was to so much as ask Dad, he'd never do it – even if it were the best investment ever." Vern went silent. His relation with his dad had never been easy. Got worse after he left the farm and even worse when he started the earth-moving business. He thought about saying the right thing to his wife about a reconciliation. She was right, but Vern didn't know what the right thing to say might have been.

"Do you remember that time when we were so poor and had to hock your wedding ring to squeak by the down-payment for that first back-hoe. Baby, that was the happiest time of my life. Well, not the happiest –I'm happy now- but the most exciting. I just ain't ready to slow down."

They were contentedly quiet for a while. Vern could almost hear her thinking. Sherrie loved to decorate. He read all manner of expensive snooty magazines about architecture and decorating and such. He took down old and put up new curtains for her, paid to have floors done & redone, tried to follow her explanations of co-coordinating colors; he failed. On the few occasions when there was no other work to do, he brought some of his crew home and had them shovel and grade the yard and plant trees and hedges. More than one of his friends had told him his house was a showplace –or more accurately, the wives of his friends said so.

As often happens in a marriage, Sherrie said what he was thinking. "Or how about a bigger house. Real-estate is going up and up. We could move to that nice neighborhood over west of town and build nice house with a big barn right next door – like you have now. I know your barn is very important to you." She giggled. "I heard they're called 'man-caves'."

"Ya, it's also a big part of my business. Besides Robby and I have some great moments out there." He tossed back the last of his drink. "As I was coming home from Kevin's this afternoon, I figured out why I buy equipment the way I do. If the bubble breaks –and I may be the only one in the county who thinks it will- anyway, if it breaks, I can load up my equipment and move it to where I can either find work, or I can sell it.

And for that matter, the biggest asset a man-camp owns is trailers. They can get moved down the road as well –when the good times end. Honey, if you really want, I'll build you a bigger house, but Beth will be in college in a five years and Robby will be out of college in eight years – or ten years if he has to spell."

Sherrie giggled into her wine glass. A good sigh in Vern's mind.. "I've stuck it out with you this far. What's a few more years?" She got up to go to bed. "Don't stay up too late."

Vern set down his empty glass and picked up the operating manual for the water treatment plant that the lawyer had given him that afternoon. He skimmed the table of contents, made a mental note get back to the disclosures and cautions later, (he suspected were written by the company's lawyers), and found a diagram. He liked diagrams. This one started with an Input Pipe (from river or well) and ended with a Supply Pump. So far so good, but in between, there was a Settling Unit, a Flocculent Unit, with two Flocculent Dosing Units off to the side, a Sludge Discharge –Vern was dang sure you didn't want sludge sitting around un discharged- a Clarification Unit, a Sand Filter Bed, and finally, a Disinfection Unit at the output end. All the pieces and parts apparently came out of a semi-tractor trailer and had been put together with big pipe wrenches. Not nearly the same as the air, fuel, and oil filters on his heavy equipment, but Vern was interested in spite of himself. This was something he could do –with or without a degree in chemistry, but it would take a little study.

Chapter 9

Despite her afternoon nap, it had been a long day and she was determined to be back in the GED classroom in about 6 hours. She remembered to plug in her engine's block heater after she dug the extension cord out of the crusty wind-blown snow before she trudged around back of the house to her little garden-level apartment. It was a tiny place. A single bedroom / living room with a kitchen stuck in the corner and bath just beyond. She had been fiddling about with cheap fabric from Walmart and hung sheets of it from the ceiling to make 'walls'. She knew it was silly. Her mother would not approve –in fact, she would undoubtedly be snotty about it, but it pleased her. Coming home was always a good thing. She had heard the word "cocoon-ing" somewhere and it seemed just the thing. When she got home she wrapped her cocoon about her she was content and warm.

Comfy cozy or not, she got all pensive and thoughtful when she was tired. Why –for example- was it so important to her to put herself thru the agony of high-school math to get the damn GED anyway? She was making good money. She has just under $300 in paper money in the hip pocket of her jeans. Good tips tonight -for for a week night anyway. Three lap-dances and five sets on the stage –two of which were Tonia's by rights, but the money was going into a mason jar that she kept hidden under the bottom dresser drawer that didn't close quite right anyway.

Half her money went home to her parents in a little town outside of Saint Louis. She declared the other half, paid axes, and lived off it. Rent was far and away the biggest expense for everyone in Williston. She paid $1200 a month for a tiny studio apartment grafted into the basement of an otherwise nice house west of town. An older couple lived upstairs, but she rarely saw them. Actually it wasn't bad by the standards of the oil boom, and she lived alone and that certainly was worth a lot. Even with half her money going to Mom & Dad in and half of what was left going to rent and the IRS, she still was putting money in the bank –honest after-tax money at that. She suspected it was a lot more that a most 27 year-old girls –even those with degrees and office jobs.

How much more was she going to make when she finally passed the science and the damn math tests anyway? College maybe? Seemed a long way off as dreams go and then what? Nursing maybe. She thought it might be fun to do something with fashion or design. Her mom had been a teacher's assistant, but one of the other girls she worked with said that they did background checks on prospective teachers and exotic dancers were not likely to pass muster.

Her mom's associate's degree got her the teacher's assistant job, but she called herself a teacher. Her work no longer gave her any pleasure –if it ever did. Janet wondered if her mom ever took pleasure from anything but general purpose bitching. Her dad had most of a degree in literature but hadn't finished. When her mom had too much to drink, she berated him for never finishing –like she had. Finishing a two year degree was evidently better that finishing three years of a four year degree, at least in her mom's view.

Her dad was an insurance inspector. He spent his days driving around Saint Lewis with a tape-measure and clipboard. When he had to wait for a home-owner to keep an appointment –which he often did- he read the classics. When Janet was a little girl, he read to her after dinner. It would make her dad so happy if she were to get her GED and enroll in college somewhere. Maybe even study literature like he had. Her mom never missed a chance to give her shit about dropping out of high school. The old woman was pretty good at pushing her buttons, but Janet cared less and less as time went by. But it would really make her Dad proud.

Beyond that, there were times she wanted… what did she want? A white picket fence? The song from that old musical went thru her head: 'Someone's head resting on my knee -as warm and tender as he could be?' She giggled when she remembered the next line –'Warm hands, warm feet, warm face, wouldn't it be lover'ley' That would be nice. What might it be like to do the 'Hi honey, I'm home, How was your day? What do we have to eat? Ya' wan'na watch the game after dinner?' That might be very nice. It started out that way back in Topeka with Jack-the-Jerk, but he went from marijuana to coke when he could afford it, and finally meth. She shuddered and wondered if he was in jail –or still alive for that matter. Then she realized she didn't even care.

There was one guy tonight. He wouldn't pop for a lap-dance, but he bought her a cocktail. (Or what he thought was a $7.00 cocktail but was actually Red-Bull and soda. Her commission on it was $2.50. A pittance compared to what she earned on the stage or in the lap-dance room in the back.)   The guy was nice and cute too. A little different from the usual roust-abouts and roughnecks. He had kind of a college-boy thing going on. He asked polite question and listened to her answers. Looked her in the eye too – rather than at her chest- at least most of the time.

She put some Pop-Tarts in the toaster while she got ready for bed and thought about what life might be like with Kevin. One time he drove by his old house just to show her. She wasn't sure if it was to impress her, or make her feel sorry for him. Probably a little of both. This was the house his wife got in the divorce and promptly sold before she moved to California. Nice and it actually *had* a white picket fence. But that was then and now he lived in a dull apartment on the east edge of town.   She had spent a single night there in his bed for some seal-the-deal sex. It struck her as sad lonely place: minimal furniture, no plants, nothing on the walls. There were plenty of books, but only one bookcase –the rest of the books were lined up along the wall on the floor in the living room and down the hall. She never went to his apartment again. If there was to be sex, it was going to be someplace fancy. Nor would she let him come to her home. Never her home. They hooked up the time he took her to Vail. Wonderful three days and all, but despite his buying her two complete outfits and a beautiful turquoise necklace and earrings, she would have been money ahead if she worked the weekend at Willy's Place.

There was another time: a first-class all deluxe few days in Bismarck, or as deluxe as Bismarck could offer. She tried to just enjoy herself and his company, but it was still North Dakota and he was pre-occupied with work. He told her the work was beneath him, but the people he was working for –'consulting' he called it, needed his expertise and were paying him very well. She got the feeling he needed the work. There was talk of anther ski weekend, or maybe a trip to Hawaii or maybe Las Vegas. Someplace warm had more appeal than skiing.

Chapter 10

The next day dawned less cold and gray than Mike might have expected given all that he had had to drink the night before. For one thing it was less gray because it was still dark out, being as it was it was early December. Williston at the far western side of the central time zone, and about fifty miles south of the Canadian border. Plenty of dark to go around there.

As he drove by the man-camp office up the hill, he noted there was a light on so he stopped in. The odd little New Zealander who checked him in a couple of days before was now a tall woman a little younger than he was. She wasn't unattractive and he thought she might have been a looker in her youth. An imposing looker. She wasn't fat, but nor was she willowy. If the XY chromosomes had stacked up differently, she would have been a tackle or maybe a defensive end. Matching pants and blazer, dark hair pulled back, the least little but of make-up. It struck him that she had small eyes. Or it might have been the lack of makeup. He didn't know. He had a fleeting notion he might ask her out sometime, but her businesslike attitude made him dismiss the notion. There was also the supposed twenty men to one women ratio he had heard about somewhere. He supposed it applied to older women as well as the women that young oil-field workers might find interesting.

After introductions and the 'How may I help you?'s, Mike explained his problem. "I have found the guys in trailer 4-C very nice and quite educational, but I'm wondering if you might not be able to recommend a trailer with a more mature crowd. Actually, I also have a couple of questions: What are the rules on booze, and what about women visitors?"

The woman sat behind the desk leaned back thoughtfully, "I'm not sure about the maturity of the various trailers, and we have no rules about drinking, but have no tolerance for drunken nuisances. Nor have we views on women visitors."

"I am trying to be tactful here. I mean… well, I'm talking about call-girls."

The woman shrugged. "Prostitution is –of course- illegal and therefore the owner does not tolerate it, but nor is there much that can be done about it. As to another trailer, we might have a room left in the staff trailer. It should be pretty quiet."

Mike agreed to check in later that day and drove off to work. He knew there was a cloud of blue smoke coming out of his little truck's back end, but it was dark and the wind was blowing to hard it disappeared right out of the tailpipe. The sky was just lightening to the east as he hit the traffic light where 26th St. veered off to the east from Highway 2. The wait gave him the opportunity to enjoy the sunrise.

Before class started, he hit the Xerox machine in the teacher's work-room to run off a bunch of worksheets. Over the years he had written many worksheets that he felt were better than anything the textbook publishers sold. Or at least they fit his notion of how to teach math to adults. A bunch cheaper than what the textbook publishers wanted too. One of his -and his student's- favorite worksheets involved mixing cock-tails. It involved scaling up a single cocktail to a whole pitcher –for example- a pitcher of margaritas. Lots of fractions, ounces to pints, and other scary stuff, but his students enjoyed it a lot more than crap like *Bobby has 12 apples and wants to share them with his two friends*.

After "Good mornings" and role (necessary to keep the funding coming in), Mike segregated the advanced students and got them started on the cocktail problems and some multiplication drill for the struggling students. There were two new students: A young man with thick dark hair, an open honest face, tall, and with a chest like an oil-barrel. There was also a middle-aged non-descript woman. She explained that her children had grown and she was finally tackling some personal goals. And she said she hated math. No big surprise there.

There always were new faces, given the drop-in / drop-out nature of GED programs and given his student's jobs and families and whatnot. So he pulled a couple of his home-made diagnostic test out of his black bag and gave one to each of the two new students. He also gave them a short and well rehearsed lecture that there would be a lot of practice tests here in the GED classroom. *Not a bad thing –taking tests was a skill and like any skill, one that could be improved with practice –quite separate from the material in the test.* He had come to realize that there were many reasons people ended up in his GED classroom, some quite poignant & heart-breaking, some walking indictment of public education, and some other rather mundane & sadly predictable reasons. Mike was quite sure that test anxiety was responsible for more than a few of his students being there.

Then he set out to get to know the rest of his students. He compared their scores on the state's official test to where they felt they needed the most help. Usually they had pretty accurate ideas of what was what, except in one area: the multiplication tables. He decided that a good quarter of them needed to nail down these pesky little facts as a very first step- the 6's, 7's, 8's and the evil 9's in particular. He'd be damned if he was spending class time on this task, so he gave some of his student's a stack of blank business cards he had brought with him from the Bay Area. He instructed them on making their own flash-cards. He promised them that math was simply more fun if these tedious facts were burned into their memories. "Put then on your dashboard and every time you hit a red light, pick them up. You will know them in no time."

A big slow-moving guy –a new student ambled up and handed his diagnostic test to Mike. "That was quick." He sat down and slapped the key with its little holes over the multiple choice answers. It took only a minute and he was impressed. The guy had aced it. "Nice work…" he checked the student's name in the blank in the test. "…Jeff is it? Sit down. Doesn't look to me that you need a lot of help with math."

"Nozur. I'se 'ways been goo' at may-uth an' sech. I's written'n 'glish where I fells d'o-un."

Mike paused before asking the big guy to repeat himself. His first thought was that the guy hard of hearing or maybe he had a speech problem. He certainly wasn't retarded –at least not in math –but he certainly sounded… off. Took a minute to translate. "Where you from Jeff?"

"Lo-zanna. Way up'erds in t'swamp."

"Do you speak any other languages than English Jeff.?"

"French, but nary t' fancy French. They's some what calls it Creo' but my peoples more Cajun 'en Creole."

"Well, we can help you with that too. How do you feel about helping out teaching the math?"

"Fine'ze as fogzear."

"Fine as frog's hair?"

"E'yup"

Mike paused for a second. "Jeff, do you mind if I help you with your English – your accent. We don't get a lot of Creole up this far north –certainly as well seasoned a Creole as yours."

Jeff laughed and Mike was confident they would get along just as fine as frogs hair. "Jeff, you know how to make red beans and rice."

Jeff grinned. "Damn straight"

"Jambalaya? Etouffe?" They both laughed and Mike reached out to shake Jeff's hand. "Welcome to class Jeff. We are going to have us some fun. Now set yourself down and write me a one page autobiography. Just so we can see where we have to start."

Mike stood up, stretched, and walked over to check on the students doing the Margarita problem. The pretty girl from the day before was confused about the whole thing and seemed a little angry. He had had high hopes for her given the previous day's class. She seemed to have a good grasp on functions, but was lost with ratios. He tried a quick review of fractions to jump-start her to the cocktail problems. No luck, but he was seeing the glimmer of a possibility in classroom management. "Write me a one page biography and let the math go for another day."

"I write just fine, I need help with math."

"I know. Humor me." Within an hour he felt he had a good enough idea as to who was where. Enough of an idea anyway that he had a plan for the following day's class: two worksheets for two different groups: one on converting back and forth between fractions and percentages, and another one for division practice. A little one-on-one with the most advanced students, and drill on the multiplication tables for the struggling students. If he were to set up a little competition -boys against girls, they would have fun -even as adults.

Jeff, the new guy, and Janet finished their essays at about the same time. As expected, Jeff's was a mess. Spelling –such as it was- was phonetic –and highly accented phonics at that. Grammar a little better, but a there was a surprising amount of organization and the least little hint of poetry and eloquence. That is, once Mike ran it thru his mental Creole-to-English translator anyway. Janet's was dry and predictable, but handwriting, spelling, and grammar were all nearly perfect. He had a notion that she had been a perfect student as a little girl when they taught these subjects. But somewhere along the line –and given her beautiful face and stature and –no other word for it / them- her figure, Mike guessed it was shortly after adolescence that she came to find school a distraction from boys. Or perhaps more accurately, boys came to find her a distraction from their own studies and it rubbed off on her. There were any number of studies on the effects of puberty and academic performance –but none –as far as he knew- that considered breast size as a contributing variable. Maybe someone needed to do this study.

He brought himself back to the matter at hand with a start. He was too old to concern himself with his student's boobs. But he wasn't dead either. Both students were sitting at his table. Jeff trying to ogle Janet without appearing to, and Janet ignored him. "As I suspected. Let me introduce you to one another. Janet, this is Jeff. Jeff, this here is Janet. Janet, Jeff is very good at math, Jeff, Janet is an excellent writer and her English is perfect. Can you guess where I'm going with this?"

Jeff was understandably enthused about the idea. Janet less so. "I just want to get thru the math test. I've passed some of the other ones. Why can't you help me?" A brief look of disappointment crossed Jeff's face.

"You are not ready to pass it now. Do you have any plans to go on to college Janet?"

"Yes, someday. Maybe. I guess."

"Then you are going to need Algebra and I simply don't have time to take away from the other students to get you there. I will keep an eye on your progress, but I think Jeff can get you over the top and well into the territory you will need to do college level work. And there is the other side of the equation. Jeff needs help with his writing. And his accent is more than a little rough around the edges too. If you two were to work together, you both would benefit and not just in the areas where you think you need help.

Like they say, the best way to learn something is to teach it. Jeff, your math will improve for helping Janet and Janet, your own writing will improve for helping Jeff." Mike didn't add *And maybe you can learn to add a little description to your own plodding narratives.* but it surely occurred to him.

"Think about it. Discuss your schedules and logistics –where you each live and all. If you were to stick around after class and put your heads together for even an hour every day, I am quite confident you both would be pleased with the results."

All in all it was a good day. Some solid progress with the multiplication tables – or at least some of his students made a commitment to think about planning to consider the possibility of taking up the problem. You took what you could get. The mid-level student's were working and probably learning. He was sure he had made Jeff's day –if not his entire week. Only a couple of smallish flies in his ointment; One -Janet was not happy with his proposal, and two, Jeff was entirely too pleased. Given things they way they were in Williston, Mike hoped he had not started something that might end up with his needing to testify in court.

Chapter 11

Kevin had mixed feelings about going to the strip club. First, he got to take his rich-guy persona and go see Janet. On the other hand, the guy who summoned him -and a right scary guy he was– would want to know how things were going with the investment made by some even scarier people in Kansas City. Kevin had never met these investors, but had signed documents with himself personally as the general partner AND one of the limited partners as partnerships in a holding company. Perfectly legal, but back-ass-ward for the general to be a junior limited partner as well. It was also the sort of thing the IRS looked at very closely.

It had all changed after the divorce. Everyone was getting divorces. Except of course, apparently not everyone in North Dakota –or apparently not any of his Lutheran farmer clients anyway. And, yes, she had put him thru law school, and yes, she had stayed home to raise the kids, but the kids were out of the house now, and no one could blame a successful middle aged professional money-man for one little fling. Except of course it wasn't just one. And except of course, apparently they could. She took pretty much everything but the partnerships. Not much she could do with them anyway. A license to practice law was not strictly speaking necessary, but there was a lot of work to be done even if it much of it was depositing rent checks that came in like clock-work from about half the oil field service companies on Fortune Magazine's list of the biggest oil-field-service companies. There was even one big oil company that hired the service companies. Most of the money went back out anyway, but equity was a-building –as he liked to remind is clients.

The divorce happened as he was beginning to fund the man-camp partnership. His ex hadn't been bashful about airing the dirty linen and the farmers got bashful in their own way. Damn it, they were getting great returns on the Butler buildings, but… A few came thru, but not as much as he needed so he decided to take a large equity position himself. All he needed was money but she had it all. So he started taking on new clients for the first time since he started doing the partnerships and went back to work doing simple CPA stuff. He did a little consulting, some tax defense work, and lived like a pauper for about a year.

One of these new clients was the putative manager of one of Williston's two strip clubs down by the railroad station. He was hesitant to be seen there, but he was certainly curious about such a business. He concluded he didn't have much to loose reputation-wise and for that matter, what –exactly- would one of his Lutheran farmer clients be doing at such a place anyway? Melvin was a short compact man given to wearing western-cut sport coats over pastel-colored cowboy shirts and lizard-skin cowboy boots. He had a Brooklyn accent that made his small size and dress almost comical. But Kevin was careful to respect the guy, and as he learned more about him and his business, he was increasingly careful. It was an interesting business. Lots of cash from drinks and cover-charges. One of the minor income streams was the fee dancers paid each night to dance. The dancers paid these fees willingly to be able to harvest astounding amounts of money from the horny & lonely oil field workers.

It was probably a very good thing that Kevin was both a lawyer and an accountant. He more that expected that all the cash that came thru the door did not make it into the businesses' books and the IRS knew nothing about some of it. Melvin never went so far as to mention money laundering, but it was quite clear that a lot of money went somewhere out of state. He asked about ownership and never got a clear answer. Melvin was the owner, but lease payments for all manner of bar equipment, the music system, lights, furniture, and even the two stages and stripper poles all went to different businesses, but all at the same address in Kansas.   Kevin didn't need to know the actual value of it all, and he didn't ask, but there was no way in hell that these payments were reasonable for a smallish one story building with the minimum required facilities. As lawyer these irregularities could be overlooked –maybe even ethically- as a part of rigorous advocacy on behalf of his client. Accountants, on the other hand, were supposed to represent the client, the public, and -God help them- the IRS, All at the same time.

The man camp went ahead, but he took some shortcuts, did it in stages, and it went slowly but the boom just kept on booming. He had saved up just barely enough to leverage his way into a majority position on the man camp, when in June of 2009, several things happened at in short order. First, the earth work had been started when city got backed out on a commitment to pipe water and sewer to the man-camp. Second, his earth-moving client Vern mentioned he had done the prep work for a small water purification plant to augment a shallow water-well for another man-camp way out in the sticks. Next, Mel at the strip club asked him in an off hand kind of way, what he –Kevin- did for investments and what he –Mel- might consider to enjoy some of the boom outside of the naked-girl and watered-down-booze business. Finally, Mel introduced him to one of the girls that worked at Willy's Place.

Within a week, the water problem was resolved with a loan from Mel's people in Kansas and he had the most extraordinary weekend of his life in Vail with Janet.

And now –about three months later- Kevin was both the general partner and a limited partner in a man-camp with a vague scary foreign holding company as the senior limited partner in that partnership and a small water treatment plant as collateral to that senior position. If he hadn't drawn up the contracts himself, he wouldn't have believed it. So on this cold afternoon, the local representative of the senior limited partner asked for a meeting. Nothing to do but straighten his tie, grab his briefcase, and head over to that side of town. He stalled till about 4:PM when he thought Janet might be working.

The doorman / bouncer seemed unimpressed with his tailored three piece and said "That'll be $10 cover."

"I have an appointment with Mr. Koptick."

The big guy didn't even look up from his the newspaper spread out on the counter and picked up a phone. In the time it took for the guy to press a couple of buttons, mutter something about an appointment, and wait for an answer, he seriously considered turning around and walking off, and phoning Mel to complain. It came down to playing the insulted professional who had better things to do, vs. the humble borrower who owed about $200,000 to some scary people. It was close, but staying won out.

"OK, you can go in" the bouncer mumbled; still not without bothering to look up from the sports page.

Kevin stood directly in front of him and waited until the jerk looked up. "You will remember me?" The guy gave him a surly nod. "I beg your pardon, w*ill* you be able to remember me?" He leaned closer, "Is there some way I can help you to remember me in the future?"

There was a pause, but Kevin won. "Yes sir." Such was the power of the suit. A small win to be sure, but given what he expected lay ahead, he was grateful for the win and passed thru the sparse late afternoon crowd to Mel's office in the back. He even largely ignored the little Asian girl on the stage who was down to panties and bra. A bit beneath his dignity to wait for her to get more naked.

Mel's office was small, but surprisingly nice. Oak desk with matching credenza behind and a love seat in front. On the couch was Janet. She was sprawled out casually in a green sweater that matched her eyes, soft and tight to emphasize her girls. Incongruously, she was wearing black sweat pants and bedroom slippers, but Kevin was sure there was something considerably nicer under it all. She seemed happy to see him, but her manner -as always- was a bit aloof.

Mel on the other hand, was effusive. "Welcome Kevin. Come in. Come in. Can I get you a drink? How about a beer? Janet, would you get our councilor a drink?"

Janet got up and smiled at him with just a little more warmth. "What would you like Mr. Ahmundson?"

"Coffee would be nice. Cream, No sugar." Kevin was just barely self aware enough to note the stiffness in his own manner –after the fact. Was he an adolescent pretending to be a grown-up. God, she was lovely, When she slipped past him he could smell her perfume and was –for the moment- back in bed with her that glorious weekend in Vail.

When Janet shut the door behind herself, Mel's attitude cooled noticeably. "What shall I tell our associates about their investment in the man-camp.?"
"Nothing yet, well, not nothing, good cash flow and good write-off. I do not know what

your… associates want for a return, It is returning 9%. In this economy, that's great."

"Be that as it may, our expectations in this investment were higher. 9% was only acceptable for a limited time, and callable at our discretion. It looks to us like the place is well occupied and should be returning at least 12 if not 15%. Frankly there is some concern that someone is skimming."

A chill went up the lawyer's spine. "You can not think I am skimming."

Melvin simply shrugged. "There are some talented people from Chicago who might be able to clarify the issue."

"Clarify it? How?"

"Nothing worrisome –think of them as private detectives. One such individual is –in fact- already on the scene in our man-camp."

Kevin relaxed a bit as Mel continued. "But Councilor, please understand that if the situation is not corrected, and corrected soon, my associates will become quite insistent on calling the loan." He got very un-relaxed once again. There was dead silence for a moment and then with timing so perfect he wondered if Mel did not have a button under his desk, Janet came in with a cup of coffee and the scary little guy's mood changed to collegial good will. "How are things looking for Willy's Place numbers?"

"You are doing fine. I have been doing a little research on how businesses with a lot of cash income can protect themselves from predatory IRS audits and so forth. I haven't come up with anything workable just yet."

"Well carry on –goodness knows we get a lot of cash and the poor girls earn most of their money as tips. The IRS has been most unfair in this matter of late." Mel got up from behind his desk. "If you two will excuse me, I have to check on the delivery of some liquor. No rest for the wicked." He chuckled at his own little joke. Janet followed him to the door and made a show of locking it behind him.

She knelt on the floor in front of Kevin and put her palms on his thighs and looked at him for a moment, "Can we talk?"

He cleared his throat, "You want to take another trip together?"

"Sweetie, you know how much I loose when I don't work."
Kevin knew all too well. The ordeal he had just survived left him feeling wrung out and he found himself uncharacteristically blunt. "Janet my dear, I can pay you for another weekend if you like…" and he knew would if it came to it, "…but isn't there something else I could do for you? Perhaps a little equity position in an oil lease? And I still want to find a good way for you to invest your money without… well, without giving up a bunch of it in taxes first." He knew –or strongly suspected- that most of her income was cash and she certainly didn't declare all of it. Nor did he blame her, but was she ever going to acquire real wealth or security by stuffing in under her mattress no matter how much she stuffed.

"How much money is an oil lease?"

Kevin realized Janet had little to no idea as to how money worked; especially the time value of money. For her, all money was right-now money. He thought for a moment about how he might teach her how to become a reasonably savvy investor. As much as he loved her body and having sex with her, and as much as he wanted to have some more & have it soon, it occurred to him it might be fun to sit down with her, side by side at his desk, or at the kitchen table, or even in bed afterwards, and do the whole teacher / student thing. "An oil lease –or any lease for that matter- is an income stream. It's like paying rent, only *you* get the checks."

"Then how do you know what something is worth if you don't get the money first? My friend Tonia turns tricks sometimes and she always says you have to get paid first –right away."

"Oh. That' easy. You do a present value calculation. I can teach you that."

Her eyes flashed and she leaned away from him as she tilted her head like a dog trying to understand what it sees. Something was wrong here. She stood up and her gaze was direct and a little threatening. "So it's math?"

He nodded with mild confusion.

"And you can teach me?"

He shrugged, "Well sure." He smiled trying to break the tension. "What's the matter? You don't like math?"

This was apparently the wrong thing to say. She went to the door, unlocked it and said, "I have to go." She left without another word.

Chapter 12

After class Mike stopped in his boss's office. "Hi Linda, How are things in administration land?"

"About the same. How are things in the classroom?"

"Getting there. Two steps forward and one back. About what to be expected. One student has passed her math test. Two other students are helping each other. He is helping her with math and she is helping him with his writing. They started a little rough, but much learning is happening now –on both sides" Mike paused, "Linda, I simply can not live on what you are paying me –a single class a day. The hourly pay is fine, but I need more hours. Can you tell me honestly when the powers-that-be are making kicking off the night class."

'It looks like it will be by spring semester -late March."

He nodded, turned and was walking out when Linda said "I'm sorry" to his back. He didn't see much point in continuing the conversation.

On the way back to the man-camp, he stopped at Bakken Staffing. The business was in what appeared to be a converted gas station about a block from the train station. There was a long counter along one side and a few cheap round tables with miss-matched chairs scattered about. The focus of the room was a big screen TV above a table with a big coffee urn. Mike looked around while his eyes adjusted to the gloom. There were half a dozen men sitting at the tables, some his age and some younger. None dressed in anything but jeans and sweatshirt hoodies over various bland jackets or greasy parkas. One or two had thick padded coveralls unzipped to the waist. A more careful study of the men was not encouraging. The guys his age were a sad and desperate looking lot. Mostly unshaved –a couple with sunken blood-shot eyes –one seemed to have the shakes. The younger men were not much more energetic. They all stared dumbly at the TV except for a few who were dozing with their arms folded and heads down.

He stepped up the counter and waited for a woman to finish tapping on her computer keyboard and notice him. "How may I help you?"

"Well, I'm looking for work."

"What do you do?"

"I'm a teacher, but I'm flexible."

"Do you have a CDL?"

"CDL? I guess not. What's a CDL?"

"Commercial Driver's License."

"Oh. No. No need for teachers?

"We need drivers and construction workers. You never know what we might get a call for, but not teachers. Can you do anything in the construction field?"

"I'm a little old aren't I?" She just shrugged. "May I leave a resume?"

She didn't even answer the question, but pulled out a stapled stack of papers. "Fill this out and we will see. Come back tomorrow at 1:PM for orientation."

What else could he say but, "Thank you." and he walked out. As he was waiting behind a long line of tankers for a green light to get out of town, he flipped thru the packet. Pretty standard stuff, but there was a long checklist of job skills, things like welding, sheet-rock, nursing, short-order cook, carpenter, fork-lift, 10-key, and he read down the list with a sinking feeling. He had none of the skills they listed. How the eff could he have lived more than 50 years and end up with no marketable skills. He had gotten a job on a framing crew out of high-school and had –from time to time- pounded nails in various ways and durations for various degrees of income –usually just-barely-in-time income, but it had been a lot of years.

He remembered the sad-looking men watching TV or sleeping in the plastic patio-chairs. He guessed some of them were sent out to do physical work, couldn't keep up, and then weren't called back for another day's work first thing the next morning. So they sat in the sad waiting area all morning hoping there would be a call for less demanding work –or warmer work. Some might be talented and well paid specialized tradesmen –welders and electricians, and as such, they might have to wait a day or two to be called for comparatively higher wages. Some might still be called that afternoon, but he wondered how many of them -and this was the sad part- were there to stay warm. He stuffed the papers back onto his black bag. He wasn't there yet. Might not be long before he got there, but not yet. It would probably do him a world of good to do a few weeks of physical labor. If the work didn't kill him first. If the cold didn't kill him second.

He stopped at the man-camp's trailer office. The same woman he had spoken to the previous morning was at the desk in the converted 'living room.' "Good morning. Sara Mahon, isn't it?"

"Yep –and you were asking about a quieter trailer as I recall?"

"Yes mam. Nothing wrong with most of the people who are in the trailer you assigned me to previously, but there is one young fellow… well, no matter. It appears to be a company trailer for Slumberton as it is. Anything else come to mind?"

"Well yes. We have a room in the staff trailer. This is where our maintenance guys live. Our old cook used to have a room there, but he disappeared. The new cook lives in the kitchen trailer. Should be pretty quiet. What are your hours like?"

"I teach mornings for the time being, but expect to be teaching an evening class as well, starting sometime in the spring I guess. Other than pounding on my lap-top, I am a quiet guy. For that matter, if you needed some help afternoons, I could help out with the maintenance –or cooking for that matter?"

"Had any experience with either?"

"I used to be a carpenter –did a little of this and that along the way. I'm good with tools and all. I am a hell of a cook, but I haven't cooked more food than necessary for a nice big dinner party at any given time.   Pretty sure I could pick it up quickly and be helpful."

"You teach In Williston? At the college on the east side of town? Could you do some shopping coming and going?"

"Sure."

She nodded, turned to the side, and dug thru an open filing cabinet. "Fill out an application and I'll check your references and all, but yes, we might be able to help each other out." I can't pay much, but I could give you a break on rent." She handed him a stapled packet of forms. He glanced at it as he put it into his black bag next to the one from Bakken Staffing. A small improvement, but an improvement none the less.

"How much is… 'a break'?"

"Um… Free if you give me 20 hours a week."

Mike did a quick mental calculation. Given what he was paying to live there, the deal wasn't half bad. "One last thing, how is the internet connection in this trailer?"

"It's one row over and three trailers down, so it should be pretty good. The router is next door."

"I'll go back to my trailer to get addresses and phone numbers for the application. Be back in half an hour?"

When he returned with the forms, she gave him the key to the other trailer and promised him she would have an answer about the job by the next day –provided she could get in touch with his references. Things were looking up. He was confident his friends and previous employers would support him, and he wasn't sure his credit card could stand another week's room charge. The image of the men sleeping in the Bakken Staffing waiting area crossed his mind. Momentarily he wondered if any of them were going to be spending a cold night in their cars when the place closed. He packed his clothes, books, & computer back into banana boxes and put it all in the back of his little pick-up. He drove up nine trailers and over one row. Fifteen minutes from starting to pack in one room to being unpacked and moved into a room that was identical to the on he left behind. And like the previous day, he was alone.

Chapter 13

Jeff worked 12 hour shifts in Slumberburton's warehouse at the north side of town. He had been a roughneck off-shore when he lived down in Louisiana and worked with big heavy steel things as a matter of course. In Williston, part of his job was to fork-lift these things off big steel racks and onto trucks heading out to the field. As big as it was, this equipment was usually smaller than the stuff he was used to seeing on the big jack-up rigs out in the Gulf of Mexico. There was also a lot of silly stuff like fire-proof cover-alls, engine air filters, and office supplies. Curious that the guys out on the rig were better able to communicate with the computer to order the correct right-handed-smoke-shifter while the administrators and office dorks always seemed to need to return this form or that ream of copy paper for a different color. More paperwork for him and the other warehouse guys. And the rig workers were usually nicer too.

After 14 days on, he got 7 days off. It sounded like a long time to enjoy doing this and that, but the truth was that the first day or two he had off, he spent catching up on his sleep and another day or two after that usually got eaten up with laundry, shopping, and all the hundred little things that most folks did on the way home from work. But not those folks that worked from 6:PM to 6:AM.

They had wanted to make him a shift supervisor –he had been at it for a year now and that made him senior. Lots of guys and some gals came and went from his little three man crew. Some of them got canned because they couldn't hack the hours without drugs or they otherwise screwed up. Some just couldn't face another 14 days straight and didn't show up at work after seven days off and the long stretch of week started again. Then there were some who left because they got training and moved on to better jobs. His boss had started the process for Jeff to get the training till it came to the point he had to fill in the paper-work about when and where he graduated high school. He had to leave it blank. There hadn't seemed to be much point in staying in school in Louisiana when he was making $60,000 a year working off-shore.

This was back when oil was going for north of $100 a barrel. Things slowed down '08 when oil dropped back to $30 a barrel but they got a lot worse in 2010 when BP's Deep Water Horizon offshore rig sprang a leek. Obama shut down all the offshore drilling and a lot of people had to get by on their savings. Some folks had savings, but not many and not Jeff. He had a lot of fun, a nice wardrobe, and big-ass pick-up that was only half paid off. And not a lot else. There was also one parish he avoided very carefully. A small matter of the sheriff wanting his ass for some trifling speeding and reckless driving tickets he didn't pay. And also the rumor of a newborn that he might have had something to do with. All things considered, he decided to make the move to North Dakota. Froze his ass off, and did shit jobs, but he stayed alive, learned how to stay warm, and eventually got back into the oil game. And now he worked inside.

And he had a reason to be especially happy about working the night shift just now. His boss told him that Williston State College had a morning GED prep thing going on and he thought what-the hell –he could put off bedtime for a few hours after getting off work and check it out. The teacher seemed a nice enough guy, but the big news was the stomping hot girl the teacher had asked him to help with math. Janet was about his age, and tall –not nearly as tall as he was, but tall for a woman. Tight ass. Long black hair. She had a kind of a sophisto-bitch thing going on, but she had the face to pull it off. And her boobs. Sweet Jesus -high and proud.

He had noticed that when a woman caught his eye, those things that made her what she was, seemed to him to be his all time favorite. Cute little cuddly chicks one day, skinny redheads the next. Blonds of every shape and size seemed to cross his radar regularly, but now he was sure tall leggy brunets with spectacular boobs were now and forever his all-time very favorite.

He was about to have seven days off and then it was shift change. He had hoped to seal the deal with her soon, not just because he wanted to seal the deal, but also because after his week off, he would be working days and he wouldn't be able to see her in the mornings for a little while anyway. He figured his best bet was to move things along to the point that they could get together some other time of the day to study together. First he would have to catch up on his sleep though. He always needed a day or two, but the past week had been particularly punishing. He hadn't missed a day of class. Twelve hours at work, a little driving to and from, and 3 hours in class every morning didn't leave much time for eating and sleeping.

It was still dark when he got home to the little house he shared with five other guys. All the other guys were either off at work or asleep, so he made himself a sandwich, and stretched out on the beat-up couch in the living room. He pulled a blanket over himself, and just barely finished the sandwich before he nodded off. He felt it a good omen that the thought of Janet that woke him up in time to grab a shower and get to class just at 9:AM. The teacher was happy to see him. Janet not so much. She was sitting in her usual place in front and off to the side and didn't even look up when he came in. The other students were either reading or chatting at the coffee urn. He put his book bag down at Janet's table and returned her indifference by getting himself a cup of coffee and joining the inane conversation about how cold it was.

When he sat down Janet favored him by glancing up at him briefly. "Morning Janet. How are 'em pesky fractions treating you?"

"*Those* pesky fractions. And I don't get how a fraction can be less than one, but it can also be more than one –you called it an improper fraction or some-damn-thing."

"Oh. Ya, 'at's a ponderment, in't it?' He caught himself as she started a correction. "*That* is a ponderment, is it not?"

Mike strolled up about then and Janet asked, "Is it good English to say something is a 'ponderment'?"

"I think so. A little old fashioned maybe. Or vernacular. Is friend Jeff seasoning our bland mid-west patois with a tangy bit of the deep south is he?"

Jeff laughed. Janet didn't. "Tell Janet how a fraction can be both less'en one and more'en one."

It took Mike a few minutes with a number line on the white board to sort it all out for Janet. Then he left them alone so Jeff could help her add up various fractions – proper and improper –greater and lesser than one.

In Jeff's estimation, this was all fine and well, but completely sterile. They sat side by side for an hour or so, heads together, talking quietly, and she smelled good, but the damn math got in the way. This morning however, he had taken steps to get a reaction one way or another.

Mike had assigned him a paper to pick someone living or dead, real or imaginary and write about them. It was to have an introductory paragraph, two main descriptive paragraphs –one objective and one subjective and finally, a tight summary paragraph. He chose this study-buddy Janet. He spent all of his 30 minute lunch hour on a rough draft the night before and refined it during idle moments in the wee hours of the morning.   The objective paragraph was easy. Well. not easy exactly –he had to take a couple of runs at it to get what he thought was the right tone of vivid description without dwelling on her ass and boobs, but he thought he got it right. The subjective one was harder. He was aiming for a sensitive view of her as a nice person who had to protect herself from a cruel world that saw only her beauty not the real person. The concluding paragraph was the hardest of all –and again, he was pleased with how it came out. Just a hint of how he imagined she would come to care for a descent guy and live happily ever after.

When she was running out of math patience and energy –and it only ever lasted an hour, he pulled out his paper, slid it across the table.. "See what'chu make of this. Ya' want some cawffee?"

"No thank you."

He left the table so she could read it alone, but he watched her carefully from the coffee urn across the room.   He wasn't able to see any reaction. He took his time with his coffee. She was marking up spelling errors when he sat down again.

"Well?"

"Grammar is a little better. Spelling is still bad. And I don't understand the third paragraph. All about how this woman feels about other people and what she wants in the future. I just don't get it."

With out further discussion she was off explaining nouns and verbs and how they had to agree. Some stuff about who and whom and not putting prepositions at the end of sentences. Jeff didn't understand a lot of what she said under the best of circumstances, but he was so disappointed that she didn't get the point of his writing that he barely heard anything she said.

"Well, thank you. I… um… I'll keep trying." He opened up a grammar workbook Mike had given him and puzzled thru the rules about pronouns –what ever the eff they were. It was beginning to make some small sense, but he just couldn't get past Janet's having missed the point of his writing. Any plans he had to ask her out were put aside.

After class, and after Janet left, he walked up to the teacher. "Mike, I know class is over, but could you'all read som'ing I wrote?"

"Sure" He sat down and give it a thoughtful read. He sighed and read it again. "Well, Janet's corrections are spot on. That's not the issue is it?"

"Can ya' tell iz 'bout her?'

"Yes. Pretty obvious. Actually, setting aside the spelling and grammar, it's pretty good writing. You aren't asking me to… I don't know… give you advice on your love life are you?"

"No'zur. She di'nt seem to realize it wuz 'bout her. I thought I did a better job'o writin'… kind'a… what do you call it 'subtle'?, and all."

Mike nodded. "I can only say it's pretty good descriptive writing, well organized and thoughtful. Almost poetic in places. She has done the spelling and grammar corrections for you. As to Janet's reactions or feelings, what can I say? She is a pretty girl and here in Williston, pretty girls are scarce –particularly given the number of men here. Jeff, I will say this. Her writing is pretty literal –and she strikes me as a pretty literal –straight-forward young woman. Happy to see my student's getting along in an academic kind of way. And even in an adult kind of way, being that this is adult education and all. But you have to know I can't help you in otherwise."

Chapter 14

It was a nice day for Williston -cold but clear and no wind. Above zero -close to freezing even. When Mike drove back to the man-camp, there was just the beginning of wet water on the roads –particularly those roads with dark asphalt that had soaked up full sunshine all morning. His poor little truck started that morning, but he figured it only had a limited number of starts left in it and he didn't want to waste even one grinding start, so he parked in front of his new trailer and walked back to the office-trailer. There was snow to the east of each of the buildings. Probably a lot more had fallen, but the eternal wind out of the west blew it away. Blew it all the way into Minnesota for all he knew.

t was a nice enough day for a short walk –weather wise, but the footing was bad. Seemed gravity was a little stronger every year and nice even ground underfoot was increasingly important to him. The dirt between the trailers was still frozen and deeply rutted. Clearly it had been mud, then driven thru, then frozen –perhaps repeatedly- until finally it stayed frozen. Going to be a hell-of-a- mess whenever it thawed out. Perhaps sometime in May or June.

The tall –slightly scary- woman from yesterday was sitting at her desk when he came in. "Good morning. Sara isn't it? Or do you want me to address you as Mrs. … I'm sorry –I forgot your last name."

"It's 'Mahon' and it's Ms., but call me Sara."

"So am I an employee?"

"I haven't heard back from all your references yet, but the cook needs some help today. I will need you to do a regular time card and I-9 for taxes and all. Even though you aren't getting paid. Taxes are up to you. We will not be doing withholding for you."

"How do you do withholding on no income?"

"It's called 'in-kind pay.' Ask your tax guy. In any event, we aren't doing it.' Are we in agreement that three hours a day will pay for a night's lodging?"

"3 hours on Saturday as well as 3 hours for Sunday?"

"Ya, but if you want a day off, you can work more than 3 hours on another day. In fact, if you could work a long day, the cook could have some time off. That would be helpful."

"We will have to see how it all sorts itself out –schedule wise, but I'm sure we can make it work."

"Good." She turned back to the file cabinet and dug out a folder and pulled the various tax papers. "Here, fill these out." She punched a few numbers into her phone while Mike started the name, address, SSN thing. There was a long pause. "Hello Chef. Did I wake you?" She didn't wait for an answer. "I told you about that guy who wanted to help out around here. I am here with Mike Williams. Do you need some help now?" She fiddled with her ballpoint. "An hour or two? That's fine. He can help out with the laundry for a little while first." Pause "Good. OK. And give him the shopping list for tomorrow. He goes into Williston every morning." Sara looked directly at Mike for confirmation and he nodded understanding & agreement. "Good. Thank you."

Sara hung up. "OK. Chef isn't ready for you yet. I suspect he was sleeping. He needs about an hour, so there is a pile of laundry in the next room and four washing machines & dryers. It's all whites. Half a cup of detergent at the start and a cup of bleach once the water is full. Fold things up when they come out of the dryer. Don't try to start more than one machine at a time or you will blow a fuse. And if you can, don't run more that three at once. Try to be loading and unloading and folding while the other three are running. Any question?"

"Nope. I'll just pop off and change clothes first?"

"Good. Off you go. And write your hours and what you are doing. Good records should not be a problem for a math teacher, right?"

During the walk back to his trailer, Mike examined his own thinking. Two majors and a minor, another year of post-grad work to be get a teacher's credential, in not one, but three subjects, fifty some years old and he was a washer-woman here in fucking Williston, North Dakota. On the other hand, who knew him here in North Dakota? He was not likely to run into anyone from high-school who had gone on to be wildly successful while he was here measuring out bleach. For that matter, he had to admit to himself that he had been something of an ass in high school and college too for that matter. If he did run into someone from back in the day, he would probably deserve a ration of shit. Or worse, deserve a heaping-helping of polite bemusement & surprise. Mercifully, the days of chasing women by first trying to acquire the expensive things that impressed women were long past. He was a little curious about the withholding tax on no income thing. Sadly, he didn't have a 'tax-guy' to ask. Not much need for an income tax guy when there was no income to tax.

For the moment, he was –or would soon be- living within his means. Hadn't been that way in a while. A long while. He doubted the Prozac had had a chance to do its work quite yet, but he decided he felt good about the whole thing. Who knew, if he did a good job as a cook's helper and laundry guy, there might be some future in it. Or maybe whatever damn committee that made these decisions would decide there needed to be an evening class and then –please-Jesus- maybe even an afternoon class as well.

He paused at the foot of the five steps up to the trailer and pondered his little Japanese pick-up. If, and it was a big if, if his transportation remained reliable. His little white truck was twenty years old and burning oil. It was usually happy to start, but not enthused about doing so in these cold North Dakota mornings. After changing clothes, he checked the oil level. A little low, but he had most of a gallon jug of motor oil he carried all the time. Simple matter to add about a pint before going on to do laundry. He made a mental note to check the owner's manual on light-weight winter oil.

When he got back to the office / laundry trailer, he had emoted one dryer and was about to empty another when he remembered Sara's instructions about not over taxing the circuits, so he unloaded a washer into a dryer, started it, reloaded the washing machine from the pile on the floor, and started it up. All told, it took him about two minutes to noodle out the math of optimum use of the machines and his own time. He began to cast about for other things to do while on laundry duty. Nothing occurred to him other than some general tidying and organizing, but he felt his attitude was on the right track. He made another mental note to ask Sara about what else might need doing between the loading, unloading, and folding. Tomorrow would be soon enough –after he had gotten more of the lay of the land.

He was finishing the second wash-dry-fold go-around when Sara came in and checked up on him. She didn't say anything, but she seemed to note how tidy and organized he had gotten the laundry room. "Rudy is ready for your help." She paused thoughtfully. "Listen. This guy is good and we are lucky to get him when the previous cook quit rather suddenly. He is a little…, well, you will find out what he is… spooky maybe. But please be sure to stay on his good side and do what you can to make sure he stays happy. 'K?"

There seemed to be no one there when he got to the cooking trailer. Something was in the oven and it smelled good. It was clearly the cooking trailer. Where the other trailers had a couch and small dining table under a big screen TV in the 'living room' this one had shelves all along the wall where the TV would have been otherwise. There were boxes piled on the floor on the wall opposite the front door and a small counter just under the window. There was no couch, but a big work table, and while the other trailers had two refrigerators, this one had three lined up on the wall opposite the sink. Otherwise it had the same counter-top, stove / oven, and dish-washer as his trailer.

He was poking thru boxes on the floor –staples mostly- when he heard footsteps and turned to find what had to be the hairiest little guy he had ever seen. It wasn't that his hair was long, or even that he had beard, but his hair was thick, jet black -blue almost, and his brow had a deep widow's peak nearly reached his eye brows. Correction: his single eyebrow.   He was about 5'4,"whippet thin and Mike was sure he was also whippet quick. "You must be Mike? You are here to help me, right? You will call me 'Chef'"

"OK" They shook hands, but it was an awkward thing. Chef seemed hesitant to do so, but for a little guy, he had a crushing grip –enthusiastic or not. "What needs doing?" Mike decided this was going to be his mantra. – *What needs doing?* Good attitude and all.

"I understand you are working for lodging?"

"Yep, three hours a day."

"And you are filling out your hours and giving them to Mahon?"

For just a moment Mike was put off by the guy's attitude. He considered suggesting to the cook that it was none of his concern, but he stopped himself. He was getting into his new self-image as a simple easy-going blue-collar worker, and the cook was is boss after all –or one of them. "Ya, well, no. She has me emailing her a description of what I do every day. I did have to do the W-9 and all, but no with-holding and no time sheets. Pretty informal."

"You are living in what they call the staff trailer with some other workers?"

"Yep. The maintenance guy lives there. Has for some time I gather. Sometimes the other guy who runs in the office when Ms. Mahon is off – he sleeps there, but I think he has a place in town. There is a girl who makes beds and tidies up the trailers has a room. But I've not met any of them. Pretty quiet all in all"

"How many of you are working for your lodging?"

"I'm not sure. The maintenance guy I think."

The cook nodded. "Empty the dishwasher. Figure out where to put tools and pots & pans as you go along. Dishes, glasses, and silverware and all go to the dining-trailer next door. Stack them up on that counter under the window. Then open the window, go around outside, and carry it all into the dining trailer." Without another word, the guy turned and walked back down the hall and shut the door behind him. Mike figured it was his bedroom or office and clearly off-limits.

Mike finished with the assigned tasks and gave the counter & sink a thorough tidying & cleaning and noted the time. It had been just over three hours, so he knocked on the door where he heard the cook's voice. "Sorry to bother you Chef, but I've run out of things to do Sara wanted me to work just three hours."

"Get tomorrow's shopping list after dinner."

That seemed to be about all he was going to hear, so he went back to his trailer to check his email and take a nap.

Chapter 15

Jeff figured it had to be this morning. This was the last day of his week off and tomorrow morning he started the day shift. No more morning GED class and no more Janet. He had made it to class on time and stayed till the end all the past week, but he had to give up on a little of his end-of-the-week catch-up sleep to do it. No doubt his writing benefited from Janet's help. He also felt he was ready to start taking the GED exams. The teacher said he was ready for math and perhaps science. But not writing just yet.

But as productive as this time had been academically, if was a complete bust as far as Janet was concerned. He had asked her to lunch –all casual like- after class and was shot down dismissively. One way or the other he was going to move things forward with her and it had to be today. He got to class before she did and sat himself down at their usual table off to the side of the classroom. Then he got up nervously and got himself a cup of coffee. He was staring out at the early-morning glare of the sunrise in a cold crystalline blue sky when she came in and dumped her books on the table. "Having a bad morning are we Janet?"

"Ya. Been working too many late nights."

"Where do you work anyway?"

"It's not important. Can you help me with these story problems?"

Despite his infatuation, Jeff was getting a little tired of her cool dismissive attitude. "Janet, I tol' you I am goin' to be working morn'ens starting tomorrow. If we are go'n to keep he'ping each, we are going to need to find another time or place."

"Then I guess we will have to stop. I can't take evenings off. Just simply can't."

Jeff said nothing for a moment –just looked at her as she took her books and papers out of her backpack. She was the very picture of businesslike indifference. "And I suppose you work seven nights a week?"

"Yep. Pretty much"

Wasn't much he could say now. He took a deep breath and stepped over to the table where Mike was talking to some of the other students about the American Revolution. He listened for a minute. If he ever knew it, he had forgotten that there were some fine and decent colonists that sincerely wanted to stay subjects of the crown and there were some English guys living in England who were just as convinced that war was a waste of time, treasure, & lives and the crown should pull its soldiers out of that quagmire that was the American colonies. Jeff had a much older cousin who had served in Nam, and when the old boy had had a few beers, he heard all about it. It reminded him of his cousin's rantings, but it struck him that only a couple of the older students at the table understood what the teacher was getting at.

When Mike wound down, he turned to Jeff and did their shtick. "Morning Jeff. Hoz' ever' lil' thing?"

"Fine z-frog zair. Looky here teach, I'm starting the day shift 'morrow. Won't be coming in for a spell."

"I understand. There might be a night class starting shortly, but it's 'still in committee'." Mike did the air quotes thing to indicate 'shortly' might be anytime in the next hundred years. "But I think you are ready for the math test. And if you are not ready for the science test, you can easily get yourself ready for it by reading the workbook every evening for an hour or so. Will you and Janet be able to find a way to keep working together?"

Jeff simply shook his head.

Mike grimaced sadly and nodded resignation. "That's a shame; I think you have been able to really help one another."

He gestured to Jeff to walk with him over to the table where Janet was sitting. "Good morning Janet. I understand you and Jeff will be setting aside your partnership for a while?"

"It's not a partnership." Janet snapped and Jeff made a point of looking very carefully at a far corner of the room opposite from where Janet was sitting.

Oops… thought Mike to himself. …touched a nerve here, didn't I? He remembered paper Jeff had written about Janet and decided to tread softly. "Let's do this. How about some practice tests and we will see if you have helped one another enough yet. Always a good thing –a practice test. Is this a good plan?"

Janet and Jeff both nodded -Janet perhaps a little less enthusiastically than Jeff. "Give me a minute to dig out a math test for Janet and a writing test for Jeff. You can sit in the empty classroom across the hall. I'll set the timer in this room –better for concentration and all, you know.

Forty five minutes later the timer dinged and it took Mike another 10 minutes to grade the tests with the Swiss-cheese cardboard template for the multiple choice questions. Reading Jeff's essay took another five minutes. He debated speaking to each privately, but decided that he might be justified in doing a little academic match-making –or at least trying to keep the match he had already made matched-up. The tests made it clear it was a good match. Perfectly reasonable for the teacher's role to try to keep things going and equally reasonable for him to be oblivious to what was… what? A lover's spat? None of his concern, but he sat back and looked at then both as he gathered his thoughts. They did make a good looking couple, but that was completely beside the point.

He gestured for them both to come to his little desk in the back of the classroom. He had to stifle a grin when they both came up to his desk ignoring one another. "Well good news / bad news kind of thing. You both have improved remarkably in a short time. Nice for me to see I was right about your complimentary skills and needs. Bad news is that Janet, I don't think you are ready to take the math test. And Jeff, you are not ready for the writing test. Well, Jeff you are ready for the math, but we have talked about this. You each owe one another a debt of gratitude." No response here. None what-so-ever. "I'm not sure if Jeff is the better teacher, or Janet, you are the better student, but Janet, you have improved slightly more. I'm pretty sure I can't take credit for either of you. Other than for putting you together, that is."

With a curt nod Janet went back to her seat while Mike and Jeff sorted out the details of the test schedule, cost, and registration. Janet was damned if she was going to give anyone the impression she cared one way or the other about the breakdown of the 'partnership.' She could do it all herself. She had come this far mostly on her own, damn it. Only a matter of carefully reading the book, mastering the vocabulary and following instructions. So she flipped back to the beginning of the chapter she had planned on working on with Jeff, and read everything. Twice. Then she tried to make sense of why $Y = mX + b$ could define a line. Apparently it had something to do with thermometers and converting American Fahrenheit to metric Centigrade. It didn't take. She found herself looking around for Jeff, caught herself and quickly went back to the book. He had evidently left and she told herself it was just as well. But the big dumb hick really could make her see things in the numbers. She went back another chapter and read that one too. Tried once again to think up an equation in the form of something to convert this to that. She sat at her desk till class was over at noon wrestling with math that seemed not to have an answer. Or had more than one answer. Or the answer was an incomprehensible string of letters and numbers. Adding and multiplying and even long division she could do. Careful and methodical, she almost always came up with the right answer. Mike had told her that grade school was all about what he called 'answer getting' but high school math was about much more. It was about finding ways to get the answer *and then* getting the answer. God only knew what college math was all about. She wasn't in tears when she left, but it was a close thing.

Janet drove home trying to convince herself that the way it worked out with Jeff was the only reasonable option. She got a few hours of sleep before heading into work. It had taken almost a month, but she was finally used to sleeping a few hours in the afternoon and a few hours after she got off work before she went to class. Still, it was a struggle to get down to Willy's Place for her first set of three dances starting at 6:PM. At 5:30 she was in the dressing room wearing her under-bust corset –the one that so perfectly displayed her girls- under baggy warm hoody. As she was finishing her make-up in the grim little room by the back door of Willy's Place, Tonia came bouncing in.

"Hi girl. How's tricks?"

"Same ol' same ol." replied Janet. *Holey crap!* Was she talking like Jeff now? One more reason it was best that she not study with him anymore. "How are you Tonia? Still seeing that farmer?"

"Yep. You still seeing the accountant?"

"Meh. He has gotten weird lately. He hasn't come up with the money I need to get me to spend more time with him."

"Sweetie, swear-to-God, you let my boyfriend Tom make you a web site and start doing escorts, you can start raking it in. Just dates. You fuck them -you make way more money. I mean I know you do great here with tips and all, but why not pile up as much as you can. Did I tell you Farmer Bob endorsed another royalty check from Exxon over to me? Almost $1000 this time. I had to take it to the bank but they wouldn't cash it and all. I had to open an account and shit, and the manager says I will have to declare it to the IRS and all, but money is money isn't it?"

"I know. But I have another problem. Did I tell you about that guy I was studying with? He was helping me with math?"

"I thought there was a teacher. Like you go there every morning. I don't even get up before noon and you are in class? Shit girl. I don't understand you."

"There is this old teacher and he's OK, but he has a lot of other students. There is this big dumb dork from Louisiana or somewhere and the teacher got us to work together. I was really understanding math and I was helping him with his writing."

"So? Is he cute?"

"I suppose. He's big fucker. But he is an oil field looser all the way. Anyway, he is going on day shift and we aren't going to study anymore. He wanted us to study evenings or something."

"So what's the big deal? If you don't like him, but you are getting what you want out of him, what's the big deal. Does he like you?

Janet didn't answer. She just looked at Tonia in a way that meant this was a dumb question.

"Ok, so he likes you. Even easier. Have him come here, or there, or where ever and get the help you need. You can lead him around however you want him, can't you? It's not like you are back in Omaha where there are enough women. This is Williston girl!"

"Topika." She folder her arms. "I don't want him coming around."

"What do you care? And how do you know he hasn't come by before or isn't out there now? Are you worried he might make a scene or something?"

Janet didn't answer. Tonia was usually naked 10 minutes after getting to the dressing room, or at least had her boobs out. Janet thought maybe Tonia was concerned – or at least interested- in the study-buddy thing. Janet hadn't realize she wanted to talk to someone, but she found herself trying to figure out what to say. Tonia had more smarts – street-smarts maybe, but more smarts than a lot of people she knew.

"I suppose it would be nice to get it on with a young guy, especially a big one like him –I mean he's got to be about 6' 4" and 250. Maybe just once in a while. He' kind'a cute, and he is not dumb, but sure sounds like it when he talks."

"What about the lawyer guy? Over with him?"

"No. he's just busy –tax season he says, but he says he wants to help me with money and I guess there is math involved. I'm thinking about having him help me. Have you ever had a boyfriend –well, you know, a client, help you with things?"

Tonia shook her head adamantly. "Never. You let them think you need them and it changes everything. They don't want to pay you anymore. But it's cool to let them think they are smarter'n you and shit. Just don't ever let them do anything to get out of paying you."

Janet had a thought. "Maybe I could get him to help me with my math? It would be worth a few fucks to get thru this damn test."

"Maybe. But I think you should fuck the big guy too. What's his name?"

"Jeff. It might be kind'a fun at that. But what about studying together? And what if my lawyer guy gets it together and wants to take me to Las Vegas or Hawaii or somewhere nice. Or shopping? I just don't want the hick hanging out around here, and it's such a pain when I want to… you know… get rid of him."

"Why are you so hung up about him coming here. I mean the lawyer guy has seen you stripping hasn't he? That worked OK for you didn't it? Guys are even more stupid around us pros than they are around regular women. You aren't thinking about meeting his mom and everything are you?"

"God no. But I was kind of bitchy to him this morning."

It's Tonia's turn to give Janet the 'Are you kidding look?' "Sweety, let him glance at the goods and it will be all nice again. I promise."

"I guess I could leave a note for him with the teacher. He is a pretty cool old guy. He seemed bummed that we were not studying together anymore. No damn it. My lawyer is a better investment. I'm going to talk to Mel."

She pulled on a sweatshirt, left the dressing room, and knocked on Mel's door.

"Come-in. Hello Janet. What can I do for you?"

"I need to start an hour later today."

Mel was not enthused. "Why"

"I need to go see Amundsen. Something personal."

Mel leaned back in his chair behind his desk. "Janet, as you know, the councilor is important to us here at Willy's Place. I am generally in favor of your... keeping the line of communication and good will open with him. But I can not help wondering if you need this time for personal matters rather than the needs of the club."

"What do you want me to do Mel? I don't know dick about finance."

"No worries my dear. I'd just like to know what you make of our friend's outlook, his mood and such. I'd also like to know that he was happy and committed to us here at Willy's Place."

Janet's instincts were not as keen as Tonia's, but she caught on. "What's in it for me if I fuck him?"

Mel's expression changed. "Ah Janet dear girl, are you happy working as many evening shifts as you like as well as weekends?"

"You know I am Mel."

"Splendid. Bring me back a report of our friend's… *erotic contentment*, nothing salacious, and perhaps some sense of how his finances are going, and you may work what ever shift you like. Nothing specific. Perhaps just some pillow talk. Men do like to brag about their money don't they? Or they do like a sympathetic ear when things are going the other way. Mmmm?"

Janet took a moment at a red light to look up 'salcious' on her phone while she drove the few blocks to Kevin's office at the Pioneer Building where he had taken her a few weeks earlier when he showed her his office. Then it was in the evening, but now it was different. She hadn't bothered changing out of her sweats and stage makeup but the hallway and stairs to his office were mercifully empty. Her confidence and resolve were still intact when she found the door to " Kevin Amundson Esq, CPA" but there was a middle aged women just inside the door of who did a double take when Janet came in. She felt her confidence slipping, but she decided to brazen it out. "I need to see Mr…" and she forgot his last name. "Kevin . It's very important."

The secretary got as far as, "Mr. Amundsen is…" when Kevin came into the outer office.

"Thank you Beulah. It's OK. " He kept a professional expression and turned to Janet. "Won't you come in?" It was as if she were an expected visitor –an important client. He gestured into his office and shut the door behind them. Janet immediately pulled off her sweatshirt revealing nothing underneath but a red bustier trimmed in back lace. Kevin went pale, and without talking his eyes off her, cracked open the door. "Beulah, that will be all for the day. Have a nice evening."

"You said you could help me understand stuff. First you have to help me with Y=mX+b. You want any of this…" she gestured at herself, "You have to make me understand."

An hour and a half later, she was back at Willy's Place. She was able to inform Mel that Kevin was 'erotically content,' but she had nothing to report about his state of mind regarding his finances. Nor did she tell Mel that the whole Y=mX+b thing now made perfect sense. Jeff or her teacher Mike might have done it better, but –by God- she understood. The understanding was far more satisfying than the sex.

Chapter 16

The warm feeling after the session with Janet on his desk the week before stayed with Kevin only till Monday morning when he got another call from Mel down at the strip club. Mel wanted him there that afternoon. He checked his appointment calendar: "I can make at three."

"That is not acceptable councilor. We will be meeting with an associate of mine from Kansas and the only mutually convenient time is right after lunch." Mel spoke in his quiet voice and any small vestige of calm that Kevin might have had evaporated.

"Will twelve thirty be soon enough?"

Mel snapped a curt, "One will be fine" and hung up.

This gave him a few hours to pull himself together and –more importantly- pull together the latest numbers from the man-camp. The papers had been sitting on the corner of his desk for a few days and he had been putting off looking at them. The brief chat he had with Sara Mahon when she had dropped them off late the previous week was not encouraging. She said that things were going well, staffing was a problem, but this was only to be expected in the Bakken. Occupancy was running between 60 and 70 percent and receivables were a tad high, but otherwise, all was well. 'All was well' from the view point of the woman who ran the day-to-day operations at the man-camp, but not what the account needed to meet his agreement with Mel's people in Kansas. So like the ostrich with his head in the sand, Kevin set the papers aside telling himself he would look at them later. Later was now.

The Mahon woman was right. The place wasn't full. *What the...?* Every man-camp within a hundred miles was running 90% occupancy and the missing 10% had more to do with the tedious and time consuming process of evicting someone who wasn't paying rent than it had to do with demand. Perhaps a little marketing? But that would cost money and what small cushion he had built up over the last month or so had gone to Vail when he and Janet took their erotic little vacation. Some money came back to Williston in the shapely back pocket of Janet's jeans. Maybe, if Vern didn't go for investing in the water treatment plant he could convince Janet to invest? God forbid, had it come to that?

He was the son of a middle class farmer, a good student, but a poor one, a struggling new professional getting started and never had money back then, but nor had he ever lost sleep on the subject till after the divorce and he decided to do the man camp on his own. Now he owed money to some names in Kansas and was seriously thinking about conning the stripper he was occasionally 'dating.'

It was small consolation, but the bouncer at the door of Willy's Place was almost polite. Kevin didn't even notice who was dancing, as he walked straight thru to Mel's office, knocked, and went in. There was a third man in the room: a smallish guy -30 something- with way too much dark hair.

"Good afternoon Mr. Amundsen, this is Mr. Smith."

The guy stood up, faced Kevin, and made a slight bow from the waist. Kevin held out his hand to shake hands, "How do you do Mr. Smith?" The offer of his hand was ignored. The hair on the back of his neck stood up and his mouth went dry.

"Please sit down Mr. Amundsen." Mel gestured to the chair in front of his desk and sat himself behind the large desk. 'Mr. Smith' sat to the right. "I believe I might have mentioned that my associates in Kansas had sent something of an expert out to explore the situation at the Bakken Lodge. Mr. Smith is that man. Shall we hear what he has to say?"

He tried to speak, and failed. He cleared his throat and tried again, "Yes please." Better, but still pitiful.

Mr. Smith looked past him as he spoke. "A ground level survey indicated nearly 95% occupancy."

Kevin interrupted, "But the numbers…"

"Shall we let Mr. Smith continue uninterrupted councilor?"

Kevin got quiet and felt the sweat start down his back. "My survey certainly has some margin of error, but I am confident it is more accurate than anything you are getting from your on-site manager. I am equally certain that she has been embezzling from the partnership for nearly the entire time of her employment at the camp. My research runs as follows. There are at least two, perhaps three, employees working part time in exchange for free rent, but the partnership is paying them –or being charged to pay then- for 60 hours a week at more than twenty five dollars an hour. With overtime, these employees are costing you $3500 a week and one has been working for more than a month and the other just about a week. I suspect there have been more in the past. As near as I can tell, these employees are innocent dupes, but there has been no withholding. I do not need to tell you, councilor, what will happen when the IRS brings this home."

He shook his head numbly.

"I thought not. Do you believe it is worth the effort to unravel the ultimate beneficiary of these monies?"

Kevin shook his head again and croaked a single "No."

"I thought not. My research is not complete, but it seems clear that there have also been bills paid to fictitious vendors –or vendors who are –as they say- kicking back. One such vendor is the company -or companies- that pump out your sewerage tanks. We find councilor, that the number of people living in a given facility can be calculated with a high degree of accuracy by considering the amount of sewerage that needs to be processed –or hauled away as the case may be. You have been paying for far more sewerage removal than you would need if you were running a mere 70% occupancy. You have been paying for far more than necessary for even 100% occupancy.   Once again, do you think it is worth the time and effort sorting out which of these two companies is fictitious and who is the beneficiary of these monies?"

"I….no."

"But the biggest issue is the rents that have been going to two Bakken Lodge Partnership credit card accounts. One here in Williston and one in Minneapolis. Mr. Smith did not ask the question, he simply paused and looked pointedly at Kevin .

"I had no idea."

"It looks like a little under two hundred thousand dollars."

Kevin wasn't quite up to the mental math, but it was clear that this money would have fit his financial predictions perfectly and left him in the position to pay off the un-named people in to the south. "What do we do now? Tell the police?"

Mr. Smith and Mel glanced at each other and Mel's lips twitched into an almost smile. Mel took over. "Only if you want to wait years to recover only some small portion of this money. I fear that my associates are not this patient. Do you have the where-with-all to cover your obligations without recovering this money in short order?"

The trickle of sweat down his back stepped up a level or two, and he was barely able to suppress a shudder. "Not really. Do you have any… suggestions?"

"Mr. Smith has considerable skills in collecting embezzled funds… um –what was the expression you used Mr. Smith? 'Extra-legally'?".

Mr. Smith simply nodded and Mel continued. "There will be certain things you need to do before Mr. Smith can begin the recovery. There is the matter of your meeting your obligations to our associates."

He felt a glimmer of hope. $200,000.00 would more that meet this year's payment to the guys in Kansas. Perhaps even a bit of marketing with a little left over for Janet's hip pocket. If occupancy went up to the 90-95% he expected, and without further embezzlement, there would be enough cash-flow to make the following years payment as well.

"And there is the matter of Mr. Smith's commission."

It was an effing roller-coaster ride.   First some glimmer of hope, then the little guy with the Brooklyn accent took it away. "Um… it is perfectly reasonable that Mr. Smith should be paid for his efforts." Kevin was surprised he got out a complete sentence.

Mel nodded. "Mr. Smith's extraordinary talents require extra-ordinary payment. I believe your usual commission is fifty percent of the recovered funds is it not Mr. Smith?" He paused and glanced at Amundsen, but did not wait for confirmation. "There is also the matter of some indemnification to Mr. Smith should his efforts lead to some liability. I believe it is called a 'hold harmless' clause in your world. I am sure you understand such matters, do you not councilor?"

Kevin nodded. Mel went on. "Time is -as they say- of the essence." He slid a single legal page across his desk to Kevin and placed a pen on top if it. It was only then that Amundsen noticed his desk was otherwise completely empty. "I think it is your best interest to engage Mr. Smith as soon as possible in this matter."

Kevin started to read the contract when Mr. Smith spoke up. "By all means councilor, take your time. There are perhaps other means at your disposal to recover this money and satisfy your creditors out of state?"

He forced himself to look at each word but was hardly was able to make himself understand them. How many times had he urged his clients to at the very least read *and understand* contracts carefully and –better- let him look them over? Here were two very dangerous men waiting for him to do something –something that might very well save his ass –or help to save it, but the paper they wanted him to sign, God help him. There were phrases indicating he would 'direct the agent in all matters pertaining to….' and 'pay all legal costs of defense in criminal matters., and the big one, 'shall be considered solely responsible for…' He signed the document.

Chapter 17

When Vern took the time to think of such things, it seemed to him that of all the things that made it worthwhile: falling asleep holding Sherrie, winning a bid for work when it had plenty of profit, trying out a new piece of equipment, and the Con / Agra Heavy Equipment Convention in Las Vegas on those rare years when he could get away, the best one was going out to the pole-barn to work on a piece of equipment with his son. The kid was a pretty good mechanic –indeed a damn good mechanic for a thirteen year old.

It wasn't always easy to watch the boy struggle with a task he could do himself in a fraction of the time, but increasingly he had learned to explain things carefully and just stand back, or go do something else entirely and leave Robby alone. Somehow the work got done. He might be working in the cab tracing out an electrical short in the dash-board while he had Robby puzzle out how to remove and replace something in the engine compartment. It had started with simple things like the air filter and had progressed to things like diesel injector pumps for big 12 cylinder engines.

He thought about the times he spent with his own dad working on the farm equipment. Not quite the same though. His dad was never satisfied; there was always something he did wrong or did too slowly. He was a year or two in the navy before he noticed that the petty officers and chiefs that ran things tended to give him the tough jobs and he realized that maybe he wasn't the incompetent his dad always made him out to be. Vern was damn sure he wasn't going to treat his own son that way. They would talk – often about how engines worked or why & how a given piece of equipment did what it did, and sometimes the conversation was less technical.

He and Robby had been working on the hydraulics on an old loader. As he was reviewing the maintenance log for the machine, he realized he had come to a decision. Struck him as silly, but damn it, if he could keep this particular old machine running *and running profitably,* he could do the same with the water treatment plants at Ahmundson's man camp. Sherrie had left it up to him. He wasn't a particularly religious man – certainly not as religious as his dad, but he decided to leave it up to God. Or fate. Or something. That morning he had gotten an email from the guy in Denver with the Caterpillar D-9'er he had his eye on. It had been sold. He would have a chat with his banker, and then let Kevin know about his decision. Once the decision was made, he felt good about it. Now to concentrate on the important things like his son.

"Dad, when can I learn to drive? You got to drive when you were my age right?"

"Ya, but it's not like you think Robby. I was about your age when I helped your Grandpa with harvest. I drove an old truck alongside the combine while it filled up with wheat and then I drove to the elevator and back to the field. Over and over again. Did this from dawn to dusk and believe me –it was fun for about an hour. It wasn't like I got to –what do you call it- go cruising for girls or even down to the store for a cold soda."

"Oh." Robbie screwed up his face thoughtfully. Sherrie said he did it just like Vern "I still want to learn to drive. You let me drive a backhoe that one time."

"Make a deal with you –if you bring your English grades up, I'll teach you to drive some of the equipment this summer. You can't drive on roads, but we will be doing some work for oil companies out in the field. Maybe even give you a job –you know with pay and everything."

"How good a grade do I have to get?"

"You get A's in math and science –I think a B in English sounds about right."

"OK"

Yes, he loved both his kids the same and all, but it was SO much easier with his son, than with his daughter. Every so often, he just fell into a situation that worked perfectly with Robby. To achieve any sort of satisfactory end with Beth took planning, co-ordination, coaching from his wife, and no small amount of luck. And even then, despite everything, it often disintegrated into melodrama that left him wondering just what the sam-hell had just happened.

The matter-of-fact way Robby agreed to pull up his grade was the boy's way. Perhaps the stern stoic Norwegian ancestry from Vern's side of the family was showing thru –perhaps even more in the kid than in Vern. Generation skipping an all. He had been considering getting the boy out in the field anyway. He was pretty confident Robby would get the grade so it was a double win.

"Dad, why don't you ever go with us when Mom takes us to visit Grandpa?"

But then again, the lad also had an astounding way of noticing things –things well beyond his age- and asking sincere but uncomfortable questions. "Oh Robby, I am usually busy catching up on work on Sundays."

Partially true –after the family got back from church Vern was often at work, but he cherished the morning's quiet time when they went off to church, Sunday School, and lunch in the church basement. Shirley called it his 'ME-time' Sometimes he even had himself a nice nap. No way in hell he could do this during the rest of the week.

"Grandpa says it's a sin to work on Sundays."

"Grandpa has some strong opinions." Sometimes the lad could be diverted with a question coming going back at him. "What do you think about working on the Sabbath?"

I think some people have to work on Sundays, don't they? Nurses and police and all. Maybe it's OK to work if you also go to church and do family stuff."

"I think that puts it pretty well Robby."

"But don't you like Grandpa?"

Nope –the diversion didn't work. Vern owed the kid some kind of answer. Maybe some dilute honesty? "Your Grandpa wanted me to work on the farm when I grew up. I decided to join the Navy. I wanted to see the world. You know about this, don't you? I didn't see the world, but I did see lots of little islands in the Pacific and I got to drive a lot of earth moving equipment. So when I got out of the Navy, I met your Mom, we moved back to North Dakota and we started the business. My dad still wanted me to come work for him. He is still sort of angry that I didn't." Vern thought to himself '*And he is really pissed that I'm doing well without his help.*'

The man-door by the big overhead door open and Beth ambled in, "Dad, mom says dinner is ready and you have to wash your hands. She is not waiting. It's your favorite: roasted chicken with 'em little baby cabbage things you like so much.

"*Those* little cabbage things -and they are called 'Brussels sprouts'. Thank you honey." He looked at his daughter as she made a face at him. She was once again –and for the moment at least- his little girl. "Let's go Robby –this will wait." He realized once more that he was a very lucky man.

Chapter 18

That Wednesday when Mike left to go teach his morning glass there were two police cars parked in front of the office. He was curious, but didn't have the time to find out more. He would figure it out –someone would have the story- when he got back that afternoon after he dealt with the food shopping list. Nothing he could do anyway.

After a week of teaching mornings and helping around the man-camp, Mike took some small pleasure in noting that he had only used his credit card once for gas and would shortly be making a payment that was marginally larger than the minimum amount. Food was free and he had no other expenses.   'Marginally larger' was very marginal, but it was a start. The three hours he worked to pay for his room worked out to be only a little time out in the cold, but almost entirely in the kitchen. Could have been worse. Could have been 8 hours or more out in the cold. The oil field workers he met told him that 12 hours was a typical workday, and that most of it was out in the cold. Even so, it took a deliberate effort on his part not to do the math as to how much they were making: 12 hours, 6 days a week and $15 or $20 or $25 per hour plus time-and-a-half overtime or even double overtime. The sad afternoon he spent in the Bakken Staffing's waiting room had not crossed his mind since that day.

The time in the kitchen was easy. A little chopping and a little stirring. He was doing more and more of the actual planning and cooking when the cook was gone, and the cook seemed to spend a lot of time out of the kitchen. He was either on the phone in his room, or somewhere off in his car. Mike thought the guy was very interested in the comings and goings around the man camp. On one occasion Mike was walking back to his own trailer when he saw the guy walking between the trailers one row over. He appeared to be taking notes. The cook had a room in the kitchen trailer, so Mike had no idea why he would be out in the cold, but decided it was none of his concern.

In addition to taking on more responsibility, Mike was also working more than the three hours he needed to do to earn his lodging. That afternoon, as he was sautéing some onions per written instructions, the cook showed up. "Excuse me chef, any idea what the excitement with police was all about this morning?"

The cook shrugged. "Evidently, the office was burgled."

Not a very satisfactory answer, but by now Mike had learned not to bother trying to have a conversation with the guy. "Oh. By the way, Ms. Mahon wanted me to work three hours to earn my keep. I put in almost five hours yesterday and it's probably going to be at least that much again today. I'm not sure what to do here. Do you want me to stop at three hours, or save the extra hours up and take time off at the end of the week?"

"You will have to ask her. I need you to get the food out regardless. How do you pay for the groceries you buy in town?"

Another unsatisfactory answer but it would have to do for the moment. He told himself it was all part of being the simple working stiff, and answered the cook's question. "A credit card Sara… Ms. Mahon gave me." Something was not quite right here. He signed a receipt for groceries at the restaurant supply place that said something about net 30 days, but he also paid with the credit card Sara Mahon had given him. Struck him as odd, but what would the working man do? He hadn't thought to ask the Mahon woman at the time and as for now, he decided to just keep stirring.

"What's the name on the credit card?"

Mike stopped stirring, "Come to think of it, I never thought to look. I take it out of one pocket and put it back in the same pocket with the receipt –so not to mix it up with my own money you know."

"And you do all this shopping at grocery stores?"

"Mostly I pick stuff up at this restaurant supply place, and sign a receipt and then pay with a credit card. Sometimes I go to the big chain store or the grocery store north of town if I can't find what you order at the other place. There I just use the credit card. Ms. Mahon wants me to buy as much as I can at the restaurant supply place even though prices are a little higher than the other places.

The cook nodded absently. "Thaw out the chicken-quarters for tomorrow." Then he turned around and went into his room. A few minutes later the cook left the trailer.

Chapter 19

After serving breakfast, the next day, the cook and starting three large crock pots of beans, left a note for his helper –the teacher-putz- outlining how to roast the three big bags of chicken with Italian salad dressing. He put on his warmest coat and left the trailer. He had a few maps –one was mostly downtown Williston, one of the whole state –both fairly worthless- and a county road map that might be useful. He climbed into his rental car and took off –after a longish grind on the piece of shit rental car's starter.

It was cold; colder than New Jersey. The sky was perfectly clear but the sun gave no warmth nor energy beyond a blazing brutal glare. He preferred the north-west Dakota's otherwise regular gray sky so he started by driving west –away from the glare. Horrible gravel roads with washboards that made driving more than 20 miles an hour annoying at best, or at worst, risked breaking something –and he was damn sure he didn't want to break down in this country-side.

When he thought he was far enough out in the country, he circled to the south till he came over a low bluff and saw a long line of trucks heading east –bumper-to-bumper & barely moving along a two lane paved road. He checked the map and figured it was Highway 2 heading east into town and the tie-up was where Highway 85 joined it coming from the south around the Missouri River. Way too much traffic and activity for his needs so he turned right at the paved road and heading further west. Traffic was moving in this direction past the intersection and he got to 146th Ave NW and drove off to the north. Effing ridiculous a little no where town having 146th Ave. It wasn't anything but empty, but still not desolate enough. Lots of traffic –big trucks mostly.

He could see some interesting bluffs off to the south, but too far off. Otherwise there was nothing but rolling prairie: some few buildings, a rare farm house and several tank farms with their nodding oil pumps. He came upon a single oil drilling rig on the horizon and as much out of curiosity as anything else, he found the road leading to it. It got bigger and bigger the closer he got, but before he got close enough to be able to see human bodies and get a real idea of its size, he came to a fence with a little guard house and what he took to be a rent-a-cop with a clipboard stepping out of the little building. He stopped well shy the fence and the guy with the clipboard, smiled, waved, and turned around and went back the way he came.

He headed south again and after he crossed to the south side of Highway 2, he found one place behind a bluff and close to the road that might barely have served his purposes. Not a lot of topography in the prairie and not a single tree to be seen anywhere. Privacy was essential. He parked within sight of the road, but half behind the gentle raise where he could watch traffic but not stand out. He pulled out a magazine and sat there for an hour. Three pick-up trucks passed –one non-descript dirty pick-up, and two relatively clean ones with crew cabs and petroleum-service company's logos on their side. One great lumbering tanker-truck passed going one way and another one a short time later going the opposite direction. He guessed they were tending to what he thought might be what they called a tank farm: a collection of from eight to twelve twenty-foot tall cylinders each about eight feet in diameter lined up by a bobbing oil-pump thing. There was just too much traffic and he suspected it was no less busy at night. Possibly if he were to move further out into the county he might find the space he needed, but being too far out created another set of problems. He would have to rethink his plans.

He drove further west and found more of the same. When he passed the sign welcoming him to Montana, he muttered a WTF? to himself, gave up, and headed back the way he came. It took him 20 minutes to get thru the intersection at 2 & 85 and continue on around town to the north past the man-camp where he was staying. The city –such as it was- went a lot further north than he might have expected: businesses selling pizza, gas, ammunition –only in North Dakota could you buy gasoline, Hostess Twinkies, cigarettes and thirty-ought-six rifle ammunition all at the same check-out counter. The ammunition was often piled up in neat little boxes right next to cash-register and chewing tobacco. There were also businesses selling or servicing earth moving equipment, farm equipment & cranes, oil-field equipment, as well as hoses, snubbers, sand, mud, pipe, LNG & propane in big tanks, cable, welding equipment, pumps, hydraulics, and God only knew what else. A little further north out of town be passed a huge trailer park –not unlike the man camps, but rather than manufactured homes lined up in rows, there were row upon row of travel trailers –acres of them with pick-ups parked between each. When finally he made to the country-side, he found it much like the country to the west, but a little flatter and emptier of anything remotely interesting. But there seemed to be even more trucks coming and going.

By late-morning he had worked himself around to the land to the east. It wasn't much different from the countryside he had already checked out, a little less oil and a little more farming, but he began to consider a whole new plan. All these damn country roads looked alike: dead straight, perfectly north-south or east-west, washboard gravel ranging from bad to horrible. The cook missed the road back to the man-camp. He was one road too far north and didn't figure this out till he was one county mile too far west. When he got his bearings, he found himself driving down a road he had only passed, cursing this God-forsaken empty part of the world. Empty of everything except effing trucks.

Out the corner of his eyes, he passed something that didn't look quite right and stood on the brakes and backed up. It was a row of squat metal tanks about 100 feet off the road. They were not the perfect black cylinders precisely lined up next to the ubiquitous oil pumps, but squatter -10 feet or so in diameter and about 12 feet high. They were made out of grey corrugated metal and had semi-conical roofs. They looked a bit older than the oilfield tanks and it struck him that they must have had to do with something agricultural. The short drive off the road was actually better than County Road Number Give-A-Damn. He got out of his rental car, and noted the sparse wind-blown snow along the drive and around the tanks. He knew himself to be not particularly skillful at maters of nature, but it seemed to him that there were no tracks and no one had driven nor walked there for a time. For that matter, he would leave no tracks himself. Nor would his guest, when the time came.

There was about eight foot of rusted farm something laying in the weeds between the three tanks. The top was a knee-high framework with a hitch, and an array of pointed metal parts pointing down. He figured it must have had done something agricultural to the ground. One of the three tanks had some sort of machine piped to the side with what might have been a blower –perhaps it had something to do with loading or unloading the tank with something –something dry. There were no electrical connections available, neither was there a gas or diesel motor to be seen, but he thought he could see where one might have been hooked up. All in all, it confirmed his thinking that nothing had gone on here for quite some time.

All three of the tanks had a door, -or more accurately, an access hatch about three feet high and two feet wide. Big enough for a person to crawl thru for some unknown purpose of maintenance or what-not. One tanks' door had a pad lock. He pounded on the side and it rang hollow. He guessed it was empty, or largely empty anyway. The next tank was not locked, but rock-hard frozen dirt obstructed the door from opening more than a few inches. Not an insurmountable problem, but the third tank's hatch opened easily and all the way. It had a good strong hasp, and he bent down to look inside. More frozen dirt, with a thin layer straw stuff and a six inch sheet-metal pipe that ran from the middle of the circular floor to the side of the tank –presumably for loading or unloading the thing with the help of the blower gizmo outside. He crawled in and looked more carefully around in the dim light coming in from thru the hatch. There wasn't a lot to see. He kicked at the galvanized sheet metal around the edges and satisfied himself that it was firmly buried in the rock-hard frozen ground. A little light came in from under the eves at the junction of the roof and sides, but otherwise, it was a perfect prison cell.

He crawled out, got back in his rental, and started a mental shopping list. Most of what he needed was buried in the bottom of his luggage. What was the line from the old TV show? Somebody "loved it when a plan came together."

Chapter 20

After the meeting at the strip club with Mel and Mr. Smith, Kevin was not a happy camper. It got a little better Monday morning when Vern called and said he was willing to buy the water treatment plant. He almost asked Vern how quickly he could write a check but bit his tongue. Better to let things unfold as they needed to. Vern said he had discussed it with his banker and the banker wanted a meeting with the three of them –at the bank no less. It was probably nothing, but in the past, Kevin had this particular banker –and a couple of others- come to *his* office for similar meetings. Perhaps for meetings wherein he was an uninvolved third party advising their mutual client, rather than his new role as the guy who was getting the check. The meeting was scheduled for later in the week, and the bank would need time to do their own due-diligence –as if bankers knew jack-shit about water treatment plants, but it had to happen. As far as getting good funds, funds he could pass on to the guys in Kansas, he new from experience it might be weeks.

Tuesday morning he was going over the numbers from the man camp a very careful study. He had to give his manager Sara Mahon credit, everything looked good – on paper. Mr. Smith was evidently a pretty good accountant –or detective- to have found the graft. It remained to be seen how good he was at the *extra-legal* recovery side of things. His impulse had been to confront the thieving bitch and get her arrested, but he kept hearing Mel asking if he were able to wait years to possibly get back some small portion of the money she had embezzled; he kept quiet but something needed to happen. He just wasn't sure what more what he could do.

He got up from his desk and went to the window and looked out at a gray North Dakota day. Ordinarily he would be glad to be inside and warm but today he was restless and felt like going somewhere; anywhere. His thoughts turned to Janet and where he they might go together when the money issues got sorted out. His phone started ringing and he ignored it till his secretary Beulah called out thru the open door, "It's your personal line, boss. Do you want me to get it?"

He snapped out of it. "Oops –sorry. Grab it. I'll be just a second." He collected himself, closed the door, and went back to his desk. Maybe the call was from Janet. She was one of the few people to whom he gave his personal number.

He couldn't have been more wrong. Beulah buzzed him that a Mr. Smith was on the line for him. How did the guy get his personal number? Kevin tried to collect himself again; he was not entirely successful.

"Good morning Mr. Smith. I'm sorry for the delay."

"I was given to understand that this phone was your private line councilor. Is this not so?"

"Um.. ya.. –yes it is, I just stepped away from the phone for a minute and my admin grabbed it for me."

There was a long silence. "In the future councilor, it might be best if you answered your own phone. For the next few days anyway. What is your cell phone number."

Kevin swallowed and gave it to him. "What is happening at the man-camp, Mr. Smith?"

The guy ignored the question. "I wish to confirm that the gentleman –from New Zeeland I believe- can run the camp without the Mahon woman. Is this so?"

"Ya, he does it all the time. Well, he checks people in and out and does some of the supervision of maintenance and keeps track of the keys and such. Mahon does the books and pays the bills. But… you know this don't you?" *Fuck,* Kevin thought to himself, *Mr. Smith knows better than I do how she pays the bills.*

"He is there in the office now and the Mahon woman is out. You are to call him immediately and give him this message. You would like to meet with Ms. Mahon in your office and you would like to have her bring the new cook so you can meet him. This afternoon would be good, but not essential. You are to make the request in a casual manner. Do not elaborate. If she calls to confirm, be flexible and –again I stress- be casual, but make sure she brings the cook. You would like to meet the new employee."

"Sure. Um… I'm not a good enough actor to hide my anger at the bitch. Why do I have to meet her?"

"You will not have to meet her. In fact, I doubt you will ever see her again."

Holey Fuck! "What is going to happen?"

"Do not concern yourself with this councilor. Just do as I instruct, and then forget it. If it is convenient, and after you make the call, it might be a good time for you to be seen somewhere out of town -well out of town. Otherwise, be prepared for things to happen quickly and be prepared to take a more active role in the management of the facility." And he hung up.

Kevin did exactly as he was told. For the next forty-five minutes he stared at the wall across from his desk, trying to put together a coherent thought. He jumped when the phone ring in his outer office. Beulah answered it and called to him, "It's Sara Mahon. She says they will be here tomorrow at one. Is this OK?"

He tried to speak and failed. He cleared his throat and tried again. "Yes, that will be fine."

He heard her say, "Mr. Amundsen says one o'clock would be fine, Have a nice day."

Whatever happened now, things were happening. Amundsen felt some small relief. "Take the rest of the afternoon off Beulah. And tomorrow too."

He waited till his secretary gathered her things and bustled off. He locked up his office, walked the three blocks to The Williston, and got so drunk they had to call him a cab. The next morning, he took another cab back to his car and took a miserable hangover to visit his dad out on the farm.

Chapter 21

The winter's sun was just on the horizon while Mike was waiting for his student's to gather and settle in. The college was on the edge of town and GED classroom windows looked out over the eastern prairie. Orange sunlight glared into the classroom, but not unpleasantly so. Strange he hadn't noticed it before. Much to do and much to be done –a good feeling. For some reason he remembered the end of Solzhenitsyn's ***One Day in the Life of Ivan Denisovich.*** A brutal story of a gulag prisoner in Stalin's Siberia who comes to the end of a long cold miserable day and finds himself 'almost happy' because he was productive at work. Other than the cold, life as a GED teacher and man-camp cook's assistant in North Dakota had little in common with Russian work-camp prisoners; but there was satisfaction of having a task ahead and the where-with-all to see it to a good end –particularly after his long spell of unemployment.

All in all, his students were making pretty good progress. The housewife whose kids had grown up enough that she could get after it again had passed two tests right off the bat. She mentioned that part of the reason she was doing the GED thing was to set an example for her kids. Seemed to Mike an altogether worthwhile effort. A few other students had passed the social studies test and four had passed either the science test or the literature and arts tests. None had even tried the writing test though. It always came down to writing or math.

The pretty girl, Janet, was going to take the social studies test that morning. She seemed to remember that once that was behind her, it left only science and math. Mike had to admit to himself that he wasn't doing her much good in that direction –certainly not as much as she would have liked –or expected. He had to admire her single-minded determination, but he just couldn't give her all the attention she wanted. When he tried to explain something to her, she got impatient and insisted that she just wanted to know what steps to follow to get the answer. Not that this was much different than most of his students, particularly the math challenged ones. Damn shame that big Cajun wasn't there anymore. Jeff seemed to have the patience to get her to just relax and step back and look at the whole problem. And he liked the guy.

He did the role thing, and wrote a writing prompt on the whiteboard, *When I was young, my favorite toy was...* "OK, for those of you who are not taking a test this morning, finish this sentence, and write me a nice tight essay. One hundred words, four paragraphs ought to do it. Now, who wants to take a test?" Four hands went up. "Let me see if I remember. That will be two social studies, one art & lit, and one science, right? He got agreement all around, and he nodded. "The computers are set up and Linda was going to proctor you in the room across the hall. Good luck guys. And remember to stay relaxed." They all shuffled off with what he hoped was a fair degree of optimism.

Mike figured he had given his writers enough time to give it some thought and started a casual lecture on *subjective* and *objective* attributes of something like a toy; What did it look like? vs. How did you feel about it? He asked if this might be a good way to organize an essay? A simple introductory paragraph, an objective paragraph followed by a subjective one? Or vice-versa and a then a nice closing paragraph, and the job was done. He emphasized the imperative to edit, edit, and edit. Several of his students were already writing. Getting students to actually think and plan before they dove into the writing was a challenge he had never solved.

He spent the next hour helping with grammar, punctuation, and organization when the students started coming in from the testing room. He asked each how they thought they did and got mixed responses. "I know how you are feeling. You never know how you do on a test right after you take it." Janet was the last to come into the classroom. He figured she would be the one to take every bit of the time allotted to check her answers.

His boss Linda came in a few minutes later with the printout. In California, the tests were collected, graded somewhere else and the students got the results in the mail. North Dakota was a little more high-tech; computer hooked to the internet back to the GED headquarters. "How did we do Linda?" and all eyes went to the woman; those that took the test and those that didn't. It was heartening to see how everyone was waiting for the results and pulling for one another.

She smiled. "We have a perfect four out of four. Everyone passed." Whoops and clapping all around. The test takers were more relieved than exultant but pretty happy.

"Congratulations guys. I'm proud of you. This is as good a time as any to tell you about he last day of class in…" he turned to Linda and asked "Come to think of it, I don't know when the last day of spring semester is. Sometime in June?"

Linda nodded, "The week ending with Labor Day."

Mike nodded and went on, "It's a long ways off, but not really, I need to clear it with my boss…" he gestured to Linda, "… but I propose we do a party –everyone brings food or drink –alas, liquor is not going to happen. Then we will take a good hard look at Williston State College's calendar and catalog. We will then talk all about college. Things like what's a BS, what's a BA, how hard classes are, how long it takes and what it costs, what a pre-requisite is, and we will get you all set to be a college student. Is this a good plan Linda"?

"A very good plan. And if you were to hold class somewhere else, you could enjoy a little beer or wine. This IS North Dakota after all!"

Three of the four students who had taken the test –two women and a young man- all went off to lunch together. Janet didn't go with them, but rather went to her usual spot and opened up her math book. Mike wasn't sure weather to feel sorry for her for being excluded from the happy group that was celebrating, or admire her for her studiousness. For that matter, he suspected she wasn't so much excluded, as she was aloof, but he had other students to help. He wasn't surprised after class when she asked him if she could talk to him.

"Congrats Janet. This just leaves math right?"

"Yes, can't you help me?"

"Janet, I'll give you all the help I can, but clearly I have other students. I also have another job in the afternoon. I think they may finally be starting up an evening class. Can you come evenings?"

"No, I work."

"What is your work?"

She simply shook her head. Mike had bumped into this particular stone wall before and went on. "You were making such good progress with that big old Cajun." Her eyes flashed and another stone wall went up -an even higher one. "I can help you for a little while after class, but…. You need to… you need to understand what's going on – not just the steps to follow. Why don't you set it all aside for a few days. Rest-up a little. You should be pleased you have passed another test."

She gave him a half-hearted smile, but her shoulders slumped, and for a moment he felt sorry for her. She looked up, "Can you give me Jeff's phone number?"

"I don't think I'm supposed to, but I'm pretty confident he won't mind." It took him a minute to find the class roster and give her the guy's number.

She muttered a sad, "Thank you." and left.

After she left the classroom, Janet was a little keyed up and decided she did deserve some celebration. She would worry about math later. She called Tonia and got her voice mail. This meant her friend was either asleep or on stage. She wasn't in the mood to go home and take a nap and knew that if she didn't, she would pay the price for it later, but maybe the teacher was right; she should take a few days off and sleep in a morning or two. Or sleep in mornings and work evenings at Willy's Place. Or maybe see if Mel was really as obliging as he said he would be and take a break from stripping as well.

She thought she might do a little shopping. That was always fun. But where to go? Penny's Department Store downtown was for old ladies, and Walmart north of town was for oilfield workers and some few of their dumpy wives & brats. No good reason to go to Walmart; all she ever bought there were Pop-Tarts and coffee. Shelves at home were well stocked. There were more interesting clothes at the Salvation Army, provided you had a flair for vintage and the eccentric. She found a parking space in front of the Pioneer Building where Kevin's office was. She thought about dropping in on him and seeing if he would take her to a nice lunch. She was tempted, but she wanted to talk to Tonia before she saw him again.

She window shopped her way around a couple of blocks down-town. A little too cold and frankly, she had no interest in -and even less need for- any of the things these stores sold. There were several restaurants but she wasn't in the mood to eat alone sitting at a table next to what she thought of as professional office people like geologists and bankers and such snobs all having their martinis and rare steaks. She told herself it was because she didn't want to get hit on. So she wandered her way toward the Salvation Army to see what they have had and remembered the little book store where they sent her to get the big GED study books. *Books on Broadway* was a cute little place and she thought they had some kind of bar in the back. Seemed odd that a bookstore would serve liquor, but it was right next to the Salvation Army Store so she went in. Piles and cases of books everywhere. And stuffed animals. She liked stuffed animals. The books by the front door, on tables and a prominent bookcase, where there were books about oil and history, but just beyond the check-out counter –actually an elevated clutter of more books and an ancient brass cash register, were kid's books and toys. She picked out a dinosaur book cum dinosaur puzzle and stuffed giraffe for Ricky and took them to the counter.

There was a customer in front of her discussing some book or other with the woman behind the counter. It was apparently going to be a long conversation, so she got a second giraffe for herself, and a kit for Ricky to make his own dinosaur skeleton out of pre-cut wood pieces. She was considering another book for Ricky –a brightly colored and illustrated one on how things worked when the woman finished with the other customer and stepped down from the counter. "May I help you find something?"

The woman was about Janet's age, pretty, a tad zaftig, and showing a bit much of an impressive cleavage -even by Janet's standards. Her lipstick vivid red and her eye-shadow was multi-colored. Tonia would have approved. Janet decided she liked the woman. "I'm just shopping for my…. nephew. You have some fun stuff here."

"Well, thank you."

"Now maybe a little something for myself." Janet spoke absently.

"What kind of reading do you like to do?"

She wasn't ready for this sort of question. It hit here that her college persona might be the way to go and at the same time, Kevin 's offer to help her invest her money crossed her mind. "Um… ya, do you have anything on –like the economy and investing?" God, she hated it when she heard herself sounding like a nit-wit.

The bookstore woman smiled, nodded, and thought a minute. "Yes, we have a popular book called *Freakonomics* –it's fun to read and I've heard some smart people say it's pretty good –it gets a lot of stuff right. Or there is Thomas Sowell's *Basic Economics.* I read this one myself and I am NOT a math person. It's long, but real good."

As the woman lead Janet into the next room, Janet wondered if it was just coincidence that she mentioned math or if she had some kind of super salesman's intuition. Regardless, she decided to trust her recommendations. She also found that the bar wasn't a bar, but rather an old soda fountain and Janet smelled good coffee. Together, both women found the books and added *Investing for Dummies.* By the time she was done, Janet had spent just over one hundred dollars. A few dollars more for some coffee and some pastry in one of the little booths by the soda fountain would be perfect so she put on her black horn-rimmed glasses and did her college-girl thing with the books.

Mike the teacher had once lectured the class how to read a book. They all knew how to read, and it seemed silly, but it occurred to her that no one had ever told her how to do this in school and she decided to take his advice. He said the first thing was to look at the copyright date and see when the book was written. Then she read the tables of contents. There were some interesting topics in the Freak and Dummy books, but they were still intimidating. But before you start with page one, he said you should look at the pictures. Kids do this and they do it for good reason; to get their minds going in the right direction.   The dinosaur book had interesting pictures, but the best ones were in the How It Works book. The books on economics didn't have pictures as much as graphs and tables. Fuck math. She couldn't get away from it.

No point in putting it off anymore. She had the coffee shop to herself and thought she was in the right frame of mind. She dialed the number the teacher had given her for Jeff.

"Yo."

"Is this Jeff?"

"Ah-yep."

"I've changed my mind. I want your help."

"Who is this?

"Janet. From class."

"Oh. Din't 'spect to ever hear from you. How are you?"

"Fine, thank you. When can you help me?"

"Oh, um…, well, anytime 'ceptin 'tween six in the morning and six in the evening. And I likes to get a little sack-time in som'ers there. Maybe seven or eight in the evening. Wha'z your ske-jule?"

Janet thought she could get Mel to let her off at that time. She did sets of three dances every hour or two, depending on how many other girls were working. Between sets, she either hustled drinks, of did lap-dances in the dark little room in the back. Seven or eight was just a little too early for the profitable lap-dances to begin. The men needed to get a little drunk and needed to see her on stage before they were ready to start spending hundreds in the lap-dance room.

"OK -that will work. Where can we meet? How about the McDonalds or someplace on Second Avenue?"

"Janet dear, I work a twelve hour shift and when it's over, I want to take my boots off and have a beer. Now if I'm he'ping you, don'chu think you might could make it a little easier for me and come to my home. I live on eighteenth –off yonder by the college."

"Do you live alone?"

"Nope, they's four other guys lives here. Are you worried someone's gon'na attack you?"

She thought he meant it as a joke, but she didn't laugh. He seemed to have no idea she was as stripper and she wanted to keep it that way. If he lived with four other guys –and if they were oil-field workers, one of them was bound to have been to Willy's Place and seen her. "I just want quiet so I can learn it and pass this math test."

"Oh, well, it's usually pretty quiet. Most of us kind'a wonder thru the kitchen on the way to our bedrooms. And they's all pretty decent guys at that." But hot-damn, he thought, wouldn't they all be jealous as a puppy when the cats is fed to see him head to head with this woman even if it was only at the kitchen table.

"Ok. I guess that's OK. I'll call you when I'm coming over."

"Fine as frog's hair. I'll have a cold beer waiting for you."

"I don't drink beer. Good by." And she hung up.

As she left the little bookstore, she wondered if she might have been just a little too bitchey.

Chapter 22

He had been involved in a couple of abductions; one for an unnamed friend of his Uncle Julian's, and one strictly for his uncle. He planned the logistics for the first one but two other men provided on-the-ground help; the muscle actually. The guy they grabbed –a minor flunky who had violated some rule or trust- was bound & gagged and driven off in the trunk of one of the big guy's car. He never knew what the poor schlub had done to deserve it nor did he know what was going to happen to the guy. He really didn't want to know.

The second one was his show all the way and he did it alone. He preferred it that way, but it was more complicated and risky. Much of the careful planning involved a tricky matrix of risk minimization. First and foremost, his own exposure; the target was not a pitiful boob like the first time –he had some teeth –muscle of his own and he was thought to carry a gun. There was also the exposure afterwards. If his uncle chose to let the guy live, there was the possibility of revenge. On top of that, there was the eternal problem of the police. Finally, the risk to the target when guns came out needed thought and planning. His uncle insisted he be delivered in one piece. It had taken him weeks to set it up and organize chloroform, burglar alarms, restraints, a van with removable non-descript signage on the side as well with a hidey-hole big enough for a large man –just in case he got pulled over for some chicken-shit traffic matter. Once it was all in place, there was another 4 days waiting and watching for the perfect moment. It all went off as planned, but what a pain-in-the-ass.

Abducting Sara Mahon –on the other hand- was stupid easy. An hour after he had called the lawyer, and precisely on schedule, she called him. "Good afternoon chef. I have to go into town to meet the owner. He would like to meet you. Is now a convenient time?"

"Yes it is. Um –I have to get gas, may we take my car?"

She agreed and he stopped at the office trailer a few minutes later. As he got out of his car, she came out of the trailer and stepped down the wooden steps. He looked at her carefully. He suspected she had been a looker in her youth. She was a tall women; imposing and in her late forties. Dark brown hair cut in a business-like short style. She was bigger than he remembered from their few interactions; she sat behind a desk for most of their dealings that were not the phone. She was hefty, but not obviously fat. She looked strong, but some of the bulk may have been her clothes. He would have to be careful not to have to get physical with her. He was confident that he could handle her but he might break her in some inconvenient way if it came to the rough stuff. It was about to be bad enough for her as it was, and injuries –his or even hers- were apt to complicate his life as well. And he hated rough stuff.

.   She was wearing a long puffy down coat over pants. No hat nor gloves, but she carried a purse and he suspected she might have more cold weather wear either in her purse or the pockets or her coat. No matter.

He opened the passenger door for her and she commented, "What a gentleman ."

He wasn't good at small talk, but needed to keep her comfortable for a few minutes more, "One does try. My mother was a stickler for manners." He was an only child of a single mom who was a waitress and didn't give a damn about manners when she dragged herself home in the evenings while he was doing his homework.

"I come from a big Italian family. My mother and aunts & uncles taught me to cook." This was almost true. His mother was always too tired, but his aunt taught him a little. Most of it he learned on his own. It was the need to feed himself dinner six nights a week that taught him to cook. The seventh night –when his mom had a day off work and after she had a chance to catch up on her sleep, they went to Uncle Julian's house for dinner.

These were some of the few happy memories of his childhood. His cousins were nice to him –certainly nicer than the kids at school who were bigger than he –which was all of them. His aunt a great florid zaftig lady who -in his mind- was always either laughing or stirring something on the stove. She was the opposite of his mom –her sister, who was skinny and morose. He understood from a young age that his father had died because of some involvement with his uncle but he was never to ask about this, nor was he ever to ask what his uncle did for a living. When things got too close to the bone in their grubby little apartment, his mother would say, "Let's ask Uncle Julian. He can help us." Once when she was drunk, she added, "He damn well owes me."

He would come to understand some small part of his small family's history only as an adult. After his dad died, his uncle got his mom a job as a cocktail waitress at a popular nightclub. Over the years, too many cigarettes, too much liquor, and too many late nights, began to show. She lost the night-club job, and went to work at an up-scale steak-house, then at a family restaurant, and finally at Denny's. She was beautiful in the wedding picture she kept on her dresser. The man standing next to her was a cipher. She said he looked like his father, but he didn't remember him.

They drove thru the rutted parking lot to the top of the top of the hill and turned left onto the washboard of country road Number-Give-a-Fuck. He needed just a little more small talk as they headed toward town, "I'm guessing your people are... what? German?"

"You would think so wouldn't you?" She then went off on a long, and he suspected a well practiced explanation of her Scots ancestry. She was so involved that she didn't notice he had made another turn between the man camp and the drilling rig in the distance. It was only as he was making the third turn into the little graded place by the three grain silo things that she notices and asked, "Where are we going? We really don't have time for this. Mr. Amundsen is waiting for us."

He parked behind the three squat metal cylinders and pulled the small automatic out of the pouch in the driver's side door. "Oh my God. What are you doing?"

She didn't scream -a small thing but it saved him the bothersome need to slap her. He turned to her and leveled the pistol at her face. "Get out." This was the most dangerous part of his plan. If she got out and ran, he would have to run her down. He was counting on shock to keep her where he wanted her.

"I demand to know what you are doing. Who do you think you are?"

He got out himself and stood in the open driver's side door. He leaned in, "I said get out" and he shot once into the frozen ground. The sound was little more than a loud pop that didn't carry in the wind, but inside the car, it was impressive and had an impressive effect. She turned to the door, and as she fumbled with the latch and got out, he walked around to her side. He took her arm and led her to the middle farm thing.

"Are you the police?" The mascara had started running.

"No. Give me your purse."

She hugged her purse to her chest. She was now weeping and blubbering; right on the verge of hysteria. "Why. What are you doing" Who are you?"

He slugged her in the gut- just once and not hard. She gasped a long wheeze and fell to her hands and knees and began to retch. He was able to pick her purse up from under her and grabbed the collar of her coat and part dragged and part steered her to the hatch of the gray metal building. She was just getting her breathing under control. "Are you going to kill me?"

"That is largely up to you. Now get in there." She hesitated so he put his boot heel against her ass and shoved. She fell in most of the way and he shut the door hard on a protruding ankle. She screamed and jerked it in after her so he could shut and bolt the hatch.

When he figured he was about midway between the man camp and the oil rig, he stopped and rolled down the window and listened. It was not a terribly windy day, but he heard nothing. He was sure she would start screaming at some point, probably after the shock wore off, but if she were doing so now, she was wasting her breath.

Back at his parking space by the kitchen trailer, he took a minute to wipe down the door handle in his car and anywhere else he thought she might have touched. It was probably unnecessary, but he knew the smallest omission could screw-things up royally. The whole thing took twenty-two minutes; from the time she stepped out of the door of his trailer till the time he locked up his car.

The final step was a little tricky. He walked the three rows over and two trailers up to the staff trailer and went in. The little guy from New Zeeland was at the desk. "Have you seen Ms. Mahon?"

"No. I just got here. She asked me to cover for her for a couple of hours. Said something about going into town."

"We were supposed to go together." The cook shrugged. "It's not important."

The guy asked, "What's for dinner?"

"Chicken roasted with new potatoes, salad and vegetables. Pine-apple upside-down cake for desert.

The other guy made a waffling gesture with his hand. The cook smiled. "I don't blame you. I'm thinking of ordering a pizza myself. Tell Ms. Mahon I came by." He went off to finish cooking dinner for about 65 people.

Chapter 23

Vern was out west of town checking on the progress his guys were making on a drill pad: the acre or two of perfectly flat ground where someone –the grading contract had been signed by the secretary of some partnership or other- planned to drill a few wells. The pad had to be flat because once one well was drilled down a mile or two to the oil bearing formation, the bit would be turned off for as much as mile of horizontal drilling. Then the derrick would be laid down and the rig would be moved out of the way and the well fracked. If the geology looked promising, the rig would be moved 30 or 40 feet away from the first well, the derrick was stood up again, and another vertical hole drilled. Once at depth, the bit would be steered off in another direction. In this way, one drill pad could actually hold as many as four productive oil wells. The tricky part for Vern and his guys was scraping the topsoil off to one corner of the pad and the underlying soil to another. This allowed them to put it all back together to the satisfaction of the environment crowd.

He was almost back to the shop when his cell phone made the annoying little chirping noise it made when it had something to tell him –usually that he had missed a call -like it was his damn fault. Vern decided to wait, but when he got back to the shop, his shop-guy mechanic and sometimes unofficial girl-Friday, told him Sherrie had called. His wife rarely called him at work, and when she did, it was for a very good reason, so he called her before he went thru the little chore of extracting a message from his damn cell phone.

"Hi honey. What's up?"

"Your sister called. She wasn't able to get a hold of you and called me. She is pretty upset about something your father did. Of didn't do. She wants you to call her right away. And I suspect you had better be ready to drive out to see her."

"What's the problem?"

"She wouldn't say. She seemed more angry than worried or upset."

"All right. I will take care of it –what ever it is. Don't hold dinner for me."

If Vern's damn phone had worked the way the phone company said it was supposed to, he could have saved himself about an hour of driving. He had been within a couple of miles of the family place when he was out checking on the rig-pad earlier. Such was the reality of a community that had grown from 20 or 30 thousand people to somewhere around 100 thousand and every man, woman, and child had a damn cell phone. Not enough cellular capacity. It wasn't that he was out of range, it was that the phone company was cheap. He tried calling his sister as he was driving back west. No answer, so he left a message telling her that he was on his way.

As soon as he pulled into the drive, she was came bustling out of the house with out a coat. He rolled his window down as she came up to the side of his pickup. "Pull around to the side, I don't want… I don't want anyone to see you."

"What's gotten into you?"

"Just do it and come inside. I'm freezing."

He didn't say *You might have taken a second to put on a coat*, but he was thinking it. When he got into the living room, the three and four year-olds were watching cartoons, and the baby was having a good cry. Vern remembered the times his children were at the crying age. It had been tough with his daughter Beth -less so that with Robby- but still. His sister Veronica looked more than a little frazzled. She was wearing sweat pants and a rumpled tee shirt, and her hair was a mess. He could still see the girl who had been the Williston High prom queen and dated the big son of a Swede who was also the captain of the football, the basketball and the baseball team, but it wasn't easy. It was all a few years after he graduated and was in the Navy.

"Dad has a girl friend."

"Nice to see you too. So he has a girlfriend. Good for him. Mom died six years ago."

"No, you don't understand, a 20 year old *girlfriend*. Asian. And I'm pretty sure she was naked."

Vern gave her his don't-try-to-fool-your-big-brother look. "Maybe you had better start from the beginning."

"I got the kids down for their naps and decided to take those mason jars over – the ones that he had been pestering me about. I know he always wants me to call first, but I didn't want to wake the kids. And it's not like he respects my privacy the least little bit, so I let myself in and was putting the jars in the pantry, when he starts hollering. 'Whose there?' I holler back and walk into the living room. He is sitting there all flushed and really pissed at me. So he's cussing and hollering and this little Chinese woman peeks around the corner in the hall but only her head, like she is naked and doesn't want anyone to see it, but she is kind'a smirking."

"Did you see she was naked?"

"I didn't have too, what with dad hollering at me about not coming into his house with out his permission and all. My God Vern, we grew up in that house. So I got the hell out and have been trying to call you ever since."

Veronica never cursed so Vern knew she had been pushed to her limit. "My God Ronnie, he's a church elder. You can't be saying things like this"

"I don't care if he's the Archbishop of Canterbury he…" She stopped and collected herself. "You are right. I don't know. And I'll not be one to gossip –especially about my own father, but what I do know is that I will not be spoken to like that. Ever again."

"I understand."

"I have three kids and a husband to look after. I'm not going to all the stuff he is always having me do for him anymore. Let the little naked Chinese girl run errands and make sure he has food and a do thousand other things for him. I'm done."

"Ronnie, I kind'a saw this coming. Not the girlfriend, but your burn-out. Sherrie and I were talking about it. Can't say I blame you one bit. Sherrie too, as comes to that. You want me to talk to him?"

She shrugged her shoulders. "When was the last time you even spoke to him?"

"We sort'a talked coming out of church back a week or two. Let me think on it a bit. You have anything else of his needs going back to his house?"

"There is some mending he had me doing." She muttered, "It's not like he hasn't got enough money to buy a whole new wardrobe. Why do you ask?"

I'm thinking that if I were to drop it all off -everything, it might make it clear that you were making a clean break of it –you were not going to be his little helper anymore. Collect it up and I'll think on it overnight –you do the same- and I want to talk to Sherrie. Is this OK?"

"Ya, Sherrie's good people. I trust her. And tell me the truth; it was her who told you I was getting stressed wasn't it?"

Vern smiled and nodded. "Yep –ya' caught me. We will do something tomorrow. Give us a hug."

He spent a few minutes on the floor with the older kids watching some mindless cartoon about –as near as Vern could tell- a dumb square underwater creature and its friend, an even dumber starfish. On the drive back to town, he couldn't help himself being almost proud of the old guy. Darn sure he would need to have this attitude well in hand before he and Sherrie talked about it all. He supposed some of the domestic stuff would fall on Sherrie, maybe some on him, but perhaps it was time for him to sort things out with his dad anyway. Maybe past time. His brother in Minnesota couldn't do anything, but for that matter. Yep, it might be time for him and their dad to sort out their issues.

Chapter 24

It had been a busy day for the cook. First there the small matter getting the embezzler tucked away in the grain silo thing that afternoon. Then there was getting that night's dinner into the oven, but his helper did a good bit of it. This was perhaps the easiest part of his day. He checked in with the Kiwi in the office and they agreed that the missing manager must have been around somewhere because her car was still there. Business as usual otherwise and the little Kiwi was happy to sit at the desk.

He drove to town and let himself into her apartment with the keys from her purse. Burgling was always nerve-wracking –even if whom-ever lived there was safely elsewhere –assuredly so in this case. He spent a very fruitful couple of hours going thru her personnel files; bank statements, brokerage accounts, mortgage paperwork, and the like. He was pleased to find she was pretty well organized and astonished how little she had done to cover her tracks about the embezzlement. There was even a ledger that took the same general form as the accounts he read thru when the burgled the office trailer. Except of course, this listed the money she had actually embezzled. It had dates, amounts and a running total, and it struck him that she took no little satisfaction from her own personal score sheet.

He was back in the cooking trailer just in time to serve dinner. The Kiwi stopped by –not to eat- but to bitch about the fact that he had to stay at the front desk all afternoon and on until the eight PM closing time. The little guy was just beginning to worry that something might have gone wrong, but his biggest issue was how it impacted him. Lots of overtime though.

After he set up the diner at seven o'clock, the cook made a thermos of hot coco, bundled up, took a softball bat, flashlight, and a folding lawn chair out of his car, and walked across the prairie to the grain silo things. It was cold –a little above zero, but not as cold as it could get, and three-quarter moon made for an almost pleasant walk. He unfolded the chair by the hatch and unlatched it.

"Come to the opening Ms. Mahon." He tapped the bat on the ground just inside the hatchway on the ground where she could see it. "Please note the baseball bat. If any part of you sticks out of the door, I will use the bat. You have what I'm sure will be a trying interlude ahead of you. Let us not make it harder than it needs to be with broken bones." He saw her legs in the door but she made no effort to bring her face down to the level of the low hatch where they could see one another. "Can you hear me?"

"Yes" she croaked. "Why are you keeping me here?"

He ignored her question. "You are wise to stand Ms. Mahon. Sitting or even kneeling will cause you to loose your precious body heat to the ground. I also note the hoarseness of your voice. I imagine you had a good scream this afternoon? Didn't do you much good did it?"

No answer. "Now, as to the matter of your stay here and how you might come to leave, quite simply we are going to arrange for the money you have embezzled from squire Amundsen to be returned to him. It will –of course- need to take a somewhat circuitous route, and therefore take some time, but it will be returned."

"You will never get away with it." Her voice was little more that a scratchy whisper. "Someone will find me."

"Perhaps. For all I know, the farmer who owns these structures will be come by tomorrow morning with a load of wheat or oats, or whatever they are to hold. But the odds are not in your favor. I don't imagine you noticed the snow when we come here? You were… distracted, I'm sure. But the only tracks were tracks that I made a few days ago. I checked –the first snow was back in the middle of October. No one has been here for a month now."

He gave her a moment to reply. Nothing. "There is also the possibility that someone will hear your screams, but I suspect there is not much screaming left in your throat. If the wind carries just right, and if someone is close enough, and if the gas flare down the road stops it's noisy burning, and if indeed your voice holds out, there is the chance someone will rescue you. But again, the odds are not in your favor."

She sobbed. "Please. I'm so cold."

"Oh yes. This brings us to the matter of cold. I've done some research. Remarkable what you can find on the internet these days. It is going to dip just a little below zero tonight, but there is a serious cold front coming from Canada in the next few days. Your new…" He paused to think about what to call the grain thing, "…*home* provides protection from the wind, and that is a nice coat you have on. I'm afraid sleep is out of the question tonight, unless you can sleep standing up. Even if you were to lean against the steel walls, you would loose body heat to the metal. Death by hypothermia is interesting but it is a slow death. First come sporadic shivering –then uncontrollable shivering. It turns out that dehydration is also a problem. We find the body has to make a choice between healthy thirst leading to proper hydration on one hand, and on the other hand, staying warm. Staying warm wins –at least initially. The end game turns out not to be so bad. Well, you die and I suppose that that is bad, but it's not a particularly painful nor gruesome death. We find that *extreme lassitude* is how the experts describe it, followed by sleepiness. It is when the shivering stops that you have to worry, The body temperature really starts to drops and… well, it's then that the heart gives it up and that is pretty much that."

"Now as to your situation, you are not a small woman –more body mass to hold onto the heat- so that goes in your favor. But nor are you particularly fat. So sorry to bring up this subject to a woman, but I think we are past the point of social niceties, aren't we?"

Still no answer and he didn't expect one. "So, how shall we see about achieving a mutually satisfactory end; my client recovering his money and your getting out of this… um, well… alive. I suggest we begin with your local bank where we find you have a little under twenty seven thousand dollars. You write a check for twenty five thousand made out to KC Holdings. I will dictate a number for you to write in the memo, and I'll leave a thermos full of hot and calorie laden coco with you to comfort you during the coming night." He tossed her checkbook thru the hatch followed by a ballpoint.

"Fuck your coco."

"Now now Ms. Mahon, you *will* need the calories tonight, but it's up to you of course."

She tried another tack. "If you try to cash the check that size, my bank will confirm it with me. And besides, the police will be able to trace it back to you. You are going to kill me aren't you?"

"Good question Ms. Mahon. Always a pleasure to deal with someone who understands the challenges of embezzlement as well as you do. I suppose I would do well to outline my plans a little more carefully. I expect it will take a few days to recover the money. I can do things to make your stay here less unpleasant; a sleeping bag, hot food, maybe even a book or two to help you pass the time. But I will do so only if we make good progress. As you may have guessed, I have a pretty good idea of where the money went. We will do things step by step. Think of the coco simply as a very expensive purchase you are making."

"As to the police, I fear going to them would necessitate your admitting to the original embezzlement. Or if you were to come up with a good enough story –one that hid your own role in this little melodrama, you would find that the police would view it as a white collar crime and not nearly as important as busting drunken oil-field workers and their drug suppliers. In good time, they would do something, but by then I would be long gone and the money would have bounced from bank to bank, both on-shore and off. Given time, an expensive forensic accountant might sort it out, but –here again- your original embezzlement would also come to light. I must mention that Canada is what?, twenty miles to the north? I will release you, or I will see to it that you can get out of your new home once I am well away from this God forsaken country."

"And as far as that goes, I would suggest you follow my lead and get out of out of town too. In a few days time, our mutual client Mr. Amundsen will report to the police that you are missing as is a great deal of his money. By the way, I hope you don't think any of the information in my employment application is accurate do you?"

Still no answer. "Now then. Are we ready to write that check?" She was sobbing as she wrote the check, but he cook doubted the tears were was genuine. No matter. "Now write the following in the memo *Lot #23-9.* Do not tear the check out. Toss me back the whole checkbook and the pen." She did as she was told. "Now step back from the hatch." Again she did as told. He set the thermos on the frozen dirt inside the hatch, shut it, and latched it. He considered leaving her the lawn chair too, but decided that the coco was enough and a bad night would put her in an even more cooperative mood the next day. Instead he folded it flat and stuck it under the farm implement where it would not blow away and added the bat. No need to give anyone the need to wonder why a guy was carrying a lawn chair across the prairie in the dark.

The moon had gone behind a cloud as he walked back to the man camp so it was not as pleasant a walk as the walk out, but he was pleased with how well things were going –or at least started. He decided he would serve steak the next night for no particular reason.

Chapter 25

Janet had gotten a few hours of sleep and woke as much from habit as from being actually rested. She hadn't quite decided about heading off to Willy's Place to add a bunch of twenties to the Mason jar hidden in her dresser. Back in Topeka she needed the money and it would have been an easy choice to go to work but then it was mostly ones and a few fives she folded into her jeans. Things were different in Williston but the decision to skip work didn't come easily. She was still on the fence when Tonia called.

"Hi girl, what'chu doing?" Tonia didn't wait for Janet to answer. "I've had the weirdest day. Let's do something and I'll tell you about it."

"Cool, I called you earlier 'cause I wanted to get your advice on something, but your phone was turned off. What you want to do? Where do you want to go?"

"You know what, I don't want to go out. I'm up to here with men today. Can I come over to your place?

"Sure honey. Is Tom bugging you?"

"No more than usual, he's just always here on the couch. I'll get us some Irish Cream and we can just hang. We can do a slumber party thing –we'll just get all comfy and drink and talk. And drink."

Janet giggled, "Super! And I have something to tell you too. I have something to celebrate."

"Be there in a flash." and Tonia hung up.

She started tidying up her home, but here wasn't much to tidy. It was basically a room in the corner of the basement of a larger ranch house: one window by the front door, and another over the counter in the kitchenette which was backed by the bathroom. The only interior walls were the two that enclosed her bathroom. Janet had draped a colorful piece of cotton over what should have been the closet door. She liked it so well, that she hemmed more fabric to drape over both the little round kitchen table and two chairs with matching fabric. She decorated one 'bedroom' wall with a large free-flowing 'sculpture' made from fabric scraps, ribbon, and dried flowers. All in all, she was pleased with her home and proud of what she had done with it. But it was her bed that pleased her the most. She pushed her bed into the corner and hung a large piece of dark velvet behind and then she hung pale blue cotton sheets from the ceiling to make a canopy on the two open sides. She filled it with pillows and a fluffy comforter. She supposed it was sexy, but it was not for sex. It was her cozy refuge and intensely private little space.

She hoped that when summer came, the garden would bloom and it would be

83

even nicer. Imagining flowers in December was difficult, but she remembered helping her dad in his vegetable garden. She went so far as to think about asking her elderly land-lords who lived upstairs if she might do a little gardening of her own.

When the few stray clothes had been tossed into her dresser and a couple of kitchen items put away, Janet called the club. Mel didn't answer and she was a little relieved. She left a message that she wouldn't be coming in that night and started pulling treats out of the cupboard and fridge. She hadn't gotten very far when her phone rang and she guessed it was Tonia. "Hi honey, what did'ya forget?"

"Um. Janet this is Mel."

Oh fuck. "Oops, sorry Mel. You got my message?"

"Yes. We have enough girls in tonight so no worries there. But I wanted to chat with you about our friend."

"Oh?" Janet hadn't given much thought to Kevin since she considered having lunch with him earlier. Was Mel expecting her to report in every damn day?

"Janet, I appreciate you efforts in this matter, but it might be best if you were to back off –let him concentrate on other matters for a short time. And I trust it goes without saying you are not to discuss it with your co-workers."

"Sure Mel, but why is it a secrete?" She had been planning to discuss that situation w/ Tonia –among other topics.

"Various reasons. Not the least of which is that our arrangement to let you have a stage whenever you like. At the very least, this is likely to lead to bad feelings among the other dancers. And there are some people who have money invested with our friend. These people take things very seriously."

A shiver went up her spine, but until further notice, she was off the hook. "I understand Mel. Tell me when you want me to spend more time with Kevin."

"Very good"

"Is there anything else?"

"No. Call me when you are ready to come back to work. Good night Janet."

"G'night." She wasn't sure if Mel frightened her or just bugged her. Probably a little of both, but she damn sure was going to run it by Tonia despite his insistence on secrecy. Besides which, Tonia already knew about her deal with Mel. Fuck him.

When Tonia arrived, it struck Janet that she had only ever seen Tonia at the club where she was mostly naked to one degree or another. Janet was a little relieved that she was dressed from head to foot; sweatpants, sweater, hoody and parka –pretty much what Janet was wearing -minus the parka. Clearly it was going to be a warm comfy girl's-night-out. Or girl's night-in.

Tonia handed a large bottle of Irish Cream to Janet and started talking immediately as Janet did the ice and glasses. "So I was out at the farm today seeing my old farmer? We are doing what he calls 'bible study' when someone comes in the back door. He freaks, and jumps up –'bout dumps me on my ass, and he starts screaming. I'm nude so I run down the hall and hide in the bathroom and he is screaming and then a woman's screaming, but my clothes are in the… get this –he calls it the 'parlor'- so what am I gon'na do?"

Janet poured a generous glass of Irish Cream and hands it to her. As Tonia takes a long gulp, Janet uses the silence to say, "Hoooooold on a minute. *Bible study, naked bible study*? Wha…? What? I mean WHAT are you talking about?"

"Didn't I ever tell you what the old guy wants? OK. So I go out there and sit in his lap for an hour or so. Sometimes he wants me to wear bra and panties, sometimes he wants me to strip down all the way. Then he reads me the bible. Or prays. Or I guess reads prayers from the bible. Sometimes he wants me to read parts of the bible to him. Then he pays me and I get dressed and leave. Or he gives me one of them royalty checks from that oil company. But I told you about the oil checks didn't I? That time I tried to deposit it."

"Ya, I remember. Ok, naked bible study –that's a new one on me."

"Me too, but it's a lot easier then getting pawed by some dirty oil-field horn-dog. But anyway, I'm not sure what's going to happen. After the hollering, she went away and I came out and got dressed and everything. He was pissed, but not at me. He was pretty mad at her and embarrassed to me –or about me –or something. What ever – his face was all red –I mean redder than usual. The little stack of twenties were on this little lace doily on the table like they always were, except when he gives me a check. Ya know what?"

"What already?"

"I think it was his daughter. I couldn't understand all of what they were hollering 'cause I was in the bathroom and all, but I thought I heard her say something like 'my own father'."

The thick sweet cocktail seemed to go down Janet's throat very easily. "Wow. So you think it over with him?"

"God, I hope not. He is actually kind'a sweet. Weird, but sweet. I'm just not sure what I can do for –what do they call it, *Damage Controll* ?"

Janet took another long thoughtful drink. "Maybe play the religions angle? I mean is he trying to save your soul or something?"

"A little bit. Maybe. I guess. I kind'a hinted he should take me to Rome to visit the –wha'dy call it? the *vatical* or something."
"You mean the *Vatican*?"

"Ya, that's it. I figured if he wanted me to get all religious, that would be the place to be. But this was so the wrong thing to say. He said something about the filthy papists. Did you know that the pope guy in Rome is only for Catholics? The other religions –like what ever one my farmer belongs to- they think the pope is a bad-guy?"

"Ya, I did read about that somewhere. I guess a long time ago the pope was like a general and killed a lot of people who didn't believe the right things; sometimes even other Catholics."

Tonia shrugged. "Who knew. He said he's a Lutheran. Where is the Lutheran headquarters? Is it somewhere exciting? Maybe with shopping?"

"I don't know. I don't think it the Lutherans have a pope or special city. I'll ask my teacher. OH ! I forgot to tell you. I passed the GED science test today."

Tonia squealed and hugged Janet. "Oh sweetie, that's terriff. This calls for a toast." And she topped up Janet's drink and they clinked glasses. "Are you a graduate now? Going off to college and everything?

"No, I still have to pass the math test."

"Bummer."

"Actually, that's what I wanted to talk to you about. You remember the big dumb Cajun that was helping me with my math?"

Tonia poured herself more drink and topped up Janet's glass. "Ya. You still hung up on him?"

"I'm not *hung up* on him." She did the air quotes around *hung up*. "I just don't want to get involved. I want to keep my life as simple as I can, make money and get this damn GED thing behind me. Then I'll figure out what's what."

"OK?"

"So I had my lawyer friend explain some algebra to me. I got it, but I had to fuck him. OH –that's something else, Mel wants me to fuck him, and find out shit, and report back to him and keep him happy, and he will give me the all shifts at Willy's Place I want, but I'm not supposed to see Kevin till he tells me to again and I'm not supposed to tell anyone, but I already told you so don't tell anyone else. OK? And what about Mel? The guy creeps me out to the max, but Kevin is loaded and in love with me, and I think I have a good thing going with him, but I'm not going to fuck him for help with math. I want money. And I want the Cajun to help me with math and I don't want to fuck him either. So what do I do?"

"Holey crap girl. This will take some thought. And have you eaten? You are sounding a little drunk for just a little Irish Cream."

"Nope. I got Pop-Tarts. You want a Pop-Tart?"

"Ya, and you had better have one too. Maybe more than one. Le'me think."

Tonia sprawled out on Janet's bed. "I love what'chu have done with your bed. So what guy do we talk about first? The Lawyer of the hick.?"

Janet dug around in a cupboard and pulled down a box of Pop-Tarts and put two in the toaster. She grabbed the bottle and joined Tonia. "The lawyer first. You told me to not to let him to do things for me. Why not?"

"Not quite sweetie. I said never to let a man get out of paying by doing things for you. Men must always pay. It's OK if they do things for you that make them feel smart or strong –you know –all manly and shit."

"Oh. I guess I understand."

"Ya, if you fuck them just because you want to, you end up with a guy like my Tom who spends my money of computer shit and toys. I mean I love him and I like fucking him, but he's costing me too much money."

Janet took a thoughtful sip and Jack-the-Jerk back in Topeka came to mind for a second. She munched on a Pop-Tart. "I like Tom I guess, but I never understood why you were with him." Then she thought that if it was anything like the Jerk, maybe she really did understand. A little.

"You know, I don't either. I'm going to bail on him when I get a little further ahead –or get a better offer. Do you see anything happening with the lawyer? Like marrying him or something?"

"Hell no. I mean if he took me to live in New York or Los Angeles or something maybe, but I'm out'a here. Sometime. I've been saving money and so I'm gon'na keep getting while the getting is good."

"Hear that. So what about the hick?"

Janet reached over and put a couple more Pop-Tarts in the toaster. "So I called you to get your advice on him. But when you didn't answer, I just decided to go and call him and tell him I wanted his help with studying. Ya know what was weird? He didn't seem all that happy about the whole thing. He's been hitting on me pretty hard in class and I thought he fall over himself."

Tonia giggled, "No worries sweety, he's just playing it cool –trying to *play* you. So if you keep it professional with your lawyer, you can use the hick to study, right?"

"Ya, I suppose, but he's not really a hick. And for some reason I don't want… I just want.. I want to kind'a use him just for math and shit."

"Janet, do you think he's cute? Do you want to fuck him?"

"I dun'know. Maybe."

"Any future with him?"

"Tonia, I have to tell you a secrete. You must never tell anyone." Tonia nodded, crossed her heart, and spilled a little Irish Cream in her lap. Janet went on. "Have you ever wandered why I always wear the bustier?"

"I thought it was to keep your boobs up?"

"No they stay up by themselves, thank you. I have a son. He lives with my parents back in Kansas."

"Wow. I didn't see that coming. How old is he?"

"He's almost five. So whatever I do, I do with him in the back of my mind. I want to be back with him, and I don't want to keep stripping –I don't know how much longer I'll be able to do it. And this is why I work so damn hard to get my diploma. And saving money of course. Someday I want to get a regular job and live somewhere with my son with a regular life."

Tonia sits up and faces Janet. "What's his name?

"His name is Richard William. We call him Ricky. He lives with my parents in Missouri."

Tonia starts to say something and fails. She reached out to Janet and gathered her into a hug. Tears came to Tonia's eyes, "I dun'know why I'm crying, but I'm so proud of you."

Janet tenses and then relaxes into Tonia's hug and hugs her back. She puddles up as well, and the women cuddle. "Um Tonia?" pause "I'm not gay."

"Nor am I." another pause "'Richard William' is a nice name. It sounds like a king's name. Do I want to ask about his father?"

"I think so too. And no."

Janet was the first to fall asleep, but she woke up to find herself tangled up with Tonia and too much bedding, so she got up and rearranged the comforter and threw some of the excess pillows on the floor. The night she and Kevin slept together –the night she first fucked him –was before she had made the canopy and her place was still pretty grim and bare For that matter, she had to admit to herself that the sex with him that night was also pretty grim and bare. The room was cool as she was sorting out the bedding so it felt nice to slip back into bed beside Tonia in and let the fabric of the canopy enclose them both.

She warmed herself against Tonia's back, and thought about Ricky's father, Jack-the-Jerk. She was young, but not young enough to have made so stupid a series of choices. Before Jack had gotten into drugs he wasn't a bad guy. It wasn't such a stupid choice at the time. Ricky was a beautiful child and she was sure they had a future together. But Jack was a dreamer and always on the lookout for an easy 'big-thing'. A friend of his knew a guy who needed a just little cash and anther guy who needed something done with that cash. It would have paid Jack a lot of money, but it didn't. Instead he lost the money and got arrested. All their money went to a lawyer who got Jack an acquittal, but now they were in the hole. So three months after Ricky was born, she put on a bustier and he started stripping. When Jack wasn't looking for the next big-thing, he was smoking pot. Then he was smoking every morning, then drinking in the evenings, then all day, and then coke, and finally, meth. She had to admit to herself it was cliché, but –in retrospect- utterly and sadly predictable. He only hit her once, but that was enough. It took her a week to arrange things with her parents to look after Ricky and she headed off to Williston.

Janet decided she would call Jeff again the next day and go see him as soon as possible. Tonia was probably right, even if he or one of his roommates knew her from Willy's Place, what did it matter? As she fell asleep, she imagined a meeting between Jack-the-Jerk and the Jeff the big Cajun hick. 'Iz'is guy bother'n you may-yum? Ya' want for should I pop his little ha'id off'n his scrawny pencil neck?' It was a nice image.

She quietly –and a little drunkenly- giggled herself to sleep.

Chapter 26

There would probably be some grumbling at breakfast because the cook didn't bother to do more than make an urn of coffee and put out pastries and cold cereal for breakfast. No big deal; he expected to be gone in a few days. Let the new cook worry about it. Perhaps the lawyer could put on aprons and do the job with the teacher. He giggled at this image and caught himself. Clearly it was time to finish the job and get the hell out when he started giggling at his own idle thoughts. He left the breakfast stuff for the teacher to clean up and got in his car. He figured it would attract less attention to drive than it would to set off across the prairie on foot –at least during daylight hours. The three silo things were in a row so he could park hidden from the road. But the real reason was the need to take the first check to town and over-night it to his uncle. There was also the need to do a little shopping in town. He had to keep the lodgers happy and didn't have time to fiddle with anything more elaborate than steak, baked potatoes, and pre-made pies for desert. To hell with the expense for the time being. He grabbed a box of cornflakes and made another batch of hot coco and put it in a jug. He'd have to remember to get the thermos back. In the meantime she could warm her hands on the hot container. Better for her write another check with warm hands.

He had decided to see if the Mahon woman was ready to write the second check –drawn on her bank in Minneapolis –this one for more than $65 thousand dollars. He had gone on-line and printed out the bank's form for closing an account. Once this was done, it would be just over $90,000 of the $200,000 he planned to extract from the woman was almost ready to be send off to his uncle for laundering. Made for a good start.

As he drove behind the silos, he gave the horn a polite toot. He had thought of announcing himself by banging on the side of the corrugated metal with the bat, but figured it might give her a heart attack. No point in being rude. He pulled the lawn chair out from under the farm thing, made himself comfortable, and unlatched the hatch. "Good morning Ms. Mahon. Same rules as yesterday about your coming out the door. How was your night?"

Silence. For a moment, he was worried she had already died, and was about to bend down and look into the silo when but he saw her feet shuffle to the door. "Please let me out. I'll give you anything you want."

Her voice sounded terrible, even worse then before. She knelt down where he could see her –well back from the hatch. She looked even worse. Her eyes were red and swollen. Her nose was red and her upper lip chapped. "Oh dear Ms. Mahon. Have we been screaming again? Or is it just a result of the cold and lack of sleep?"

"What do you want?" she croaked.

"Very well, right to business." His tone was chipper. "There is the matter of your bank in Minnesota. I think we will simply close this account and move all the funds to a holding company in… well, never mind where the holding company is, I have the paperwork for you to sign."

"It won't work. You are going to kill me aren't you? I might as well let you kill me now and that way my kid will get the money."

"Oh, we have a lot of work to do first Ms. Mahon. And believe it or not, killing is simply not my style. Nor is it necessary. Here is the deal. You sign the papers and I'll give you this lovely lawn chair. Can you sleep sitting up?" He didn't wait for an answer. "I suspect you will be able to do so if you get tired enough. The trick of course, is to sleep without loosing too much body heat and the chair will help in that direction. Also, here is another nice hot jug of coco. Did you enjoy the coco I brought you last night? Oh, that reminds me; give me back the thermos so I can bring you more in the future."

He set the jug on the ground just inside the hatch where she could reach it. "It's hot. You might want to warm your hands a little on the sides first. We need a good signature don't we? If your bank hesitates, that's just that much longer that we will have to work together, isn't it?"

"My banker will not honor the check with just my signature. He will need more."

"Ah. Glad to see that your circumstances haven't clouded your keen financial mind Ms. Mahon. You are right. I suspect you will be getting a call from your banker – probably late tomorrow. I have your cell phone and will be your very helpful assistant who explains that you are in a meeting but will be happy to take his call in…shall we say 30 minutes. Plenty of time for me to pop over here and be helpful.”

The cook giggled. “Oh my –so much to do. I had best get you some throat lozenges. We can’t have you sounding like a frog when your banker calls now can we? Please take care of your voice. Screaming simply does you no good.”

He had put the three pages he had printed out on a clip-board and tossed it to her. “Take your time and read everything over. We will be doing an inter-bank transfer after your bank gets these documents and makes whatever confirmation calls they see fit. Probably happen tomorrow. It strikes me that the bank is a little too interested in what you plan to do with your own money, so let’s be co-operative, but vague.”

He knew that most of the fiddly little blanks on the form only masqueraded as security and tax requirements. It all had more to do with the bank holding on to deposits just a little bit longer. The banking classes he had taken the year his mom died served him well, but what really finished his education, was the work he did for his uncle.

“Write *Saratoga Partners LLC* in the blank when you get to the top of page two.” He spelled it out carefully. “They also are quite anxious that you might have outstanding checks. This is of course just a banker’s fatuous policy to make it hard for you to get your money out, so we will be sending them all the unused checks to settle their minds. This is not to say you couldn’t have written a counter-check, but it might help you get out of here just a little sooner.”

Mahon thought about the mortgage payments that were coming out of her money market account. “How are you going to do a transfer without my password?”

“The same way I know the exact balance in this account is $65, 802, 29. I found the little three by five card with your passwords written down. I must commend you organizational skills Ms. Mahon, but suggest you need a little more practice at security, particularly if you plan to continue to do things outside of the law.”

She was weeping softly as she read thru the document and wiped her eyes from time to time in order to fill in the blanks. She finished and handed him the clipboard, turned to get the thermos and handed it to him too. He thanked her, stood and folded the lawn chair and passed it thru the hatch, closed and locked it. She heard the soft crunch of his tires as he drove off.

She had tried to sleep standing up the previous night. She failed. She used her fingers as rakes and gathered straw from the floor into a small pile just big enough for her torso and tried laying down on the hard frozen ground. She succeeded in falling asleep for a time, but the inch or so of straw and her coat weren’t enough. She awoke shivering and deeply chilled. She remembered the cook’s description of the progress of hypothermia so she began pacing around and around in the dark inside the silo with her elbow brushing the inside of the corrugated metal. Six steps and then she would use her toe to carefully feeling for the pipe that came thru the side of the silo at ankle level. She would then step over it take another six steps. She fell three different times. She wasn’t sure if she had tripped over the pipe, fainted, or simply fallen asleep for a moment.

But now she had a chair and was a little warmer from the jug of hot coco. She fell asleep and dreamt about her daughter and being warm. When she awoke, there was still light coming in under the eves of the bin, but she had no other idea of what time it was. She was chilled, but the shivering was only intermittent. She felt like shit – marginally well rested shit, but shit none-the-less. There was some coco left, but it was ice cold. She felt the need to pee and decided the part of the silo by the pipe would be her toilet. If she could aim under it, she would not step in her own waste when next she needed to pace. It occurred to her she hadn't peed since she left the office the day before. So this was what the harry little fucker was talking about when he told her all about cold-weather dehydration.

When she had done what little she could to make herself more comfortable, she reviewed her situation. Didn't take long. She was stuck. She turned her mind to her finances. The cook was well on his was to taking back about $90 thousand that she had taken from the man-camp. She had no idea how he knew, but the $200 thousand figure had mentioned was about what she thought she had embezzled. Ugly word embezzled, she took if from a fucking lawyer. That wasn't a crime. She used some of it to pay her daughter's tuition and that was clearly good.

Besides the money in both checking accounts, there was another $40 thousand in a managed bond account at IBS Financial. The biggest thing, her most important asset, was her house. About $80 thousand went to pay off the mortgage on her house in Minneapolis. And it took some fancy-ass accounting with a bogus family trust to get the funds into the form they could pay it off without bringing the IRS down on her head. She had certainly earned *that* money and she figured the house was safe. No way he could get by county clerks and recorders. So provided the little jerk didn't kill her, she would get out of it all with a house worth $180 –even after the '08 downturn. It was free and clear. Not bad for less than a year's work. But how much better it would be if she could keep it all, but to do that, she needed to get out and get the police involved. First the little jerk, and then the asshole lawyer.

She started digging at what she thought was a low spot in the rock-hard dirt. She broke three finger nails within the first five minutes and loosened all of about a teaspoonful of dirt. She sat back down in her lawn chair, rested, and reviewed the numbers of her dwindling wealth once again. She had to find a way to keep digging. She dug a quarter out of her pocket and tried that. Better than fingernails, still hopeless. Then she tries the little brass buckle from her fashionable belt. After an hour of effort, she has made a pile of loose dirt about the size of a teacup.

She alternated between digging and pacing. The digging warmed her arms, but kneeling chilled her legs. Pacing was better –at least for warmth. The whole time she reviewed the math of how much she would loose if she didn't get out.

Darkness came sooner than she had expected. She must have slept longer than she realized. She was exhausted. The little pile of dirt was now the size of a small phone-book. She sat in her chair and ate dry cornflakes with filthy hands and broken fingernails.

Chapter 27

After getting drunk the afternoon he summoned Sara Mahon, and then leaving town the next day, Kevin was back in his office, but admitted to himself that he was not going to get much done. He was staring out the window at another gray day when shortly after nine he heard Beulah answer the phone in the outer office. He went to the door as she said, "It's Mr. Spencer. Says he's out at the man-camp." There was a questioning tone to her voice and it took Kevin a moment to remember Spencer was the little chap from New Zealand by way of Salt Lake City that Mahon had hired to help run the place. The waiting had been hell, and no matter what the guy had to say, Kevin figured it had to be better than waiting. "Good morning Mr. Spencer. How are we today?"

"Um… Spencer is me' given name. I'm Spencer Taverell. Everyone here calls me Kiwi –coming from New Zealand and all. I'm sorry to bother you Mr. Amundsen, but I didn't know who else to call. I found your number on some papers here in the office."

"Not to worry Mr. Taverell. What may I do for you?"

"Well, it's like this, Sara Mahon has gone missing."

"Missing?   What do you mean missing?" The lawyer's mouth went dry.

"Just that. Two days ago she asked me to look after the office while she went to town for something. She's not been back. I've been sitting in the office from nine to nine. Happy to be able to do it and all, but I thought someone needed to know. There are things need doing that I'm not sure how to do 'em. You know, paying people and whatnot."

He had no idea what to do himself, so he stalled, "What did she say when you saw her the other day?"

"I didn't see her, she just called me and said she needed me to cover the front office for her for a while. I think she might have said something about going to see you. Maybe. I don't remember. Oh, and her car is gone too."

"No, I didn't see her." He was not lying yet, but he made a quick decision to go a step farther. "I don't know anything about her coming to see me. Are you sure that's what she said?"

"Not really. There is another matter Mr. Amundsen. Some guys from Exxon are checking out early and want me to close out their credit cards. They say they won't be coming back for a while. I can't find the slips where they paid."

Kevin deliberately misunderstood while he tried to think of his next move. "They won't be coming back? Have we done something to leave them dissatisfied Mr. Spencer.. um, Mr. Taverell?"

"No sir. I don't think so, they just said they had done what they needed to do here and were going back… back to Texas I think. But if I can't stop charging them for their rooms –there are three of them and they are geologists staying in the fancy trailers, they are going to be pissed when they get their bills."

It occurred to Kevin that this was probably a bit of Mahon's embezzlement coming home to roost. Nothing to do but stall. "Very well, I'll look into it. Can you continue to cover things while I try to find out what's going on?"

"Sure, but what about paying some bills, and the housekeeper is expecting to get paid in a couple of days. I am too for that matter. And I must ask if I'm getting overtime for me' twelve hour shifts?"

"Yes. Yes, you will get your money. I just need find out what's going on. I'll call you back later." He hung up without waiting for the other guy to say anything.

He knew from experience that there was no point in calling Mel at the strip-club before noon so he settled in for another bout of anxious waiting. He thought about calling Vern's banker to see if they might get together to review the water treatment plant that was to secure the loan Vern was getting. He realized that bankers –what-ever else you might way about them, were very good at detecting desperation, and he decided he was too nervous not to appear desperate. Bankers never make loans to desperate people. If things were working out with Mel's scary little monkey guy, there might be no need for get Vern the loan anyway.

When noon finally arrived, he called Mel, but before he could say more than 'Hello' Mel interrupted him. "Good day counselor. Perfect timing on your part. We have much to discuss. Can you come by the club this afternoon?"

"How about right now?" He heard the anxiety in his own voice. He hated it.

"Perfect. I'll see you momentarily."

Kevin put on his coat on the way down the hall and his gloves and hat when he was out on the sidewalk. He decided to walk the few blocks to see if he couldn't settle his nerves. It was early yet, and cold, but there were a few souls out on the streets mostly women but a few office types dressed like he was. He wondered if any of them had worries like his on their minds. He was in debt to some bad people. These bad people found an apparently even worse person to do something very unpleasant and VERY illegal to someone he had hired –and had stolen from him admittedly- but this was the kind of shit that went on in books, not in a little town in North Dakota. Not even a little oil-boom town.

The bouncer let him in immediately, but it was evident that the club wasn't open for business. The neon lights on the walls were off and fluorescent ceiling lights were on. A janitor was damp mopping the floor, and a guy behind the bar was doing things with liquor bottles. Under the glare of fluorescent lights, the place was more sad and tawdry than warm and welcoming, let alone sexy. No naked young women either, but this didn't cross his mind. Nor did Janet. Mel came out of his office behind the lap-dance room and motioned for him to come in. "So what's on your mind councilor?"

Kevin drew a momentary blank and just stared at the other guy with his mouth open. After he recovered himself, he spoke more forcefully that he intended. "The assistant out at the man-camp called to tell me that the woman is missing. And my money. What about my money? And what have you done to the Mahon woman?"

"Calm yourself. She is fine, but… indisposed for the moment. Some of your money has been recovered and is on its way to your creditors. I fear it will not be possible to recover all she has embezzled from you, but our man is still working the problem. We need now to take steps to assure that this doesn't come back to haunt you when it's all over."

"All over?" Kevin felt whatever calm he had acquired on the walk over evaporate. "What the fuck do you mean 'All over'?"

"It would be best for all concerned if we were to keep it professional would it not Mr. Amundsen? Please do not speak to me in that tone of voice."

Kevin shuddered, but replied as calmly as he could. "I didn't expect anyone to be killed. I didn't sign up for that."

Mel nodded. "Of course you didn't, but let me remind you that you did sign a document to engage our Mr. Smith to recover some money on your behalf. But as far as it goes, no one –Ms. Mahon- will be hurt. She is alive and well now and will be on her way out of town in a few days alive and well."

"Good. Thank you. I'm sorry for my tone." He shrugged. "But… but what's happening?"

"To resume, in order to make sure that everything ends up in your favor councilor, we must take steps to keep Ms. Mahon from going to the police. The fact that she has embezzled funds from you is a pretty good start in this direction –she will obviously not be anxious to do anything to bring the harsh light of day upon herself. Unfortunately, her crime is also a good motive for you too have put her in the difficult position where-in she finds herself at the moment. Let us not mince words just now councilor, she has been abducted and motivated to return those funds. I do not concern myself with Mr. Smith's methods in this matter, but I believe him to be both effective and –to some degree at least, um… may I use the word, 'humane'?"

Kevin was thinking again and remembered the assistant manager telling him that there were some charge slips missing. "The guy who called me this morning said there was some stuff missing –credit cards and accounts and such."

"Perfect. I spoke to Mr. Smith earlier. He suggests that you be prepared to call the police and report that she is missing and at the same time, report that missing documents. But not yet. We must follow Mr. Smith's lead in this matter –our man on the ground –so to speak. This will reinforce your looking like the victim, as well as reinforce her willingness to simply go away and stay away. Much the best for all concerned, don't you agree?"

He felt some relief. "It seems to me that Mr. Smith is very good at his job? I mean -he thinks of everything."

"He is indeed, very good. He earns every bit of his fee I think."

Kevin tried not to think of the 50% fee he was paying. Half of something was far better than all of nothing –nothing acquired by entirely legal means.

"What do I do about the day-to-day management in the mean time?"

"Do what would any businessman do in a similar situation. Find someone to take her place while you try to sort out what is going on. But don't call the police quite yet. Mr. Smith is quite clear on this matter. In good time, but not yet."

All in all, Kevin was relieved and felt better than he had since he got the call to begin Mahon's abduction. "Thank you sir. I will follow your instructions to the letter." Mel smiled and slipped effortlessly into his congenial club owner and host persona.

"Excellent. By the way, have you seen our girl Janet lately? I believe she is taking some time off, but will be in sometime in the next day or two."

"I have not."

For the first time thought of the woman. It was a nice thought. He almost said something about taking her somewhere nice once the money was recovered and his client Vern came thru with the investment. He caught himself. No point in letting on that he was about to have more money than the Smith guy was getting. Even so, it was a pleasant thought on the walk back to his office.

Chapter 28

Except for the long days, the cook was enjoying himself. The cooking schedule was not so bad and the teacher was a big help, but added to the various little errands and chores he had to do surrounding Mahon and banks, not to mention the visits to the silo, he was working entirely too hard. At five AM he put out pastries and cold cereal and started the first urn of coffee for the real early risers. By six, scrambled eggs, bacon, sausage, and hot cereal were added to the fare in the dining trailer. By seven he had taken sandwiches –made the day before- out of the fridge and made up a few dozen box lunches. Cheaper than the local coffee shops, and much faster than the fast-food franchisees that had pick-up trucks lined up around the block pretty much all damn day. At five bucks for cold breakfast, seven for hot, and another five for a generous –if starchy-box lunch –never mind the twelve dollars for dinner, the place should have been making a small mint as it helped oil-field workers stay warm for their ten to twelve hour work days. Indeed it was profitable, but the Mahon woman had been taking it.

He was doubtful as to the lawyer's ability to find another manager. Not his problem though. The little Kiwi seemed to be doing the job for the time being. He suspected the lawyer would have to step in and manage the place for himself.

Even more doubtful was the guy's willingness to put on an apron and scramble eggs, or even to pull another cook out of his pocket. He figured the teacher was soon to have himself a real job as a cook. The teacher was not a bad sort. Under other circumstances it might have been nice to chat about the sort of things educated people chatted about, maybe even math or accounting. But best to keep communication to a minimum. When he left town in a few days, he didn't want to have dropped even the least little hint as to where he was from or might be going.

He left another note for his assistant about breakfast clean-up and initial prep for dinner and drove to town to FedEx some documents off to his uncle's people and do a little shopping at Walmart. As he hiked thru the parking lot of pick-ups, he pulled a baseball cap down over his face. He hated the ubiquitous baseball caps, but knew Walmart was full of security cameras and the purchases he was about to make would be a forensic give-away if Mahon was stupid and if the cops had absolutely nothing else to do. Once again, he told himself it was doubtful but a cap was easy and pretty effective at obscuring his face over and above the grainy pictures from a surveillance system. And everybody and his sister wore them. He figured he would stick out more if he didn't have one on. Being a bland little fellow in a large anonymous place like Walmart was no small part of his stock-in-trade. It wasn't likely that some poor cashier would be able to remember anything about the guy who paid cash for the sleeping bag, an air mattress, cheap plastic flashlight with extra batteries, and some trashy novels after a few days of running twenty or thirty people thru her check-stand hour after hour.

After he unloaded the shopping cart and was getting settled into the driver's seat, the cell phone he had taken from the woman rang. He had been careful to keep it charged and close. He had also taken the time to input all the numbers he could find from both her local bank and the one in Minnesota. Caller ID said it was Minnesota. "Sara Mahon's office."

"Good morning. This is First Bank of Minneapolis calling. May I speak to Sara Mahon?"

"Ms Mahon is in a meeting now. This is her assistant. May I be of any help?"

"No, this is a personal mater, When might she be available?"

"I could take a message or perhaps if you were to call back in an hour? I will tell her to expect your call." The cook knew that this sort of call could not be returned, it could only come *from* the bank and be made *to* the phone number on record.

"Thank you. I will call back."

He was outside the silo 25 minutes later and knocked politely on the hatch. "Good morning Ms. Mahon. May I come in?" He didn't wait for a reply, but opened the hatch. "Please step away from the door Ms. Mahon."

He crawled in and found her sitting in her lawn chair. She didn't look much worse than the day before. Not any better, but not worse. "How are we this morning? How is the voice?"

She replied with a curt "Fine" Her voice was better, but not quite as he remembered it. It would have to do.

"Almost forgot, here, have a throat lozenge. You will be getting a call from First Inter-Bank of Minnesota within the hour. Let us review. You have written a check for sixty five thousand dollars to Saratoga Partners LLC and wish to assure your bank they are to honor it. You will thank them for their concern, but everything is in order. You are not to do anything stupid -no secrete messages -no pleas for help. Polite and business like and you will be just a little closer to getting out of here. By the way, I have been doing some shopping on your behalf. If all goes well, I will leave you with an air mattress, sleeping bag, and some novels, which –if the covers are to be believed, describe ageless romance and passionate love. See what a nice guy I am?"

"I'm hungry. And thirsty." Her voice sounded a little better. He guessed she had given up screaming and probably just hadn't had reason to use her voice yet that morning.

"Oh yes. I am sorry, but it's been a busy morning for me. I think we might get another call or two from Minnesota and, if so, I will come out straight away with the phone and some food and drink. Do you like the coco?"

"Coco's fine. Maybe a little liquor?" she said hopefully.

"Nope. Liquor is not a good thing when one is trying to save body heat. For your own good and all. Let us see how well we do on the phone today. There is also the matter of the $40,000 managed account you have with IBS. I think I might be able to use your passwords etc. to sort this money, but I will apparently need your signature."

"Let me out and I'll sign it." Her voice was getting better and better. She seemed also to be more confident today. The cook wondered why that was. He needed her to be a little more frightened –a little more resigned.

"You know that's not how we do things. Are your hands warm enough to handle the phone or do I need to hold it for you?" He reached out to hand it to her and she reached out to take it when they both looked down at her hands. She snatched her hands back but not before he noticed her broken finger nails and filthy fingertips.

"Oh. Of course. You are digging a tunnel" He laughed. "Welcome to Stalag 13. Oh dear Ms. Mahon, how pitiful. I'm very much afraid that chances things." He glanced at his watch. "We have a little while before your bank calls. Alas, I will now need to use the handcuffs."

She started to get up and he shoved her back into the lawn chair which creaked. "You break the chair Mahon, and you will be back to trying to sleep standing up. Put out your right hand." He put the handcuffs on her right arm and looked around the inside of the silo. There was nothing but corrugated metal wall panels bolted together with inward facing flanges, some brackets between the walls and the conical roof, and the pipe between the side and the middle of the floor. "Not very dignified, but it will have to do." He tried to pull her out of the chair and she resisted so he pulled harder. As he did so, she heaved herself up and put her shoulder into his chest. She was clumsy with cold & hunger and he didn't even grunt, but rather used her own momentum to slam her into the wall of the silo. She went down to the ground with her back to the wall. He stood over her, took the free end of the handcuff on her right wrist and it held against the wall with his left hand so her right arm was pinned. He simply stepped on her left hand as she was trying to push herself up off the ground. "You stupid cunt." And he began slapping her unprotected face with his free right hand.

He made himself stop well before he wanted to because he needed her to be collected when the bank called. She was passive and weeping softly. He glanced at his watch again. He had not quite fifteen minutes to get her ready for the phone call, stop the tunneling nonsense, and see if he couldn't take advantage of her cowed state to get a few more signatures out of her. He dragged her a few feet to the junction of the wall and the four inch sheet metal pipe and wrapped her right arm around it and hand-cuffed her wrists together.

It took him only a few seconds to find her excavation. It was about six inches deep and not deep enough to even get under the edge of the metal wall. He wasn't sure how deep the metal went, but it would be a long time before her hole was anywhere big for her to escape, but the question was, how was she doing it? He had checked carefully before he put her in it and there was nothing that would serve. He had brought a thermos that had a plastic cup, but he had taken it away the next morning. The lawn chair? Rounded edges and metal tubes; too big and clumsy as it was, and it clearly hadn't been broken down –it was still in one piece. The box of cornflakes? Did it come with a little shovel prize inside? It had to be something on her.

He made himself comfortable in the lawn chair and looked at her. She had stopped crying and had turned over to an awkward sitting position with her arms around the pipe. "Start counting."

"Are you going to beat me when I count high enough?"

Stupid question, but she wasn't thinking quite clearly. "Nope. I need you to be calm and your voice under control. Start counting from one, or ten or a million if you like. But start fucking counting, bitch."

She started with one and he just looked at her. If he couldn't figure out how she had managed to dig even her pitiful little hole, he would have to do a body search and he was pretty sure this would push her over the edge. She was at just about the perfect place now for what he need her to do, or would be when she had counted for a while. Her coat had fallen open and he did an inventory of her clothing. The coat had buttons and slash pockets. He would search all her pockets in a moment, but the coat didn't have the big metal zippers that were fashionable some years ago. She was wearing a blouse that buttoned. Presumably she wore a bra –she was a big woman and didn't big girls wear bras with under wires. He hoped he wouldn't need to search her bra. Her slacks presumably had a zipper, but he was pretty sure it would be too small –even if she were able to pull it of her pants. Pretty damn sure she hadn't taken off her pants in this cold to dig her silly hole. Then he noticed her belt. It was a stylish woman's belt –thin black leather with a long slender gold buckle. "Take off your belt." She could have reacted with fear as if he were going to rape her. Instead her reaction was one of resignation. He had guessed her secrete.

"I can't with the handcuffs."

He nodded. Plenty of time to deal with the belt later. "Very well. Keep counting."

When she got to 100, he uncuffed her, demanded her belt, and had her sit in the lawn chair. Her voice was getting better and when she was north of 600, her cell phone rang. As she answered it, he took a knee in front of her and simply stared at her with as non-threatening but as serious a face as he could manage.

"This is Sara Mahon"

pause

"Yes, hello Marty. How are you?"

pause

"Fine thank you. What can I do for you?

pause

"I need to close my account."

pause

"No, no complaints about your bank at all. I am making an investment and need the money."

pause

"Yes, I wrote a check to the Saratoga people for that amount. How long do you expect it to take for them to get good funds?

pause

"Now Marty, that's not acceptable, you know my funds are good and you know my credit record. Let's hurry things right along, can't we? If I hear from these people that you people are dragging your feet, I will be chatting with someone downtown. Am I clear?"

pause

"Thank you. You have a mice day too."

She tossed the phone to the cook and they both sighed. The cook was the first to speak. "You did very well Ms. Mahon."

She noticed that it was now *Ms. Mahon* rather than *bitch* and *cunt*. Other than being sixty-five thousand dollars poorer, she was thinking she might live thru it all. He had her sign some more papers that she was too wrung out to bother reading. True to his word, the cook set a sleeping bag, air mattress, and some books on the ground inside of the hatch before he left but he did take her belt.

Chapter 29

She found Jeff's home on 18th Street without any trouble. She had called him that morning after Tonia left to go home. The two girl-friends had themselves a lazy morning –blissfully so for Janet who hadn't slept in for a long time. Tonia made a point of leaving her cell on take-a-message mode and they had coffee and more Pop-Tarts for breakfast. They talked about going shopping, but neither had much enthusiasm so they cocooned till noon.

Jeff's home was kitty-corner from the college's baseball diamond. It was a sprawling brick ranch house with a couple of pick-ups in the driveway; one was probably Jeff's. The neighborhood wasn't as nice as the one she lived in out east of town. She was pretty sure Jeff wasn't the owner of the house, but rather was one of several roommates. There was a big flowerpot on the front porch overflowing with cigarette butts –it had to be the work of several smokers over a long period of time. She hadn't smelled cigarette smoke on Jeff when they studied, so she was pretty sure that Jeff lived with some number of people –probably guys, and probably oil-field workers.

He answered the door promptly. "Howdy Janet. Welcome to. . ." He had a vague idea of something witty to say, but it got away from him. "Well, I don'know what to cal it –my home I reckon is 'bout all I can say." As she stepped in she tripped over a large muddy pair of boots set beside the door. "Oops, sorry. We has a rule about taking your shoes off before you come in –but you doesn't has to. I mean being as you are all . . ." Again, a half formed funny slipped away, but Janet laughed anyway..

She was glad she hadn't put on her stage make-up yet and remembered the afternoon when she bought gas with all her make-up on and got propositioned twice in three minutes. She smiled "I'm all what?"

It occurred to him that this was the first time she had ever smiled at him. She had a nice smile. "Well, whatever you is, you doesn't has to take your boots off. Ya wan'na beer?"

"No thanks." He led her thru a large living room with three miss-matched couches facing a large screen TV and game console into an even larger family room or dining room with more couches –also mismatched- and a single eight foot Formica-topped table with three mismatched dining chairs. The all the walls were painted uniform off-white, not a single picture, book, flower, plant, or decoration anywhere. There were several large Rubber-Maid totes stacked next to one of the couches and a bong sitting on the mantel of a 50's style flag-stone fireplace.   The table had a few pieces of mail and a package with a UPS label. Janet was surprised at how neat it all was and how bland it was. Jeff pulled out a chair for her at the table. "Oh, such a gentleman. So how long have you lived here?"

"'About nigh on to a year now. I've been in Williston longer, but only moved here after a while. I like it here. I live with some nice guys."

"I live alone. How many guys live her?"

"They's four other guys; five all told. Three of us live upstairs and two more live downstairs. We also have kind'a a game room downstairs. It must be nice to live alone."

"Ya, I suppose. Do you hang out with the other guys much?"

"Well, a little. We mostly all just comes home, takes off our boots, and has a beer. I like to put a pizza in the oven, take me a shower while it's cooking. Then I eat and play video-games –maybe just for a little while, and hit the sack. I kind'a work long days and the other guys do too."

Jeff realized he was nattering on, but Janet appeared interested so he went on. "You would think that with five of us living here, we'd be partying all the time. One of us guys is a college boy –geology I think- and he tells us about all the crazy parties he had when he was in a fraternity or something. Sounds like a crazy good time and all, but now he's the first one to puss out go to bed. And it 'pears a lot of his paycheck goes to paying off student loans."

Janet nodded. "Anymore I like to just get home and get warm and sleep. Do you still want me to correct your English? I mean both spoken and your writing"

"Yep. That'd be good. And you still willing to help me with my writing?"

"Seems only fair. If you help me with my math and all."

"So we are kind'a laying down rules and all now. Right?" Janet nodded. Jeff went on. "I has the notion I daren't ask you about your work, but I think you work long hours too?" Wait a minute. 'I *have* the notion. . . –I'm not sure that's right either. 'I *has* the notion' 'I *have* the notion…'

She thought a moment and went on. "Ya, that's right. Just say 'I *have* the idea. . And I don't ask."

It struck Jeff that he was getting close to the prickly neighborhood, but he went ahead carefully. "And don't what?"

"Don't ask me about my work."

"Will do kiddo, but you got'a to know I'm more curious now n'ever."

" 'You *have* to know…"

Thirty minutes later, they had their heads together over book and paper and were making progress on related rates problems when they heard the front door open. A moment later a guy about Jeff's age walked into the family room, saw Janet, and stopped dead in his tracks -his mouth hanging open.

"Janet, this here is Steven. He is in the welding b'ness."

Janet panicked for a brief moment. She thought maybe she might have recognized him from Willy's Place, but she saw so many men that they all looked alike at the club. His reaction, on the other hand, suggested he recognized her. Women were rare in Williston, but this guy looked like he had never seen a woman before in his life. Or he had seen this particular women and seen a lot of her, and had never expected to see her in his own house.

"Hello Steven." She tried her hardest to be casual and extended her hand to him as he stood at the table. She noticed a funny look on Jeff's face as well. Was it pride? Perhaps a little bit of a smirk?

After an hour it was clear that Janet was at the end of what their teacher called her 'learning readiness' and they agreed to stop. Jeff said he would have an essay ready for her next visit. He stopped himself from asking when she would coming by again. He wanted it and she needed it. Wasn't easy, but he kept their Good-by polite and friendly. They had made good progress –both with the math and Jeff was pretty sure she had warmed up to him –just a little.

Chapter 30

While Vern had pretty much decided to go ahead and invest in the water purification plant at Amundsen's man-camp, and he had read the operator's manual but he hadn't ever seen the thing. His banker gave him the go-ahead, and he was pretty confident he had negotiated a good return from the man-camp buying the water from him as well as paying to take away what he had come to think of as the 'used' water. It was enough to pay off the loan in a few years and give him a few hundred dollars a month of taxable income on top.   The taxable part was unfortunate, but there were some nice write-offs and credits to take the tax man's sting out of it all.   If the machinery –or most of the machinery- were to outlast the loan, it would be pure gravy –taxable gravy, but Amundsen told him they would cross that bridge when he came to it.

That just left Sherrie's go-ahead. Almost 20 years of marriage had taught him that *Do what ever you think is best was* not at all the same thing as *Ok, Let's do this.* and he knew he damn-sure wanted the later heartfelt version, so he tossed the manual in the back seat, swung by home and took his wife to a steak lunch at the Williston Brewing Company. After lunch they drove north to the man-camp and checked in at the office to get the key to the building where the treatment plan was. There was no one in the trailer with the big OFFICE sign on the front. "That's odd." said Vern, "Shall we wait? I imagine someone will show up."

Sherrie often embarrassed Vern by ignoring propriety when it suited her. "If we are investing in the place, I feel perfectly justified in looking around." and she walked down the hall leaving Vern in the 'lobby'. A few seconds later she returned, and muttered, "A laundry room and what looks like a big janitor's closet. Both a major mess.", and she continued down the hall in the other direction while Vern read the notices about check-out times, hours of the dining room and a week's menu that was two weeks out of date. Sherrie came back and didn't look impressed. "The first room is someone's office with mail piled up on a cluttered desk. The last room down the hall is clearly someone's bedroom. Vern the place is a mess. I'm going to go out and look around."

"You don't want to see the water treatment plant?"

"Honey, I've seen enough of your big machines to know that I wouldn't know what I was looking at. I trust your judgment about machinery. I won't be long." And she went back outside and Vern tried to learn what he could from the various notices and posters stuck on the wall. Other than the out-of-date menu, they weren't all that different from notices on the door of every hotel room he had ever stayed at.

He as about to head out to find Sherrie and go home when a little middle aged guy bustled in with an armload of linen. "Oh, hello." The guy spoke with an accent. British or Australian or something. "I'm sorry, have you been waiting long?"

"Little bit. Kevin Amundsen told me to see Sara Mahon about a key to the water treatment building. And maybe have her show us around."

The little guy carelessly tosses the laundry behind the desk sat down. "Well now, 'at presents a bit of a problem. The Mahon woman has gone walk-about. We haven't seen her for a few days and are a little short of help. Is there something I can do to 'elp?"

"I'm going to be operating the water plant and I'd like a key to the building. Also my wife has –how did you say it –gone walk-about- to see your operation. If you have a moment, you might check with Mr. Amundsen and see if you could give her the nickel tour. Otherwise, she will have her nose into everything."

"Aye, I'm a married man me'self. If you say it with Mr. Amundsen's voice, it's fine with me." He turned to a large lock box with what looked like hundreds of keys lined up in rows and columns. He took one from the lower right corner and handed it to Vern. "Please be sure to lock it up when you leave and don't let the heat out. Bitch of a problem if it freezes up, don'chu know. Shall I pop out and find you lovely wife, or maybe you could give her a ring on your cell? I'll show her around, but t' fact is that all the trailers look alike 'cept for the kitchen and dining ones."

Vern arranged for Sherrie to meet the guy outside one of the trailers and he walked across the frozen parking lot and up a gentle slope of about a hundred feet of prairie to a small Butler building. He walked around the collection of pipes, motors, pumps, and tanks and was able to recognize everything inside the building from the manual, but it was all a little smaller than he expected. He figured that is was designed to process water, not store it. He didn't do much more that look –other than peeking into a 55 gallon drum labeled 'Sani-Tabs' and found it nearly full of white hockey puck sized tablets.

It took him a few minutes to walk the rows of trailers till he found Sherrie and the little chap with the accent. He stood quietly in the cold for several more minutes while she finished her conversation with the guy. He recognized her being in what they called Mom's Detective Mode and once they were back in his pickup heading back into town, he asked, "You ready to de-brief me?"

She chuckled. "Yep, the little guy is from New Zealand. Everyone calls him The Kiwi, and the place is hopping. Nearly full occupancy, but they have trouble keeping staff to make beds, do laundry, and cook."

"That's no different from most of the businesses around here. What else did he say?"

"He's running his ass off because the regular manager disappeared. She set off to town to met someone –the owner he thought- and never came back."

"Must have been going to see Amundsen."

"I suppose. So now they are getting by with him as full time manager –and that means twelve hours seven days a week. A fulltime cook and part-time cook's helper. Three house keepers and one or two maintenance guys.   All the full time people are working overtime and the part-time people all have other jobs and are working for rent and some of then are getting paid on top of rent. . And do you know what rent is?"

"Kevin says it's pretty high, but oil companies and drilling companies pay it."

"It's $70 a night with a month's stay. More for a week. And I think he said $120 a night if you just roll in for a single night. Meals are extra."

"So what do you think?"

"Other than the place being a disorganized mess, I think it's a license to print money. I also think Kevin should hire Beth to make beds and maybe Robby can do maintenance."

Vern didn't say it, but he was sure they had crossed over to his wife's *Let's Do This Thing* stage. "I was thinking the same thing, only Robby is gong to work for me looking after the water treatment plant. Once or twice a week. He's too young to drive, but he ain't too young to take responsibility for an expensive piece of machinery. I'll help him out and make sure he reads that manual from cover to cover."

"Good idea. They can ride up here together. Beth's driving might improve if Robby is there to um.. well, keep an eye on her."

Vern took a deep breath. "Speaking of Robby, I was thinking about taking him with me out to see Dad. Ronnie's still pretty upset and refuses to have anything to do with the old man and someone needs to do something and I guess it's me."

"You think having Robby there will kind of make things with your Dad a little easier? A little calmer."

"Ah-yep. I figured Robby could go drive the tractor around while dad and I talked."

She glanced at her watch. "Robby will be getting home from school in a few minutes.

Vern glanced at her as he waited for a green light. "So you think this is a good plan?"

She mocked him, "Ah –yep" and they both smiled at their old gag. "And you really think Dad had a hooker out to the farm?"

She got serious. "I can't hardly imagine it, but your sisters seems pretty sure that something weird was going on. He's always been pretty self-centered and ever since your Mom died, he's been running Ronnie ragged with all manner of chores and such. I doubt he realizes it himself, but I think he's simply lonelier than all get out."

"Oh Sherrie, I am so out of my depth with this kind of thing –even more so with Dad. I don't think we said twenty words to each other at Christmas last year. What should I expect to accomplish? What are we trying to do here?" He almost asked her to come with him, but knew that wouldn't have been a good idea –he was just looking for the easy way out.

"Just go be the good Christian man I know you are. I think you've always tried to be a good son to him and it hasn't been easy. That's not much advice, but it's all I can come up with."

Robby was happy to go to the farm with Vern and drive the tractor, but less than enthused about having to read every bit the water plant's owner's manual, but a little more enthused about having a job with pay and being responsible for machinery. He had tried to negotiate the need to drive into the deal but Vern wasn't convinced. Such were the trials of adolescence.

Vern parked right in front of the big window in front of the house just to make sure his dad knew they were there. No way in hell he was risking surprising the old guy like his sister had. Neither he nor Sherrie had told the kids about the situation, nor did he ever intend to, so he figured his dad and son would be OK together. "Before we go barge in on Grandpa, let's be sure you are going to ask politely to drive the tractor and if your Grandpa says no, that's no. And if he has some chore or other for you to do, you do it. OK?"

"Sure Dad."

When they walked up on the porch, Robby was about to let him self in, but Vern stopped him and knocked. Robby glanced at Vern but didn't say anything. When his dad opened the door, Robby popped out with a cheerful "Hi Grandpa."

The old guy glanced at Vern as he welcomed them into the hallway. "Hi Robert, How you doing boy?"

"Fine. Guess what? I'm going to be in charge of a water plant. I will be working for dad. You need any chores done? Or can I drive the tractor?"

Vern's dad smiled with what Vern thought was a touch of relief. "Sure Robert. The tractor is in the barn. You know how to start it. Let it warm up good. They's the straw trailer out in the south field. You think you can back the tractor and hitch it to the trailer? Then bring the whole she-bang around to the back the barn, uncouple it and put the tractor back in the barn. I guess you can take the long way if'n you like." Robby looked at his dad who pretended to consider it very carefully before he nodded permission, and the kid took off.

The men went into the parlor and sat facing each other -Vern on the couch – where he always sat growing up, and his dad sat in the overstuffed chair –where he always sat as well. Neither spoke. Vern got uncomfortable and remembered all the times he had sat there while his father berated him for any number of shortcomings. The room hadn't changed in 40 or 50 years. It was a Midwest farmhouse with his mother's touches. Dark heavy mahogany furniture, cheap framed prints of landscapes and still-lifes on the walls.   Heavy curtains that were shut every winters night against the cold, and taken down and dust-beaten every spring. Beige walls, silver framed photos of family –living and dead- on the mantle and buffet. The floor was original wood with a braided rug that Vern had tripped over a thousand times as a clumsy kid. His dad gave him a ration every time he saw it too. And if he ever forgot to put the rug back the way it belonged, he really caught it. There was no TV. Never had been one.

Vern's dad spoke first. "So I'm guessing your sister had something to say is why you are here.?"

"Yep. She was pretty shook up. Angry too."

"Tain't none of her business. Nor yours neither."

At least his dad wasn't calling his sister a liar. He nodded, "I agree. No one's business but yours and your creator."

"Don't you be telling me about the creator, boy.   How long has it been since I've seen you in church? And I don't want your sister coming here any more. Nor you for that matter with out you call first."

"Dad, I am pretty sure Veronica is not planning to come over –not for a long time any way. She has a family of her own to look after. You recon you can do your own shopping and cooking and laundry? If not, you best hire someone to come and do it for you. You can afford it, can't you?"

"Yes, God damn it, I can take care of my self. And I don't want you or your brood coming over with out an invite. You hear me boy?"

Vern knew that when his dad dropped the G-D bomb, it was time to be somewhere else, but he remembered Sherrie's advice. "Dad, I wasn't there and I don't know what happened. Don't much care for that matter. I guess I might be kind'a proud of you -in a man-to-man way."

He stopped to see if the old guy might have found a little something to smile about but no dice. It was time to wrap things up and hit the road. "Dad, you and I don't get along, my brother Mark lives in Minneapolis hasn't seen you in how many years? Now your daughter Ronnie and you are on the outs. Is this really the way you want things to be?"

His dad glared at him and shrugged. Vern stood up and put his coat on. "I'll help Robby move the hay-wagon and we will hit the road. Good by Dad.

Chapter 31

After almost three days in the silo, Mahon's musings turned away from figuring what her net worth might come out to be and turned instead to three distinct flavors of revenge. Those closest to the surface involved the fucking cook, and what she would do to him given the chance. She worked out the details of how she would get him in the silo, how she would torture him, and how she would keep him alive as long as possible. But she recognized that he was undoubtedly right when he told her she would never find him. Under the best of circumstances, he would be hours gone by the time she got out of the silo and utterly un-findable there-after. Pretty thin gruel for revenge fantasies.

Far more satisfying were the imaginings of what she would do to Amundsen. He was the better target –the more satisfying target for the simple reason that it was far more likely that she would be able to find him when –and if- she got out. She spent the cold empty hours designing varied scenarios as to how she would proceed; how she would abduct him, how and where she would secure his person, what she would do to

105

him. She devised melodramatic conversations they would have as he gradually realized he was going to die -and he was always going to die –usually after pathetic pleading and gnashing of teeth. These scenarios –these imaginings- were detailed and she thought-meticulous. None of this business of criminals and murderers always being tripped up by making a single critical mistake.

But the carefully crafted fantasies only unfolded after she had been awake for a time and after she had some of the hot coco the cook brought her. Otherwise, her most visceral fantasies involved simply being warm. When she wasn't fantasizing about killing Amundsen or the cook, she fantasized about being warm; in a sauna, or in a car without air-conditioning and the windows rolled up in August, or under every electric blanket in the world and every one of them turned on high. What a luxury it would be to sweat. She noticed she stank only after a couple of days in the silo. How could she come to stink so horribly when she damn sure hadn't sweated a drop? The only way she could keep her hands warm was to undo a few buttons on her coat a little and put her hands in her armpits and now her hands stank too.

Trying to read involved too much fiddling about w/ the zipper on the sleeping bag and buttons on her coat. A little too dark too. The air mattress was a bust as well. It took her half an hour to blow it up and doing so almost got her warm when she crawled into the sleeping bag. She stretched out was so exhausted that she fell asleep almost immediately but woke up again a short time later -her teeth chattering and shivering violently –the air-mattress felt like a soft block of ice. She was shivering so violently and her hands so cold and her mind so fuzzy that it took all her will to and fully twenty minutes to simply get up off the ground, step into the sleeping bag, pull it back up over her shoulders, and settle into the lawn chair. Even then it was an hour before she stopped shivering. She was still ever-loving cold and as she began to nod off, she remembered the cooks telling her about the stages of hypo-thermal. That night she was past caring if she died in her sleep.

Her nose ran constantly –and was a mere annoyance compared to the pervasive cold –but she woke once up slumped over a puddle of runny snot in her lap. This set off more weeping and more snot. She took to blowing her nose farmer style. She peed in the corner too, but there was no corner in a circular cell so she used the pipe as a seat, but only once. The metal was so cold that she could feel her body heat flowing out thru the skin on her butt. After that, she squatted. She hadn't eaten enough to need to take a dump, and it wasn't going to be pretty though if and when the time came.

She was aware when daylight came. She was dimly aware when it became less cold in the afternoon and aware when it became dark, but other this, time became a fuzzy notion. Intellectually she knew that outside of the silo there were hours of the dark early mornings that passed -however slowly, they passed, but in her cell –when she crawled up from a troubled sleep in pitch black darkness hearing only the wind and the rumbling whoosh of the gas flare by the oil well out across the prairie- time was meaningless –it stopped –it was infinite. A dozen times a day she cycled from fantasy to sleep and then moved again thru twilight to miserable wakefulness. Every time it was her own screams brought her completely awake.

She was asleep when the cook drove up, parked and opened the hatch. "Good afternoon Ms. Mahon."

No answer. He bent down and looked in to see her slumped in her chair bundled up with the sleeping bag pulled over her head –only her face showed. He watched for a moment and saw a small puff of her breath in the cold air. "Wake up Ms. Mahon." No response. He shouted, "WAKE UP," and he slammed his gloved hand on the side of the silo. The metal was still ringing as she screamed and sat upright.

"Wakey wakey Ms. Mahon. We don't have any business to tend to today, but I thought I'd check on you and bring you up to date. So how we doing?"

Her reply was an inarticulate "I'm cold."

"I imagine. I brought you some more hot coco and a box of cornflakes. Are you OK with corn flakes? We have shredded wheat too –or something with lots of sugar if you prefer."

"Toilet paper. I want toilet paper."

"Oh – hadn't thought of that. Let me see -I think I have a package of facial tissues in my car. In the meantime, let me bring you up to speed as to money matters. Your local bank was most cooperative and that money is now off-shore. Your Minneapolis bank is dragging their feet, but nothing we can do about it. As to your investments with IBS, this has been surprisingly easy and this money is also safely off shore bouncing around in an altogether untraceable manner. I am hopeful we will have concluded our business in a day or two and you can be on your way."

He shut the hatch but didn't bother to latch it. He backed a few steps away watching the hatch -ready to deal with her if she tried to get out. She didn't –as he expected. He watched for a few minutes more, and finally went to his car for the tissue. "Here you are Ms. Mahon. Will this be enough for a while? I plan to visit you again in the morning. In the meantime, do you have any questions?"

He heard a quiet, "No."

"May I ask you what your plans are?"

"My car?"

"It's parked off in the far corner of the man camp. You are missed there -by the way. They are managing without you, but you are missed. No one seems to have noticed your car is still there –not parked in front of the office now, but still there. I plan to bring it here when we are done." He heard her mumbled something, but it didn't understand. "Pardon me?"

She cleared her throat, "You are not gong to kill me –you are going to let me go?"

"Oh dear. Must we go down this road again? I have nothing to gain by killing you. Please note that I am now taking some pains to keep you alive and as comfortable as possible."

She croaked –it was almost a laugh.

"Well . . . as comfortable as possible under the circumstances. I will be hitting the road shortly before you get out. I urge you to follow my example. By all means try your best to recover your money if you must, but you will risk charges of embezzlement.

And besides that, you will simply not find the money. If you stay in the area and make trouble against our mutual client, you run other risks. The councilor is better connected than you might expect. Connected –if indirectly- with people who are rather more violent than I am."

Silence. All in all, he was confident she was not going to be a problem. If she had tried to dive thru the hatch and run away, he would have to reconsider, but she seemed to be exactly where he wanted her to be: cowed, beaten, and compliant.

So he latched the hatch and went back to the kitchen trailer and called his uncle. Their conversation would sound like a friendly family chat to anyone listening in, but the cook learned that the last bank was still stalling. He wanted to wrap things up and hit the road, but not yet.

Chapter 32

Vern finished up a bid for the excavation of a small apartment building going in north of the airport. He had done work for the contractor before and the guy was a pain in the butt, so the he bid high and didn't really care one way or the other if he got the contract.   Then he thought about it and added another ten percent, reprinted it, and thought that at this price he maybe he *would* like to get the job. Maybe. Then he tracked down the part numbers for the injectors for the grader and ordered a set. He deleted the usual bunch of spam and answered two important emails. Finally he called his guy on the grader out at a new oil-well drilling pad. The guy was a great when it came to roads for the North Dakota Department of Transportation. He took a lot of pride in getting things pool-table flat, but the customer in this case didn't care and was in a hurry to start hauling in a drill rig. Pretty usual morning and he felt he had cleared the deck for buying a water treatment plant.

He called Sherrie. "Hi honey. You still want to come to the bank and do the paperwork for the loan for Kevin?"

"Yes I do. I want to get him to commit to hiring Beth for some maid work or something. I'll play the bad guy. Ought to be able to get her a pretty good wage, don't you think?"

"Yep –I think our attorney is a little afraid of you. You still think you want our sixteen year old daughter working in a man-camp?"

"Beth can handle herself –or start learning to anyway. What time?"

"I don't know. What works for you?"

"Anytime is fine with me. When does our banker want us there?"

"I don't know. You want to call and set things up –fit it into your schedule?

"Ya, let me do that. I'll call you and will you call Kevin? I don't want to."

"Honey, I think Kevin would postpone a coronary to meet with us. Why don't you set it up with the bank and call his secretary and tell her when he's to be there. And come by for me. I've got my truck over the pit for an oil change."

Amundsen was sitting in the lobby drinking from a Styrofoam cup when Vern & Sherrie walked in. He jumped up, smiled, and shook Vern's had. "Hi Vern, hello Sherrie. Jack is waiting for us in his office. You ready to go?"

Sherrie sat in one of the chairs in the lobby and gestured to the chair facing her.

"Let's chat a little first Kevin." Vern covered a grin with his hand just as Kevin glanced at him.

He blanched slightly but he sat down facing Sherrie. "Sure, what's on your mind Sherrie?"

"I want you to hire our daughter for after school work."

"Sure. We need help all the time. Will $15.00 an hour be enough?"

"That's fine, but I don't want her to be alone horny young oilfield workers."

"No problem. I think she can make sure she only works with another girl… well, with another older women –making beds and such. Is this OK?"

Sherrie nodded. Kevin went on. "So let's be clear. Do you want her to work like the daughter of an investor, or do you want her to work like any other worker?"

Vern had been standing watching his wife doing her best work but now he jumped in. "I hope you know the answer to that question Amundsen. School comes first, but I expect her to work as hard as anyone working there. Maybe harder."

Kevin sat back and raised his palms in a defensive gesture. "OK –I thought so. She is your daughter and I'm sure you raised her right -but I just wanted to make sure."

Sherrie raised a second finger. "Next, I want you to help her with any social studies, history or law question she might have."

"Sure. No problem. In fact, I'd be delighted to."

Vern sat down next to Sherrie, "By the way, our son will be in charge of looking after the water treatment plant. I'll help him figure it out, but the day to day maintenance will be up to him."

"Vern, I don't now anything about the machine. I'm confident you and he will keep us well supplied with fresh water. He turned to Sherrie. "What else?"

Sherrie answered. "Nothing. Let's find our banker and get the papers signed."

When Kevin got back to his office there were about one hundred thousand dollars more in his checking account than there were when he left. The money the man-camp was going to be paying for water had jumped by a considerably amount, but Vern –or Vern's banker- had cut a good deal and he could live with –particularly without the Mahon woman embezzling funds. He was still short by about that amount on what he owed Mel's guys but it was a good start.

Mel had told him to only call about the strip club; the matters involving the man-camp were never to be mentioned on the phone. Kevin took this rule very seriously –one of many things he was coming to take very seriously. None-the-less, he wanted to talk to the guy, so he called and invited Mel to lunch at The Williston. The guy seemed surprised, but pleased and they agreed to meet at eleven thirty. He considered calling Janet, but decided to wait. He had a little time to kill before walking to the restaurant, so he checked out flights and accommodations to Vegas and Lake Tahoe. Both looked good. He would prefer Lake Tahoe and a little skiing, but he'd gladly leave it up to Janet.

Mel hadn't expected the lawyer's call. It disturbed him when unexpected things happened. He linked things to go as planned: Exactly as planned and he had been taught to plan very carefully indeed. The lawyer seemed far more cheerful than he should have been. It was an invitation to the nicest restaurant in town –indeed the only one with a decent wine-list, aged beef, and an unctuous wait-staff in black-tie. Mel had related cautiously good news to the lawyer about progress with the Mahon woman, but stalled as to the actual payday.

Something was wrong. Why was the lawyer so happy? He made a mental note to talk to his girl Janet when she came in. Clearly it was time for her to renew her relationship with the lawyer. Mel needed the sort of information best gathered by a lovely woman in a man's bed. In the meantime, he could easily get an update from Mr. Smith out at the man-camp by having one of their carefully worded double-talks. The cook took his time answering the phone, but Mel figured it was because he was involved in his 'cover' and needed time to get to a private place to talk.

"Good morning chef. Can we discuss your work in the kitchen?"

A curt "Yes. Local sources are proving adequate for our immediate needs. Suppliers from out of town are slower. The larger of the out-of-town source we discussed has been cooperative and the other one, regrettably slower. As to the long-term wholesale source, it should be no problem but will of course be an on-going arrangement. I expect everything to be done within a day or two at this end. If you need more detailed information, you will need to contact the office."

"Thank you chef. Keep me posted." And he hung up. He translated the double talk. The Williston bank had yielded up its funds, but the Minnesota bank funds were not yet forthcoming. The funds from the brokerage account were in hand and the paperwork for taking a homeowner's equity line of credit on her house in Minneapolis was in progress but drawing funds down would be a long careful process. For the better date on the banking situation, He would need to call Uncle Julian in Kansas City.

Mel figured he would be honest with the lawyer and made the decision as much on instinct as anything. They had –or shortly would have- recovered $130 from the woman and Amundsen would receive 50% or $65 thousand against the roughly $100 thousand he owed the boys in Kamas City. The remaining $35 thousand should be sufficient to keep the guy on the hook –a little scared and very cooperative.

As to the $100 thousand or more they would be able to extract from the woman's home equity, this was more difficult. Mel was sure his uncle would view it as gravy and theirs to keep. It took time and considerable on-the-ground support. They had a banker who had been a reasonably honest family man, but with an unfortunate gambling problem. He had repaid his loans many times over and did so by bending baking regulation more than by paying his money debts. The guy would eventually get caught, loose his job, possibly go to jail, and his life would be ruined, but not before he had been very useful to Uncle Julian. The lawyer's money they recovered was important, but –like the banker- perhaps less important that his usefulness down the road.

He picked up the phone and dialed. "Janet dear, are you thinking of coming in this afternoon? I want you well rested, but if you are feeling up to it, I'd like a brief chat with you when next you come to the club." Pause. "Thank you Janet. I will see you shortly."

The club hadn't opened yet and his people were either involved in setting up the bar or janitorial tasks, so he had the club bouncer drive him to the restaurant where he indulged himself in a perfect martini and enjoyed the ambiance of the restaurant's exposed beams, wood paneling, and stone fireplace with a slow fragrant fire at the between the dining room and the bar. In a town where restaurant décor ran more to fast-food chrome & plastic or truck-stop seedy, *The Williston* stood out. The prices matched Kansas City –or even Manhattan for that matter. Curious that Amundsen extended the invitation. On top of that, the guy kept Mel waiting. He was nearly fifteen minutes late when he wondered into the bar looking for Mel.

Mel stood and tossed back the last of his martini. "Good morning councilor. Would you care for a cocktail before lunch or shall we go in to eat directly?"

Kevin gestured to the dining room host. "Let's sit down. I might have a glass of wine." The host knew both men and led them to a nice table, took Kevin's order for a glass of burgundy, and withdrew discretely. The men sat quietly for a moment; he lawyer trying to figure out how to ask about Mahon and his money, while Mel wondered why the other guy had become so confident since their last meeting.

Mel began, "Well, things are almost done with our recovery efforts."

"Do we have a figure yet?"

"It seems that it stands –or will soon stand- at about $130 thousand, but it will take some time for it to work itself back our way, and let us not forget the commission our agent has earned."

Kevin found something interesting on the ceiling to study. "So she will have successfully stolen… what, $70 thousand?" I guess this is as good as it's going to get?"

The money the boys in Kansas City were going to extract from the woman with a phony mortgage crossed his mind, but he kept a stern face. "In matters like this, complete recovery is always problematic. I would say that all things considered, we have done well. And please councilor, it is always best to speak in the broadest generalities both on the phone and in public." And in the broadest generalities, he wanted this guy frightened. Why wasn't he?"

"I'm sorry –not used to this sort of thing." Amundsen took a sip of wine. "By the way, I will be able to paying off the balance of the loan from your associates with separate funds –I mean over and above whatever we finally get out of Mahon. I also plan to do a little marketing to make sure we are running at 100% capacity."

Mel saw it coming. He knew his grip on the guy had diminished. Not entirely; he still had the written agreement hiring 'Mr. Smith' to recover the embezzled funds. Mr. Smith left the credit card slips to help the police explain the Mahon woman's sudden disappearance, if it should ever be necessary, but he had also carefully left several circumstantial clues that would implicate the lawyer if it came to that. Altogether sufficient to induce the lawyer to do little favors for his team when the time came. There was much money to be made in Boon-Town Williston. But he wanted to know where the lawyer's windfall came from.

Amundsen closed the menu. "I don't know why I bother to read the menu, I always order surf and turf. What are you having Mel?"

"The same I guess. How did you find the money? If you don't mind my asking."

"I have a client who is an excavation business. You know, lots of big expensive machinery. It occurred to us that the water treatment plant is also just a big machine that doesn't move. He financed it pretty much like he financed his earth-movers.   He gets some nice write-off too."

Damn the little guy thought to himself. Imagine that? –something as simple as asking got him an answer.   A little too late, however. If he had known beforehand, he might have been able to scotch the deal. Maybe their tame banker could have temporarily screwed up the dirt guy's credit for as long as it took to finish seducing the lawyer. But only so much he could do. All the more reason to urge Janet to get close.

They ordered; Amundsen the large surf & turf, and Mel the small portion. "Well, congratulations. This has to be a load off your mind." *Now to put another load back on.* Perhaps a more pleasant one, but no less useful to Mel. "How is our girl Janet?"

"You know, I've been so busy that I haven't seen her for a while."

"I hope that has changed. She is a lovely young woman, and I suspect not to be taken for granted for any period of time, lest she…." He let his voice trail off. "Damn right. I'm thinking of taking her to Lake Tahoe. You don't happen to know her schedule -off hand- do you?"

"Excellent idea. Don't worry about her schedule. She is one of my best… most popular dancers but for a friend, I'm sure we can get by without her for a few days. Give her a call and she and I will sort it all out."

They spent the rest of lunch talking about the club. Kevin had always been a little curious that his advice on avoiding taxes was politely ignored, but he had come to realize that it was simply because they didn't pay taxes –beyond a certain point.

When Kevin got back to his office, he immediately called Janet. She was lukewarm on the idea of Lake Tahoe and skiing, but more enthused about Las Vegas. She stressed that she lost money when she wasn't at work. So he assured her he would be happy to make up the difference and they came to discuss the when and where of a trip together. It took not quite an hour –much of the time spent waiting on the internet, but they tentatively agreed on three days in the middle of next week with an option to extend their stay to five days ending on Saturday. Kevin was to pay for everything and pay her a cool five hundred dollars a day –in cash. It was still a little tentative as far as Janet was concerned, at least until she chatted with her boss at the club. Kevin didn't tell her he had just finished lunch with Mel, but clicked on the CONFIRM NOW button on his computer right after she hung up.

A few hours later Janet came thru the back door at Willy's Place and knocked on Mel's door. "Come in."

"Hi Mel. You got a minute?"

"For you Janet, always. What can I do for you?"

"I need some more time off. I know you let me off yesterday and thank you, but

I have the chance to go to Las Vegas."

"Oh. How nice. Anyone we know?"

"Well, ya, Kevin the lawyer or is he an account? . But you told me to leave him alone. At least for a while. I told him I had to check with you first."

"Oh. Of course. By all means, Go. Have fun.

Janet didn't bother to try to hide her confusion. "Mel, what's going on here? I like my job and all. I'm grateful that you let me set my own schedule and work the best shifts too, but what am I supposed to do. I kind'a like the guy. I mean –just as a guy. And he's nice to me."

Mel nodded and steeple his fingers in front of his mouth. "Nothing illegal here Janet. Kevin Amundsen and I –well, some out of town associates of mine- are doing business with the councilor. Rather a lot of business and it's important that he be happy." He shrugged as he went on. "And it would be helpful if we knew just a little about his finances. You know –if something changes, we'd like to hear about it. Nothing you are not comfortable with, just…what do they call it? 'pillow talk'? Just all part of doing business. I assure you, Our friend Kevin has done his research on us too." This last was a flat-out lie, but it seemed to set her mind at ease. He changed the subject. "How are your studies going?"

"Fine thank you. I have people helping me study. This is why I'm not coming in till seven or so. It's the only time we can get together."

"How nice. Well, off you go. We have lonely oil-field workers out there with too much money."

It was only as she closed the door to his office behind her that it occurred to her that she hadn't told him she was studying for her GED –or studying at all for that matter. Creepy. The guy was definitely creepy. She had to talk to Tonia ASAP, and call Kevin and tell him she was good-to-go for the trip.

Chapter 33

Jeff spent his lunch break writing another essay and used the odd moments between pulling inventory off shelves and putting it on trucks to check spelling and grammar. It was as tedious as shit. The way he pronounced words –the way everyone he grew up with pronounced words, seemed to have damn little to do with the way the dictionary insisted things should be pronounced –let alone be spelled. A few of grammar rules she and the teacher laid on him seemed a little less onerous. Janet tended just to say something was wrong and not explain why, but the teacher explained things like direct objects and the rules that governed their use. A little like the rules of algebra -more of them in grammer, but he supposed they had their own logic.

He remembered the essay he had written about Janet; the one wherein she didn't recognize herself, so this time he wrote a few plodding paragraphs about his job. The teacher had told him that –at least as far as the GED test went, organized bland writing with good grammar and spelling was better then interesting work with mistakes. If this was the case, he figured Janet was the perfect writing coach. So be it.

He got home in time to take a shower and dress in something besides his usual after-work-before-bed-time garb which was a hoody and long bathrobe. He even shaved. When she showed up, she didn't notice and immediately pulled out a worksheet the teacher had given her. "Here. Check this.". He gave her the essay and she seemed surprised. "We agreed this was a two way street, right Janet?"

She shrugged, "Ya sure." and started reading.

The worksheet involved converting expressions from sums to products and back again using the distributive property. Pretty simple stuff. She did fine when there were only numbers and a single variable, but when there was more than one variable she messed up. She actually found a way to make it more complicated and it took him twenty minutes to *unteach* her the wrong way and then teach there the right way. Once again, she got frustrated. "Why can't you just teach how to pass the test? How am I supposed to ever use this?"

"Janet, we've done been down this road 'afore. It's easier in the long run to learn wha'chur doing and maybe the least little bit of the why."

She folder her arms and stared at him. She looked like little brat and he couldn't help laughing. He managed an "I'm sorry."at about the same time her lower lip came out and her eyebrows dropped into a scowl. She looked even more like a like a spoiled little kid and he completely lost it. It could have gone either way, but she laughed too and Jeff felt they had had gotten a little closer. It felt good.

She had marked a few words on his essay and they went over the spelling. It turned out that he got the word right, but some of them were the wrong damn word. Things like *there, they're,* and *their* –he remembered this sort of thing from school before he dropped out to work offshore. Pain in the ass, but if she was going to learn the *why* of algebra, he was damn sure he could keep track of all the flavors of some almost-the-same words and some grammar. She also admitted it was his best writing yet..

"So you still going to class ever' morning?"

"Yes. I took a day or two off to catch up on my sleep, but I want to be done and enroll at Williston State College sometime."

"So teacher Mike is giving you worksheets?"

"Ya?"

Jeff nodded, "I don't have all the worksheets and books and such. Maybe you could get a stack of 'em and I could make sure you know what'chur doing before you waste time doing them wrong. And if Mike has a list of things you need to learn, we could kind'r sneak up on 'em. He kind'r sets the pace for us." He gestured at the telephone-sized GED workbook she brought. "I don't think y'all are getting much out of the book. You bring it all the time and we haven't' even opened it. And…and you could show Mike my writing and see what he thinks."

After Janet left, it occurred to Jeff that she had actually spent a little time helping him –not as much as he spent helping her, but it might have been a start. And they had that moment when they both were laughing. He got a beer, put his feet up and played a little *Death Watch* on the X-Box. He was about to fall asleep when a couple of his roommates got home; both a little drunk. "Well, howdy boys. Had a little fun this evening, did y'all."

Tommy –the crane-rigger- grunted –but that's all Tommy ever did. He went on into the kitchen to eat. The other guy, Steven, said a cheerful "Hi guy." And sat down on the couch by Jeff. "I got something to tell you." Jeff moved his estimate of his being a little drunk to pretty drunk. He hoped it was Tommy who had driven. "Why don'chu ever come to he strip clubs with us Jeff?"

"I dun'know. Just seems to me that looking at ne'kid women just reminds me what I'm missing." Jeff liked the guy. He was the youngest man in the house, but not as young as he came off, He was a gentle soul. He had learned to let Steven get where he was going in his own good time. "You have something on your slightly drunk mind?"

"Yep." Silence

"You want to share it with me?"

"Yep. Just tying to figure out to put it."

"Take your time."

"You know that girl you was setting at the table with the other night?"

He had Jeff's attention now. "Ya?"

I mean do you KNOW her?"

"Ya, she is a student down to the college. She's studying for her high school diploma same as me and I'm hep'in her with her math. An' she's helping me with my writing. Nary a thing more'n that."

"But she's hot, isn't she?"

"Oh, YA –right pretty."

"And a stomping hot body too, right?"

"Ya?"

"Don't get mad buddy, but I'm pretty sure I've seen her down at Willy's Place. She's a stripper."

"Oh." Jeff thought for a minute. "I recon that s'plains a lot. Don't really make no never-mind. We ain't more'n what'cju call study-buddies. She's kind'a a cold one."

Steven went off to get something to eat and Jeff considered his new insight. Back in Louisianan, when he came ashore, he and his buddies spent time and money in various roadhouses and honky-tonks. Occasionally they would drive into New Orleans and hit the strip clubs. He learned -not quickly- but he learned that cocktail waitresses were difficult to date and as far as the strippers went, they were totally impossible. Some of his buddies never figured this out and went broke. One poor hick was so besotted with a dumpy bucktoothed girl that he actually lost his job. It occurred to him that he and Janet had a nice relationship -not a sexual one, probably never would be, but it was almost mutual and getting more so each time they met. The way his daddy treated his mom came to mind. Clearly they'd had sex -he had a sister and two brothers, but they had fun together. And the look on his roommate's faces when they saw him sitting with Janet all cool and casual, that was worth a lot too.

Chapter 34

After he got breakfast wrapped up, he called his uncle for an update. The word from Kansas City was that, "Everything is in hand. We are working on the final matter

-the refinancing- per your instructions. Our friend in the banking industry has been most accommodating. It appears there is nothing more to be done at your end."

"So let us be clear. I can return things to the status-quo?"

"By all means. Are you sure the best solution is not…um, a more final one?"

The cook had certainly considered killing the woman –or leaving her to die, but simply saw it as unnecessary. His earlier involvement with an abduction for his uncle probably ended in the guy's death –and probably not a quick or easy one. While the cook was not present for the actual killing, he was troubled for weeks afterward; nightmares, thoughts of his mother's death, his own eventual end. Finally, he tried -and failed- to reconcile his Uncle's Catholicism and the old guy's willingness to kill whenever it served his ends. The cook finally decided there were some limits to his own pragmatism. He didn't go so far as to define his reticence as an ethic, such an admission would have opened a huge can of worms- but killing was not going to be a part of his tool-kit. "Uncle, I have taken some pains to assure that the other party will not step outside of our negotiated plan. Anything as drastic as what you propose would invite investigation and slow things down to a unacceptable degree. Possibly even federal involvement."

"This must be avoided at all costs. Carry on. Take some time off and come to see us when the time is right."

He hung up and immediately got the attorney on the phone. "Good day councilor. You may be getting a call shortly demanding money for the employees of the man camp. You must stall till tomorrow. It is beyond my purvey, but I would suggest that you be prepared thereafter to pay to your staff. Things are falling apart at the camp now, and are about to get worse. But I repeat, You must do nothing today."

"Um. Ya. OK. Why?"

"Do not concern yourself with the *why* councilor, just do as I ask." and he hung up.

From there he went to the office trailer at the other end of the man-camp and found the little Kiwi chap sitting behind the desk. "Good morning Mr. Tavaral. How are you today?"

"A bit stressed I am. Still no sigh of Ms. Mahon. Some of the staff is getting restless."

"Oh dear, I fear I am not going to make your life any easier. I have been expecting my own paycheck for a few days now. What can you tell me?"

"I can'na tell you a thing."

"Perhaps you should call the owner?"

"I already did. He's a wanking lawyer and used more words to say less that ever anyone I ever heard. I plan to call him in the PM about some other bills. Can I talk to you later?"

"Do what you can. I will get dinner out, but if I am not paid today, I will have no choice but to move on down the road. And get my own lawyer."

"I ain't got paid neither. You think your lawyer might work for both of us? Money is tight at my end and it 'pears we are in the same boat."

The cook nodded. "I'll ask. Good-day."

The cook was leaving a paycheck on the table, but it was a tiny amount compared to his cut of the reverse embezzlement. And there was no way to recover it without leaving a forwarding address –and a trail. Unacceptably high risk for a minuscule reward.

He returned to the cooking trailer and did his own odd version of a meditation. The next 10 or 12 hours were critical –the highest risk. He methodically imagined every step necessary to both release the Mahon woman and leave himself. Long habit and an obsessive nature had ingrained these meditations in everything he did –or everything extra-legal. It was how he made sure he made no mistakes –left as little up to chance as possible. His immediate plans were simple enough; he would go shopping one more time –some miscellaneous items for tonight's meal, as well as a shovel, pick, some candles & matches, and –what the hell, he could be a nice guy- even some work gloves for the woman to use to dig herself out. He owed her a small debt of gratitude for giving him the idea for letting her out long after he hit the road. She would need her strength so he added a hot meal to the mental shopping list. He figured it would take hours for her to chip away at the frozen ground under the edge of the silo. Plenty of time for him to be well away –even if she were stupid enough to go to the police. He had done everything he could to minimize this risk, but as far as maximizing the likelihood that she would behave as expected, she would need her car. He had moved it to an inconspicuous corner of the man-camp days before. It would be a simple matter to drive it to the hidden space behind the silos. He had parked there himself a couple of times. There was a risk of its being seen for the few hours it would be parked there, but an acceptable and unavoidable. There was also the risk of his being seen driving her car. Minimizing this risk at a low cost was simply involved doing so after dark *IF* the damn car started. It hadn't been driven in since before he had stuck her in the silo. He got up, went to her car and started it in the comparative warmth of mid-day, and let it get good and warm. The gas gauge indicated about three quarters of a tank.

This little errand was precisely the sort of thing that he knew justified his meditations. He returned to his room, got comfortable, closed his eyes, and started it all over again from the start. He found no other risks and no other possible hiccups. He packed everything he had brought with him into his own car, wiped his fingerprints from all the surfaces in his bed and bath rooms. The risk of anyone finding his useful fingerprints in the dining trailer was acceptably low given a hundred men used the plates and cutlery, and his assistant did most of the actual cooking. He left for what he was sure would be his last trip into Williston.

He had his assistant get dinner out and instructed him to postpone the clean-up till the next day. When it was dark enough, and most of the camp was either at dinner, or sleeping, he drove her car to behind the silos. He gathered the pick, shovel, matches & candles, and her purse from the trunk of her car. "Good evening Ms. Mahon. Please move away from the hatch."

He didn't wait for a reply, but held the shovel over his shoulder in readiness as he opened the hatch. He didn't bother to bend down to see her, but simply tossed in her purse, the pick, and the other things in. He carefully set a large bag of McDonalds hamburgers, fries, and coffee on the ground just inside the hatch. He even bought her a hot cherry thing that MickyDees called a *pie*.

"Let us review. Your car-keys are in your purse. As is your cell phone. The battery, however, is completely run down. You just heard me drive up in your car. It has most of a tank of fuel and your credit cards should still work. If you are stupid enough to go to the police when you have managed to dig yourself out, I will be long gone. *Long. Gone.* Amundsen has alerted the police that you are missing and that you have embezzled money from the man-camp, but he will not be pushing to get other –higher– authorities involved. The police won't be very interested, but he has been gathering explicit proof of your embezzlement. Far better you get out of town, find a motel, take a hot bath, charge your cell & make calls, do whatever you want. I don't care. When you are back home –I presume Minneapolis, feel free to try to recover the money. It will be a fruitless effort, but take your best shot. If you come back to Williston, the police will be looking for you, and what is more, someone –not me –someone who. . . who deals in more permanent solutions to various problems will come looking for you as well. Do you understand?"

A single defiant "Yes" issued from the hatch. He tossed the shovel in and closed & locked the hatch, and slowly walked across the frozen dark prairie to his own car in the man camp. He was in Denver fourteen hours later for a late breakfast.

Chapter 35

As he promised the Kiwi, Amundsen showed up the next morning with his checkbook. "Good morning Mr. Tavaral. Ya' know. I don't believe I ever heard your first name?"

"Me' first names *Anaru* Mr. Amundsen. It's a traditional Maori name –for Andrew –New Zealand and all, but me' parents were from Scotland, so Spencer is me' middle name. Long story. Most folks around here just call me 'Kiwi.

"If you are sure, *Kiwi* it is. I'm here to do what I can to keep things running as smoothly as possible. It looks like Ms. Mahon has simply taken a powder?"

"Aye,. More'n that, I dun'know. Last I spoke to her was a few days back. She asked me to cover for her while she went to town. Nary a word since."

"I have reported this to the police. They don't seem to be very interested. If it turns out she has embezzled money from the man-camp, I might be able to get the police more interested. I'll need the books, but for the moment, we need to get you and everyone else paid and –like I say- keep our guests happy here."

"I only ever checked guests in and out and organized house-keeping and maintenance. I'd not know anything about the books and what-not."

Amundsen nodded. "Well, first things first. Who all needs a paycheck?"

For the next hour they worked together reviewing the payroll; who did what and how much they earned. No doubt in Amundsen's mind that he had been paying for more people than really were working there. The Kiwi was pretty sure the three women who did housekeeping and the guy who did maintenance planned to stick around if the were to get a paycheck that day. "There's been a lot of discussion around here what with Mahon gone walk-about. I think the staff is pretty understanding. This sort of thing is nae uncommon in these parts."

The cook was a problem however. He hadn't served breakfast that morning and appeared to be gone. There had been complaints. As Kevin was writing checks at the front desk, a couple of guys in coveralls and parkas came in to ask about breakfast. They were not happy and Amundsen apologized and assured they there would be breakfast the next morning.

When they stomped out again, the Kiwi looked at the lawyer and asked, "How you going to do that? We have no cook –just a part time cooks helper."

"Can we get this guy to go full time and get food out?"

"I don't know. He cut some kind of deal with Mahon for a room. I think he might be a teacher or something in town. He only works afternoons."

"Can you get him in here soon?"

"Sure. He usually stops in after lunch. There's another wee matter Mr. Amundsen."

"Oh?"

"I've been manning the desk now from 7:AM to 9:PM for four days now. I can'na go on much longer and I figure you owe me for a little over-time." Amundsen figured the guy was not usually so forthcoming –rather he was truly getting a little wrung out. "Understood. If you can give me a just little more of your time to teach me just the rudiments of your procedures, I'll cover for you –let you get some time off. As to overtime, I agree, but I'll need some record. I'm afraid there's been way too much stuff done without paperwork around here."

They traded seats; Amundsen got behind the desk and the Kiwi got comfortable in one of the chairs in front of the desk. They spent another hour reviewing the procedures for checking guests in and out. Kevin was coached on finding things on the computer, finding keys, finding credit card forms. He sent the Kiwi off and started unraveling the books. There were bills that were unpaid and bills that had apparently been paid more than once. The material he had forgotten from his *Auditing 101* class back in the day as an undergraduate came back. Shortly after lunch he called Beulah in his office downtown and told her she was running things there until further notice. He started two lists: one of items he wanted to bring from his office and another one –a TO-DO list scheduled to wrap up at noon the day he and Janet were leaving for Las Vegas. Top of the list was to call an employment or temp agency about beginning to find another on-site manager. But it was all to be done before the plane left. If it wasn't done by then, it wasn't getting done.

He was finishing up a call to the restaurant supply store to sort out what he owed and how they could help keep food going into the dinning room, when a guy in a tweed jacket and soft lather book-bag came in. He looked confused for a moment and Amundsen gestured to the seat in front of the desk as he confirmed an appointment with the food salesman for late in the day.

"You must be the teacher who helps out the cook?"

Mike nodded. "Yep. Who are you?"

"I own the place." Kevin knew more about Mahon's absence than anyone, but only to a point. He didn't really want to know, but asked just to seem suitably ignorant. "You don't know where Sara Mahon went do you?"

"Nope. Seems to me someone said you were a lawyer?"

"Yes I am. No one else knows what happened to her either. Have you seen the cook?"

Mike shrugged. "No. He had me get dinner ready yesterday. Is he gone too?"

Kevin nodded. "We seem to have a little trouble hanging on to employees lately. Late paychecks and all."

"Good news, bad news kind'a thing for me. Good news is that I'm not being paid. I am supposed to help out three hours a day for my room. Bad news is that it's been a lot more than three hours lately and I'm… well, it's time to renegotiate the agreement."

Amundsen had lots of experience negotiating and went to default his ass-hole lawyer posture. "Your agreement with the Mahon woman is now… null and void."

"Understood. By my reckoning, I have just over a weeks stay coming to me." At the end of this time, you will either pay your going rate or I will have moved on." Mike stood up to leave.

Amundsen realized the guy was a better negotiator than he first guessed. His opening gambit was poorly done. It could be fixed, but it probably was going to make that fix more expensive. "We will see. Before you go. Could you bring me up to speed on the procedures in the kitchen."

Mike looked down at the guy. "Sure thing councilor. But first, could you bring me up to speed on the procedures in employment litigation --and do it for free?"

The lawyer bristled caught himself before he said anything. He needed the guy. He also moved his estimation of the guy's negotiating posture up another notch. The only gambit he had left was to be honest, beg a little and hope that the other guy was a reasonable man. He gave him a crooked grin and gestured to the seat. "Please Mr. Williams. Let's Talk. You clearly know I'm over a barrel and you are in the best position to help me. At least until I can replace the cook. How might we be of benefit to one another?"

Mike sat back down and considered. "Well, for starters, why don't you scribble out a receipt for services rendered indicating I'm paid up for eight more nights stay. Use lawyerly talk as you like, but let's make it simple enough."

"Fair enough."

"As to the kitchen, quite frankly the cook left most of the cooking to me. He seemed to be quite busy with other things. Don't know what. He was not a particularly outgoing fellow."

Amundsen suppressed a shudder at the mention of the cook's being *busy with other things* but lied. "I never met the man. He was a Mahon hire."

Mike went on, thinking as he spoke. "As for the procedures, and how we might get 'er done, breakfast has to be started at about five AM. I could get it on the table and head off to my other job at nine. You knew I was a teacher?" He doesn't wait for an answer. "I am in Williston State College from nine to noon. Typically, I have a shopping list of stuff to bring back for the kitchen. Sometimes it's cleaning stuff. Depends on what's cooking, but that starts at about one or two and food is on the steam tables by six. Cleanup goes on more or less continuously from seven till ten and breakfast & box lunches have to be prepped somewhere in there." He counted on his fingers. "Let's see. That makes for just about seven hours for little things like sleep. Do-able –but only for a short time. Probably a very short time –for me anyway."

"Can we get someone from housekeeping to help with the dishes and clean up?"

"Just what I was thinking. And it occurs to me that with less from-scratch type meals, and more ready-to-serve food, the labor time could get cut way down. Price probably goes up, but…"

Kevin didn't even need to think about it. "Do it. By the way, I have a salesman from some food broker or something coming by this afternoon. We are hoping to sort out our bill. Do you know something called Forbes Food Inc.?"

"Yes I do. I occasionally went there to pick up an order. Oddest thing. Ms. Mahon insisted I buy things there even when they were cheaper at Walmart –and even if I was going to Walmart the same day."

Kevin grimaced. "It is too soon to say, but it appears that Ms. Mahon did any number of things with my money that are a little… *oddest thing* did you say? But anyway, if it's convenient perhaps you could join us at two thirty?"

"Sure. This leaves the matter of my pay."

"Twenty five an hour over and above the three hours you work for a room sound OK?"

"Twenty five an hour, free bed, and time-and-a-half for anything over forty hours a week."

Both men did the negotiating thing with good grace and something like mutual pleasure. They settled on $20.00 an hour and one shopping trip per day in Mike's little pickup to pay for the room in the staff trailer. They weren't going to be friends, but respected one another. Perhaps under different circumstances…

When Mike got back to his room and before he changed into his cooking clothes, he sat down at his laptop and opened a spread-sheet. He remembered his first day in the trailer talking to the guys from Slumberburton Services when he tried to mentally calculate their pay at so much an hour with so much over-time at time-and-a-half and so much at two-and-a-half, but now he did it for himself. Most pleasing. Added to what he was earning at the college, the numbers were impressive. More than he had ever earned in his life. Even with the high cost of 'rent.' Then he projected it forward for months and years at various interest rates. Even more impressive, but not realistic so he subtracted a little every month for clothes and incidentals. He even went so far as to down-load the tax tables from the IRS and factor this vexatious little cost into things. And the cost of a new car at so much a month, or a single payment for a used car in a few months provided his little pick-up –please God- kept running just a little longer.

All in all, he spent an hour playing *what if* games with numbers. He had finally at long last fallen into what was a good thing and resolved to do a great job and make it last as long as possible. Or as long as he could keep up the pace. But everyone in Williston worked long hours –he damn sure could too. But he had just wasted an hour better spent in the kitchen. Time to get to it.

Chapter 36

She got as far as a little town about three hours east of Williston. It was that much closer to her home in Minneapolis but exhaustion led her to pull into a motor lodge. The little mid-eastern woman behind the desk looked at her carefully before she gave Mahon the registration card. "I've had some car troubles. This is why I look the way I do." It seemed to satisfy the little bitch. Sara thought she might burst into tears if she were turned away.

She had dug all night stopping only when the last of the candles burned out. It was still dark when she tried to squirm out thru a hole that proved too small. Got stuck and tore her coat trying to get back in the silo. She slept fitfully –even by the standards of her usual naps. She awoke when it was just getting light and she finished the hole and got out. Her hands were filthy and blistered in spite of the work gloves. Her hair was ragged and going in every direction. Her clothes were filthy, wrinkled, and now, torn. She checked herself in the rear-view mirror and cried. But her car started and soon she was warm –or warmer. She wondered if she would ever again feel truly warm.

Her thinking was confused; her predominate thought –her over riding drive-- was to put as many miles as possible between herself and the silo. As the miles piled up, she considered turning back and going to the police, but she kept driving east until she nodded off and drove off the road. Not a big deal in the flat prairie, but the terror and adrenaline kept her awake to the next little town –one with an actual traffic light- where she found the motor lodge.

Once she got the key from the little Nazi she drew a hot bath, climbed in, and promptly fell asleep and only woke up when the water cooled. From there she slipped between clean sheets in a real bed and fell asleep again. She woke up eighteen hours later, famished but with nothing to eat except packets of sugar that came with the complimentary coffee. There was nothing to do but to climb back into her filthy clothes and start driving eastward again. She bought gas in the next little town; ignoring the funny looks from the hicks in the store where she bought a burrito and heated it in the microwave. She got as far as Fargo at noon before she found a Walmart where she could buy clean clothes without attracting embarrassing attention. Even so, she sped thru the women's wear department quickly and picked out underwear, tee shirts, a jogging suit, and a cheap coat. She also grabbed some bread, sandwich fixings, and a six-pack of cola.

She found another cheap motel on the east side of town and checked in. The young woman behind the desk seemed not to notice -or care- what she looked or smelled like and she repeated the bath and bedtime routine much like the day before. As she fell asleep, her thoughts were like the revenge fantasies that had sustained her in the silo –but with a little more calculation and –she thought- more reality.

She got home to Minneapolis by noon the next day reasonably clean, rested, and fed, but she recognized she was not quite the same person she had been. Perhaps she was not entirely sane. She thought perhaps she did not care.

Chapter 37

It had been a long week for Kevin -getting things back on track at the man-camp. He admitted to himself that he had actually enjoyed it. He had been more productive than he had been in a long while. One of the easiest items he checked off his list was the need for a temporary manager to take the Mahon woman's place. Mel pulled a rabbit out of a hat with a little woman he knew. Amundsen would have liked to have done more than a short interview and cursory reference checks before he hired her, but Mel was pretty insistent. A little too soon to ignore the guy to whom he still owed money and besides, it was one less thing to do. Beneath it all, there was the conviction that he was doing things that would make him a great deal of money in the future. But it would be great it get away with Janet.

The trip started out a bit awkwardly. It took Kevin longer too pack that it did Janet, but they got to Sloulin International Airport on time to make their flight. The plane to Denver was a little puddle jumper regional turboprop thing and their seats were on either side of the aisle. So much for confirming reservations with adjoining seats on flights out of the Williston's international airport. The plane was also too loud for much conversation. The flight to Las Vegas less so, but Kevin did most of the talking and mostly about himself; his up-bringing and his time at school. He spoke about his marriage, but glossed over the affairs leading up to the divorce.

For the most part Janet just listened. She listened particularly closely when he spoke about his college days. She wanted to learn more, but didn't want to show her ignorance about things like BA's and BS's and graduate school. She would have to ask teacher Mike when she got back to class. It crossed her mind that Jeff might know about this sort of thing. In some ways, he was a better person to ask than even the GED teacher. They were in the same boat -education wise. Kevin's talking about exams and all-nighters and writing long papers worried her. If this guy struggled, who was she fooling about her college dreams? Janet couldn't get it all out of her mind and knew she was being a dud all thru the last part of the flight, the luggage chore, and the taxi ride to their casino on the strip.

The room was nice, but not as nice as Kevin expected. After he looked around, he told the porter to put their luggage back on the cart and they all went back down to the front desk. He complained that he had reserved a deluxe room and got a regular room on the seventh floor. The desk clerk tried to assure him it was a deluxe room and there were no super-deluxe room available. Kevin put on his best ass-hole-lawyer hat and got in the poor guy's face. "There will be a super-deluxe room available tomorrow, will there not?"

"Yes sir. I believe we can arrange that. It will cost twelve hundred dollars a night, but it will be available."

Janet thought she saw him blanch at the cost, but he recovered quickly. "That's acceptable." He turned away, smiled, and winked at Janet and they all went back up to their original room. He did not tip the porter.

123

Janet unpacked quickly and as she was waiting for him to hang his clothes carefully and arranging his toiletry articles in the bathroom just so, she discovered the mini-bar and opened a split of white wine for herself. "You want a drink Kevin?"

"Ya. Sounds like a good idea." He finished his unpacking and came out of the bathroom and saw her kneeling on the floor by the mini-fridge below the little bar. He also noticed her wine and noticed her ass. He was aware that Janet and he weren't clicking so far and it struck him that they both needed to loosen up. "Any scotch there?"

"There are a bunch of little bottles of whisky. Isn't dee wars a kind of Scotch?"

"It's pronounced du wers. Ya, that's fine." He stretched out on the couch and patted the cushion next to himself. "What do you want to do tonight?"

"I'm hungry." She got up off the floor, poured the Scotch into one of the glasses from the glass shelf above the mini fridge. She folded her legs under her in the couch facing him.

He had in mind putting his arm around her and moving things in the direction of bed, but all he could reach were her folded knees –at least with any degree of poise. It wondered if she did it on purpose. She was lovely sitting just so, poised, but a little cold. "What do you feel like? Italian, French, Steak, a buffet? They have it all."

"Italian. If that's all right with you." She tossed back her wine. "What shall I wear?"

Kevin looked at her with different eyes –less lust, but with a more thoughtful appraisal. She had worn sneakers for the flight and walks across the airports. Not a big deal in Williston –there were only a few gates behind the terminal, but the Denver and Las Vegas terminals involved a lot of walking. She had on black slacks, and a simple ecru blouse. Her hair was piled up on the top of her head in what he thought of as elegant disorder. "Unbutton another button on your blouse."

She smiled in spite of herself and unbuttoned a button. "Enough"?"

"One More"

She undid another.

She giggled as he groaned. "You need some pearls –not that any man would miss your lovely chest, but a strand –I think opera length- would lay nicely between the girls."

He got up and went to the phone by the bed. When he got the desk he asked if they had an Italian restaurant, waited a minute, and asked how long it would be before they could seat two. He glanced at his watch. "Eight o'clock is fine. Name's Amundsen. And please send me back to the front desk."

As he was waiting he turned back to Janet who was looking at him with more interest than she had shown all afternoon and early evening. He asked, "Shoes? You got some high heals?" She had only brought a pair of flats because she didn't want to be taller than him and was trying to find the right way to say it when he interrupted. "Hello desk. We need a string of pearls. Is there a jewelry store in your galleria? Good thank you. And we will need a woman's shoe boutique." Pause. "Across the street and to the right. Very good."

After Janet touched up her makeup, she was surprised when she came out of the bathroom and he told her it was not enough. She was even more surprised when he followed her back into the bathroom and took her eye shadow compact from her. "Let me see." He looked back and forth from the compact to her face. He did so with the same appraising eyes he used earlier. "OK. The blue eye shadow is fine, but let's go with some gray in the crease.   Do you have a blush that is more brown than red?"

This was completely outside of her experience. She put on the gray while he dug thru her makeup kit and looked up as she was finishing. "Take it farther out." Another appraising look.   "Good"." He handed her a different blush. "Now lay a little of this under the contour."

"Huh?"

"I'll do it." He applied the brush with practiced ease and looked at her with critical eyes once again. "See what you think."

She thought many things. She thought she looked great. Not much less that she wore in the strip-club, but it was… elegant? She thought she had never seen this in a man. Finally, she thought she liked it.

An hour later he had bought her a strand of pearls –cultured, but perfect- and they did indeed lie between her breasts beautifully. He also bought her a pair of killer black pumps. She now was at least as tall as he was –taller with her hair piled up. Once again –he looked at her with a critical eye. He was pleased and was clearly not intimidated by her height.   One more thing for her to wonder about. There had been some discussion at the shoe boutique –and mostly between Kevin and the saleswoman as to weather or not she needed a longer pair of pants. They agreed that she did, but he looked at his watch and said it would wait because their dinner reservations were coming up.

Dinner was delicious.   She drank a little too much wine. They discussed fashion and make-up, how he thought she might dress, her hair, and her makeup. She completely forgot her plan to ask Kevin about college, but she felt very much the college girl. Maybe even an extra fancy college girl. What did graduate students dress like? Was she looking like one of these elevated scholars –what-ever they were. Sounded like something she wanted to be –not quite sure what a graduate student was, but it sounded good.

When they got back to the room, she was the one who initiated sex. Initiated it enthusiastically.

Chapter 38

Too many years frustrating struggle made Mike pretty tight-fisted. Even if it was the lawyer's money he was spending, it vexed him to spend it on prepared food. He planned to get away from frozen-this and pre-packaged-that to food made more or less from scratch, but for the time being, the 'convenience' part of the restaurant supply outfit's catalog was a lifesaver. He was getting eggs and toast –mostly warm- to the dining trailer every morning as well as hot coffee, cold cereal, milk & juice and finally a stack of box lunches and still making it to teach his class at nine. He started dinner as soon as he got back from town after noon –or as soon as he got back from class and a little last minute shopping in town. In the four days since the cook disappeared, he had served pizza the first night, breaded chicken cutlets with cream of mushroom soup standing in for sauce the next night, huge heat-and-serve pans of lasagna, and finally, pizza again. It wasn't the main dishes that were the problem; it was the side dishes and salads and his own weak attempt to serve up the kind of food he thought as a *healthy*. Healthy or not, a lot of uneaten salads and vegetables were tossed when the dinner was done and he had taken the big stainless serving dishes back to the kitchen for clean-up. It seemed that starch and protein *meat 'n 'taters* were what the men wanted most. Couldn't hardly blame them; working outside in the cold simply demanded fuel and a lot of it.

But after pizza twice in four days he m decided to hang around after he had carried the food across the frozen mud between the kitchen and dining trailer and do a little casual market research by hanging around the dining trailer. He had just made his third round trip with more pizza out of the oven and was distracted with getting it out on the counter and the guy at the head of the line was distracted with getting a few slices on his plate. Mike looked up first and saw a familiar face.

"Kermit, isn't it?"

It took a second for the round black guy of about Mike's age to register, but he was still confused. "Yep, but I can't. . ."

"I'm Mike, we were in the same trailer a little while ago."

Understanding dawned. "Oh ya. You were the teacher, right?"

"Yep. Still am and just started as the head the cook here too."

"Don't no one stay unemployed here for long if they want to work."   Kermit stood off to the side of the line of guys getting food and took a bite of pizza. "So how's it going?"

"Working my ass off, but it's a good thing. How are things in the fracking business??"

"Things are changing, but things are always changing. You remember Kenny, our derrick hand?"

"Ya. What a little prick."

"Well, he's dead."

"Oh shit. I'm sorry. How…? I mean he's so young."

"What'chu call an industrial accident. He was screwing around and opened a valve."

"How… how does opening a valve get a guy killed?"

Kermit looked at the ceiling thoughtfully. "Um, it was. . . it was a high pressure line full of frack fluid. Hit him in the chest."

"I'm still confused. How does fluid kill someone? I remember you said fracking was done with mostly just water."

"A jet of water and sand at about 40,000 PSI. Cut him open like a meat ax. Knocked him off the rig, but they said he was probably dead by the time he hit the ground."

Mike took a minute to try to get a picture of it. It was not a pleasant picture. ""Oh dear. I guess this sort of thing happens a lot in the oil field."

"Well, not really. Most of the accidents in the oil field are actually traffic accidents. Same kind's a shit hurts regular folks whether they work in the oil field or in an office. We bust our asses to be safe. Classes, 'em effing FR suits that are hot as hell in the summer time, hard hats, and procedures that slow things down a lot. Kenny just go stupid. Then Rob's wife got sick and he went back to Wyoming. So they broke up what was left of out team and put us on other teams. I'm working in the shop calibrating instruments and fixing tools now pretty much full time."

"Is this good or bad?"

"Less overtime, but I'm warm all day. They send me out sometimes. It is probably temporary and I'll be back out in the field soon –maybe about the same time it starts to warm up. So that's good. Until it gets hot, anyway. How did you come to be the cook?"

"Long story. Seems the camp has a little difficulty hanging on to people. First the manager took a powder. I was helping out in exchange for a room, when the cook left."

"Ya hear a lot of that sort of thing around Williston. Is that why there was no breakfast one morning""

"I think so. There was a rumor that people weren't getting paid, but no one is talking about it. I met the owner. Seems to be all sorted out now and I plan to be here a while. Look I got'ta keep the food coming and clean-up but you want to have a drink later?"

"Sure, what time?"

"Ten?"

"Buddy, I'm sound asleep by then. I'm at work by five in the morning."

"Ya, that's about when I start too, but I get a few hours sleep in the afternoon when things are cooking."

Mike's only downtime was an hour or less between finishing up in the kitchen and hitting the sack. He continued his habit of devising and tweaking spreadsheets of how much money he was making, how long to get out of dept, and how much money he would have at the end of a year or five years or ten –but he had to admit to himself that it was not likely he would make it that far down the road. Even so, he enjoyed playing with the variables: interest rates, tax rates, and maybe the payments on a good used car when the little Mazda finally died.

Chapter 39

Morning sex is different from evening sex: slower, warmer, less passionate but more tender. And sometimes it's just fucking. Janet was not impressed the next morning. As he was finishing, it occurred to her that he hadn't given her the dollars they agreed on. Room service breakfast in bed was nice though, largely because Kevin had gotten up and was taking a shower while she was eating.

One way or the other, they were going to be together for a few days yet to come so she decided it was up to her to find a way make nice or at least to get back to of the fun they had the night before. She showered, walked out of the bathroom drying off and sat at the little dressing-table in front of the mirror to do her make up. He was sitting in the couch across from her reading and did a double-take when he noticed she was nude. *What strange things were men*, she thought. Kevin had just had her in bed, naked and willing -and now he was staring at her nude body as if he had never seen such a thing. She started on foundation and asked "Honey, how should I do my makeup this morning?"

"Hmm. Go with a single color eye shadow –beige I think. Dark mascara, neutral blush. Let me see your lipsticks."

She gathered three or four tubes, turned them lipstick parts up, and held them up for him to see.

"The dark one."

That seemed to be all he had to say, but his eyes didn't leave her. When she was done with the cosmetics, it seemed right, but a little tame. It struck her it was more lawyer's wife than college girl. Not nearly enough for stripping, but enough to get her in trouble if she were out and about in Williston. Perhaps it would be OK in Las Vegas. "What do you want to do this afternoon?"

"I want to hit the blackjack tables. You said you didn't like to gamble, maybe I could teach you?"

"It's kind'a math isn't it?"

"Well, yes. It's helpful if you can calculate odds. Just a little."

"Oh honey, the last thing I want to do is anything with numbers. When I get home, I'll have to study, but not till then." She took a last look at her makeup and got up to dress while giving Kevin a long last look at her profile. "I want to go shopping some more."

Kevin groaned. "I want to gamble." He held up the book he had been reading until she came out of the bathroom. "It's silly, but this book claims to be a system. I want to try it out. Couldn't you go shopping on your own?"

"I suppose, but it was so much fun last night with you."

"Ya, it was fun. But I still want to do my thing." He watched her pull on her jeans. "If you are going to be shopping for slacks or a long skirt of such, be sure to wear you heels. Or take them along anyway. That way you can get a good fit."

Janet didn't argue. The idea of getting out on her own was surprisingly appealing. She wasn't sure if it was because she wanted to go exploring, or just wanted to get away from the guy. She was in her pants and bra and snuggled into his lap. "Honey, I will need money."

"We'll go to the cashier and get you some money for you and some chips for me."

It was nearly noon by the time they took the elevator to the casino floor and made their way to the cage. Kevin wrote a check for five thousand dollars, took four thousand in chips and gave her ten one-hundred dollar bills and kissed her good by.

Janet went to the shopping arcade on the floor below the casino. She wondered in and out of a few stores including the one she and Kevin had shopped the night before, but after an hour, she had not found anything that struck her as being worth more than the bills she had folded in her jean's pocket. There were some nice clothes but when she tried to imagine herself in her college-girl persona, nothing worked. Closer to the lawyer's wife look maybe, but all in all, just not quite right.

Too long in Williston and too much shopping at Walmart and Penny's left her determined to buy something, any damn thing, so she left the casino, caught a cab, and asked the cabbie to take her to the best shopping in town. They drove a long block and the pulled up in front of the same store where Kevin helped her pick out a pair of shoes that were perfect for their dinner the night before.

The store was elegant; off-white walls with gold trim and blond wood floors, open mezzanines on both sides going up three levels. There were suspended staircases between each level –not at all the sort of place for people with acrophobia. She hadn't noticed it all the night before with Kevin leading her about. The store had huge volume but little floor-space and what there was, was sparse of inventory. The woman who helped them the night before was not working then, but a younger woman appeared as Janet got to what she thought was the sportswear section. As they want thru the *How may I help you?* thing, Janet sized her up. She was younger, -a few years younger than Janet, dressed more casually than the woman from last night, and wearing very little make-up. Now here was someone who might be able to help her with a college-girl look.

"Hi. I'm looking for some…" She had no idea how to describe the look she was going for. The sales woman the night before was nice so maybe this young woman would be as helpful. "...clothes for college."

"Are you in graduate school?"

"Um… no. Regular college."

"Oh." I thought you might have been a little old for undergraduate work. Where are you going?"

Janet hesitated, "I don't know yet."

"Will you be joining a sorority?"

Janet just shook her head. She changed her thinking about the saleswoman. She was a bitch. She noticed a black woman standing behind the sales woman, but was too preoccupied with trying not to look ignorant to pay her much attention. The other woman seemed to be listening to their conversation and Janet noticed in passing that she seemed to be wearing a lot of make-up and showing a lot of cleavage.

"Well, it depends on where you go of course. An Ivy League school has different styles and all. I went to UCLA and just mostly wore any old thing to class. Parties and dates were a different matter of course. Do you expect to be dating a lot? What kind of guys do you like? And of course, if it's just community college it really doesn't' make much difference. You aren't going to community college are you?"

"Excuuuuuse me." The woman bustled around the sales woman put her hands on her hips and got in her face. "You work on commission don't you?"

"Um, yes."

"Well, honey, you just lost you some." She turned to face Janet. "Hey girl. What do you say we go somewhere they have clothes for us younger women?" Janet smiled and nodded. She looked more closely at her new friend. Not quite as tall as she was. A little older. Lots of cleavage and a generous butt, but the woman had a trim waist. Her dress was too short and matched boots that were too high and a little outdated besides. But it was mostly her make-up that Janet noticed. It was like what she wore on the stage at Willy's Place back home. Not quite as heavy as that, but close and it seemed a little odd for daytime. Janet's first thought was that she was a stripper too. She let herself be lead by the arm out the door while the woman introduced herself.

"Honey, my name's Crystal. You ever been to the outlet mall? You aren't from around here are you? Want to get some coffee? My car is across the street. Let's get us some coffee and get to know one another."

The coffee didn't happen –it was forgotten in chatter and driving and shopping, but an hour later they were BFF's and Janet had bought two outfits, a pair of shoes, and two blouses, and a sweater. And a perfect pair of black wool slacks. She also still had seven of the hundred-dollar bills in her pocket and a couple of twenties over and above the two hundred in mad money she took out of her Mason jar back home. Crystal bought a pair of boots with impossibly high heels "Janet dear, I'm hungry. How 'bout you?"

Janet wasn't hungry, but said. "Sure"

"Let's celebrate. I want something gooey. CinnaBun?"

Janet wasn't sure that a gooey CinnaBun was what she wanted, but went along. "Chrystal, do you work nights? I mean, how come we are shopping in the middle of the day and all.?

Crystal stopped and looked at Janet for a moment. "Honey, I'm a working girl. You are too, aren't you?"

"Oh."

"Uh-oo. Did I put my foot in it? Are you some rich man's girlfriend or something?

"Um –oh what the hell. Ya, sort'a. How –how did you know?"

"Your too hot and, well, your makeup is not what office girls wear. But you are not from here are you?"

"Nope, I work in a strip club in North Dakota. Great money, but it's North Dakota. Not enough women and lots of lonely guys with lots of money. Not much else to do with it."

"You on vacation here in Vegas?"

"No, I'm hear with…." and she stopped.

"You here with a rich john?"

"He's my…" She almost said 'boy friend' but stopped herself again.

Crystal reached out and touched Janet on the shoulder. "Honey, I have a lot of *boy friends"* and did the air quotes thing.

Janet was thoughtful. "I have a girlfriend, Tonia, who supports a boyfriend and turns tricks and has a rich old guy who she visits a lot. They pray together. Naked."

Crystal laughs. "Honey, been around as long as I have nothing surprises me, but naked praying is new. How much to you suppose working girls earn in North Dakota?"

"I send money back home and have about fifteen thousand. In the bank of... my mattress. Been in Williston about six months. I just strip and do lap dances and all. My sugar daddy is nice, but I'm not sure it pays all that well. He is supposed to help me invest sometime, but..."

"Your friend... Tonia was it? The girl who turns tricks? She probably makes more per hour, but I bet you work more hours and have the higher income. Less risk too."

Janet had never thought about it this way and decided Crystal was probably right. "You ought to come to North Dakota. Check it out. I could introduce you to Tonia and my boss at the strop club, But he's kind'a creepy."

"I'll think about it. I'm tired of Vegas and don't have nothing holding me here. Ya, that might be a good idea."

They left the mall about four and Crystal was driving the 15 miles back to town when Janet's cell rang. "Hi Daddy. How are things?" There was long pause and Janet gradually slumped forward in her seat. Crystal noticed something was wrong and pulled off the road. She leaned forward. "Oh Daddy. How long?"   She listened for a long minute. "No. It's OK. Are you sure you don't want me to come home?"

"Yes. Send him up here. I mean to send him to Williston. I'm in Las Vegas now but I'll get home tomorrow." Janet turned to stare out the side window. "Call me when you have a plane ticket. I'll meet him at the airport.. OK. I'll talk to you soon. I love you Daddy." She put her cell back in her pocket.

"What's the matter honey?"

Janet straightened up and took a deep breath. "My Mom's cancer came back. She has to do the chemo thing all over again."

"I'm sorry, kiddo"

"I have a son. Ricky's almost five. He lives with my parents in Topeka. My dad needs to send him up to me in Williston. I love Ricky so much. I want to see him, but..." She wiped her eyes. "Fuck it. I have enough money to live on. I'm going to be a Mon. The best Mom I can me. My own Mom is a b... She is never happy. My Mom and I just don't get along so good."

"How can I help?"

"Get me home. I mean get me back to the hotel. I have to get back to fucking Williston. I have to pack and tell Kevin. I have to tell him a lot of stuff. Do you know anything about changing airplane tickets?"

"Nothing. Except I think it's expensive if you don't give enough notice and all."

"I got to get there. If my boyfriend wants to stay, that's fine, but I have to go." She looked out the side window as they passed the road to the airport. "You know –I'm kind'a glad I don't have to stay. Two days with this guy is about enough."

Crystal giggled. "I hear you there girl. Ain't no man I'd want to spend all my time with. Some are nice for a day. Or a night. But that's enough. Here." She handed Janet her cell phone. "Put your number in my phone and put mine in yours while I get you to... was it the Apollo Casino where you said your were staying?"

When Janet got back to the room, she began packing. The immediate problem was finding room for the stuff she had purchased. It was only after she had her clothes and cosmetics were all packed up did it occur to her to call the airline about changing her ticket. It took her fifteen minutes to get thru the airlines menu-hell and talk to a human being. Turned out to be a waste of time because she didn't have the reservation number. She realized she would need to find Kevin and talk to him about it and start all over again.

She also realized she would have to handle it carefully. The new slacks and pearls from last night would be the perfect look. She unpacked again and debated between her new sweater and the blouse from last night. She figured she needed a little glamour –the *Woman on James Bond's arm in the Casino Royal* look and went with the blouse. She piled her hair up on top of her head, put on a brighter red lipstick, and pulled a long swath of color to her eyelid. Before she left for the casino, she took a final look in the mirror and unbuttoned another button.

It only took her few minutes to find him on the casino floor. He didn't look happy so she slid up next to him and nudged his side gently. He glanced at her and looked back at the table then he noticed that the blackjack dealer had stopped pulling cards from the shoe and was staring at her. Everyone at the table was looking at her –the men enviously and women –not so much. Only then did he slip his arm around her waist and kiss her. "Hi sweetie. Give me just a minute to finish this hand." He looked back at the table. "Had fun shopping did we?" The dealer did something Janet did not understand and Kevin muttered "Shit. Are you ready to go?"

"Yes I guess. Are you done here?"

He said simply, "Oh ya." and gathered up a small pile of chips and led her away.

Janet took his arm and pressed her breast against him as she followed. "Did it not go well?"

He stopped and turned to her. "Nope. I don't want to talk about it." They were in the elevator before he seemed to notice her. "Did you find some things you like?"

"Yes." She gestured to her outfit. "What do you think?"

"A little… casual." He almost said *young* but caught himself. "Nice, but I think you pull off the understated sophisticate better."

Janet wasn't sure what he meant by that, but rather than going down that road, she decided to see what he thought about her doing the college thing. "Kevin, my teacher says I should be taking classes this summer. What did he call them? 'remedial' or something" . Some basic stuff and then the regular college classes in September. Isn't this outfit right for school?" Kevin just shrugged. No help in that direction. "Sweety, we have to talk. I have to go back to Williston as soon as I can."

He shrugged again. "Why? I guess I'm about tired of Las Vegas too, but why do you need to go."

She waited till they went into their room before she spoke. "I have a four year old son. He lives with my parents in Missouri and my Mom is sick. My Dad called a little while ago. He needs to send Ricky to me. I've got to be a Mom. I miss him so much."

Kevin had started to mix a drink but stopped with the bottle in his hand and looked at her with no idea what to say as she finished. He didn't say anything and noticed the bottle in his hand. "You want a drink?"

"That's all you have to say? *You want a drink?*"

He poured it neat. "I need to think about this. You took me by surprise. Where is the dad?"

"Long gone. Maybe in jail." *Or dead* she thought to herself.

He went to the window and looked down at the empty pool ten floors down. "Nothing to do but to do it, I guess. I'll see about a flight for you."

It hadn't occurred to Janet that he would not be coming back with her. "I thought…" She bit her tongue. She realized that if he wanted to stay in Las Vegas, it was all right with her. "Thank you baby-doll. I called earlier. There was a seat on a flight out tonight, but I didn't know what our tickets were so I couldn't change them, I mean *it*. I couldn't change *it*."

He tossed down this drink, turned from the window, and went to the phone. The silence was deadly as he waited for the casino operator to get the airline on the line. Janet figured it was as good a time as any. "Kevin, there is the matter of the rest of the money you agreed to pay me."

He just stared at her for a long moment and turned away as he said, "Hello. Yes, I need to change one reservation." He gestured to a small collection of papers on the bed-side table where the tickets were. Janet jumped up and handed them to him. She hoped she didn't look too enthusiastic in dong so.

He read off the reservation number and explained that the soonest flight would be best. "There is a family emergency and my wife needs to get back to North Dakota."

"Good. Seven thirty tonight?'

"How much?"

"Didn't I say it was a family emergency?"

"Fine. Put it on my credit card." He hung up the phone and turned to Janet. "The fuckers was one hundred and eighty dollars to change the reservation. I'll have to go back to the casino and cash another check. The one-eighty is on you though."

Janet simply nodded.

"I see you are all packed. Let's go."

"The plane don't leave for three hours yet. You want to eat?"

"Nope, best to be early so they don't give away your seat."

After he cashed another check and gave her exactly $320, Kevin carried her luggage to the cab stand in front of the casino. He kissed her forehead, "Have a good trip" and he turned and walked back into the casino.

What a fucker. She had at least tried to look sad about the need for her to cut short their time together. She figured with the cash and clothes, she was maybe a grand ahead. All in all, not a bad couple of days. She didn't care if she ever saw him again.

It was 72 with clear blue skies with a gentle wind out of the west when she got on the plane in Vegas.

Chapter 40

Once Sara Mahon got back into her condo in Minneapolis, she didn't want to set foot outside ever again. The first thing she did -after making very sure she was very much alone, was set the thermostat to 80. Next she went to the kitchen.
Her daughter had come home from school during a while ago while Mahon was in Williston. Nothing was in the freezer. The fridge held mixers, water, and a few bottles of condiments. There were half a dozen cans of vegetables, a large box of instant rice, and some pasta in the pantry. That was about it. Then she noticed she was uncomfortably warm so she turned the heat down to 70. An hour later she turned it up to 75

She tried to relax but thinking about Amundsen made her so restless that she began pacing. Her thoughts oscillated between revenge and her finances. While she was up, she checked the thermostat and turned it down just a little. "Better to be doing than stewing." and she spread her bank papers out on the kitchen table.   She began in inventory –an audit actually- when it occurred to her she had spoken aloud one of her own mother's many adages. She giggled. "Oh fiddle. I'm alone aren't I? Probably best to make sure." She went thru the house and checked the thermostats again -first in the living room, then in the hall outside of her bedroom upstairs, and finally the little space heater in the bathroom by the back door.

The inventory didn't take long. She made calls to her bank and broker. As she expected, the accounts had been cleaned out. Not completely, this would have rung alarm bells, but thoroughly emptied. After the calls, she checked the thermostats again, she spoke aloud, "If I lay low –and that should be easy- I'll be OK till I have to pay my daughter's tuition in September. My car payments were done automatically out of my checking account. There was enough money for a few months anyway. Plenty of time to sort things out with Amundsen."

Then she decided to do her laundry first. It took quite a while. She had to do the thermostats. She made the circuit between washing and drying, and a then a couple of times while the dryer was running. When the clothes were dry, she put them into the refrigerator.

She slept only four hours that night. There were nightmares and she woke up shivering and drenched in sweat. Maybe it was just too hot in the room –or maybe it was menopause. –but mostly she knew it was a lasting terror from her time in the cold silo. She got up to check the thermostats. Her conversation with herself was pretty much constant in the small hours of the night. She repeated "Better to be doing than stewing." with each step downstairs to review her bank and brokerage papers. Nothing had changed.

She began pacing in the near dark living room fell into a rhythm that soothed her. "Amundsen must die or he will kill me and my daughter." A dozen steps from the kitchen to the front door. Then back. "Die he must, or bust." No. She could do better. "A dead Amundsen in a silo is better that two in the bush. " Better. She would have to work on it. She carried this mantra back to bed and repeated it till she fell asleep.

The next day she assigned herself the task of improving her liquidity. "Better to be doing than stewing," but first she had to find a way to cover her tracks for the eight months she had been in North Dakota. Easiest way to do this was make up a company and then make up a job description for her resume. Then she would buy a cheap cell-phone and give it to her daughter for a very few very important calls so the girl could confirm her Mom's employment with the fictitious company. Her daughter had done it before and was pretty good at playing the HR woman who could say wonderful things about an old employee. Mahon figured it might be a while before she found as sweet a deal as the man-camp had been. Amundsen was a fool who needed to be swindled. At least until it all went sideways. Just where the fuck had this small town lawyer found the scary-ass cook who got him his money back? She would find another similar situation – she had done it before- but for the time being, she just needed enough to get by and make tuition for her daughter: it would be her senior year.

After she checked the thermostats and curtains, she considered opening the curtains to the little fenced in-patio off the kitchen in let in a little light. She decided she felt safer in the gloom. "Warmer this way too." she said aloud. After thinking about opening the curtains, it was necessary to go upstairs again to make sure all the curtains had stayed closed in both bedrooms. She rechecked the thermostats.

By the third day back in Minneapolis, her conversations between herself and Amundsen were interfering with her planning and the need to check thermostats and curtains. And the food ran out. She used the last of the instant coffee and it was this – more than hunger- that finally drove her out. She went to the window in the front bedroom upstairs that overlooked the condo parking lot and peeked out. There was nothing to see except the parking lot and after a moment she told herself she was being silly. She dressed plainly, checked the window again, took a deep breath and went out into the cold morning to go shopping. She felt reasonably safe in the store, but caught herself talking aloud three different times; each time it was imaginary conversations with Amundsen as he begged for mercy. She wondered if anyone noticed. She shrugged, "I don't care." When she got home it took a couple of trips to get the groceries from her car into the house. Strange that she felt more exposed at home than in the grocery store.

After putting away the groceries and checking things upstairs and down, she decided she needed to make a decision about the shitty little furnished apartment she had back in North Dakota. "Better to be doing than stewing." When she escaped the silo, she just got in her car and drove. She left clothes and papers in her shitty little furnished apartment back in Williston. Or there had been papers till the hairy little fucker broke into the place and went thru her stuff. It was about a ten hour drive for clothes that probably didn't fit anyway. If there was any good news from the whole damn thing, it was that she lost some weight. Then she realized that if the cook left them there, and if the fell into the wrong hands, it might lead to some difficulty with the other fucker who owned the man-camp.

In the past, she had been good at keeping track of what needed doing and getting it done. "Better to be doing that stewing." but now she felt she needed to divide her time between doing things and checking things, as well as planning what to do about Amundsen. "A dead lawyer in a silo is better that two in the bush." "What do you call a dead Amundsen? A good start."

The next day she was a little bored with checking the thermostats and thinking about Amundsen no matter how important it was to do so. She found herself wondering if she should not have brought home some wine and maybe a few rental movies. She had about decided to head out again but decided to do a little research on getting a second mortgage if worse came to worse around her daughter's tuition. Probably not be necessary, but it wouldn't cost anything to find out and then she could indulge herself with a nice bottle.

The first two finance companies she called quoted rates that were about what she expected. The third one evidently needed business and the pleasant young woman she spoke to took all manner of information and promised to call back with a 'super competitive package'.

Mahon had forgotten the whole thing and gone back to checking the thermostats when she got a call from a man at the bank. "Good afternoon Ms. Mahon. This is Tom Jones from Speedy Funding. How are you this afternoon?"

"Fine thank you."

"Sara, may I call you Sara?"

"Ya. What do you have for me?"

"I'm a little confused here, Sara. You have enough equity to borrow a little more money but we would need to start all over again."

"What are you talking about?"

"Your second was set at seventy five percent of your home's value. We could go as high as eighty five, but you would need to pay off the first second mortgage first." The man chuckled. "Oh. Pay off the first second first. That's funny isn't it?"

She felt her stomach drop thru the floor. *"What* second? When?"

"We mailed you a check last week for eighty one thousand two hundred eighty nine dollars. Have you not gotten it yet? Have you deposited it?"

"Listen closely. I did not deposit anything. I did not receive and check. I did not do a second mortgage. You have been swindled. I would suggest you call the police. I will be doing the same."

Her hands were shaking when she hung up.   If ever there was an occasion she needed a drink, this was it. She toyed with the idea of heading out to get a bottle and let her thinking clear. She glanced at the clock: three in the afternoon. She had a couple of hours to do some business. She stopped herself as she started to dial 911. Better to be careful and do a little research.

She Googled *identity theft* and found it worthless: mostly ads for protection before the fact. She found an 800 number for the Minnesota Department of Commerce that apparently did something about banking, but the menu items seemed only to offer hours and addresses and options that didn't apply to her –in fact, they were so pitifully basic that only a child would find the information offered helpful. She tried to leave a message in some bureaucrat's voice-mail but got another recording telling her the mail box was full and not taking any more messages.

She had put *Ask a Lawyer* at the very bottom of her list, and finally had no other options but to try a few. The first three she called had administrative aids that acted as tenacious gate-keepers and she got nowhere. Finally she called her ex-husband's ex-law partner. He did real-estate law, but he was a pompous ass and never answered even the most basic question with out consulting this or that and 'getting back to you," and billing who ever asked the question. She was sure that anything she told him would get back to her ex within minutes, but he was her last hope.

"Hello Ed. This is Sara Mahon." She knew that given the chance, he would lead the conversation toward how sad and shocked he was about the way things turned out, and she had neither the time nor stomach for such. "I need help –I need advice. It looks like someone took out a second mortgage on my house. What is my liability and what is the banks liability"

"Well, if it was done fraudulently, it all falls to the bank, but as a practical matter, *proving it* falls to the home owner to prove it was fraud. You have to show you never received the check and you know how difficult it is to prove a negative. In my experience, banks are very skillful at twisting it around to make it look like you could have –or should have- known and received the money. How much are we talking about?"

"It was…. that's not important. How do I prove it? What do I do?"

"First thing is to notify the bank of the situation. And best to have a lawyer do it. You need proof you told them as soon as possible. Then you might build yourself a paper trail of where you were and what you were doing during the time the disbursement was allegedly made."

"What can the police do for me?"

"Almost nothing. I'm sorry, but it comes down to you and the mortgage company. At some point the FBI gets involved if things cross state lines -I think they use forensic accountants- they are pretty good at looking into people's finances and there-by prove that you never received the money. Only then to they go after the actual bad-guys, but they don't catch them very often. Almost never in fact."

Her mouth went dry. "They audit *me*?"

"Yep –the best way to prove you didn't get the money."

"Oh God." She choked back a sob. "Ed, can you write the letter to Speedy Mortgage for me?"

"Sure Sara, it'll be in the mail first thing tomorrow morning, but under the circumstances, it is best you go elsewhere for further representation. I think we can agree that we are more than even now can't we?"

She had forgotten all about wine and started packing. As an afterthought, she backed her car up as close as she could to her front door, not out of laziness, but for secrecy. She opened the trunk, put the long flat case that held her ex's thirty-ought-six Winchester with the Redfield 9x42 scope and tossed in a couple of suitcases in on top of it. Then she moved everything back into her living room, pulled her daughter's old Buick out of the garage, and put her Lexus in the garage. Then she packed up the Buick. Her worried preoccupation with being seen had somehow disappeared.

She was on I-94 before first light. During the ten hour drive back to Williston, she had a continuous and ongoing conversation between herself and an imaginary Amundsen. The beginnings varied, but they all ended with his weeping and begging for mercy. She thought she got pretty good at doing his voice as he sank into terror. She spoke her parts perfectly calmly. She ran thru each scenario over and over -again polishing the language until she thought of another way to get Amundsen. She hadn't slept that night. Nor had she bathed the entire time she was in Minneapolis

Chapter 41

It took Vern's kids about a week to sort out the whole thing around getting to and from the man-camp with a minimum of squabbling and of greater importance, little or no involvement from Vern or Sherrie. Every afternoons Sherri had to give up her Toyota for a few hours, but she was usually so well organized that it was not a problem, and in fact it gave her a little more quiet-time -always a good thing.

Beth was just sixteen and other than a little worry about making left turns onto Highway 2 north of town, Vern felt it was a pretty safe drive. He had been teaching her to drive since she got her learner's permit and had made it very clear that big trucks could not stop as quickly as her mom's little Toyota. If you got in their way because you underestimated their speed, you would get squashed.

He wasn't sure she took him seriously enough so he described a wreck he had seen as a boy when a field-hand had tried to beat a big semi carrying a load of sugar beats. And lost. The guy had been tossed off the tractor and somehow got snagged face-down under the truck's suspension and dragged about a hundred feet down a country road. The bottom half of his face was gone, but from above the middle of his nose, he was still alive and his eyes were open and terrified. Vern and his dad put him in the back of a pickup and sped into town. The guy died on the way, but he died gurgling thru his shredded windpipe –trying to scream with no larynx. Vern didn't have to embellish much. He figured that if he overdid it, she might never want to drive at all –or even ride in a car.

Robby was too sensible and Vern only had to suggest he help his big sister judge the speed of the oncoming truck-traffic. So three afternoons a week, the kids got home from school and immediately drove a few miles north. After they parked by the office trailer, Robby walked uphill to the water treatment plant to check all the gauges and carefully record some numbers in a logbook Vern bought for him. The only tricky part of the whole process was to open a little valve and run a sample of water into a little plastic do-hicky. He and his dad had read the instructions together and worked out how to add exactly five drops of some special solution from a little plastic bottle, shake it, and then hold it up to the light so they could compare the yellow color to a scale across the bottom of the do-hickey. Robby has seen a guy do this at the pool at the recreation center out on the east side of town by the college. It looked like a pretty cool thing to do and he meant to ask the guy about uitomeone, but forgot all about it when foutreen year-old Mia Magnatta from school walked by with her fully developed breasts in a bathing suit.

Occasionally he also had to add a few tablets to the chlorinator, but this work only took ten minutes or so, so then he would to make beds, and help his sister with the laundry. At the start of the second week, Spencer, the little Kiwi that saw to the day-to-day operations, sent him to help out in the kitchen.

When he first learned that Mike was a teacher, Robby was a little uncomfortable but when Mike explained how to think of cooking as chemistry; boiling points as a function of salt concentrations, how sugar caramelized and proteins coagulated, etc., Robby came to think of cooking as science. He decided he would be a chemist when he grew up rather than an engineer, but like most kids, his plans in this direction changed often. The kid had no particular imagination nor creativity, but was a good worker. Made life a little easier for Mike.

Beth's job was to run the laundry and occasionally sit at the desk and answer the phone and take messages when the usual woman had to leave for a few minutes. The woman was new herself and did bookkeeping and reservations and was always a little bitchy –or so it seemed to Beth. She was a frumpy middle aged woman who didn't pronounce her R's. Beth wasn't sure what to make of this and thought it might have been a speech impediment. She didn't like the woman anyway and when she drove home with Robby that evening she mimicked her accent. She thought it was pretty funny, but Robby told her she was stupid and the woman was from Boston and they all just talked like that.

Part of Beth's dislike came from the woman bossing her around. The real problem was that this woman had ideas of what Beth was supposed to be doing and the little guy they called 'the Kiwi', (but Beth called him Mr. Tavaral to his face), also told her what to do. The two sets of instructions didn't always fit together too well. The Kiwi also talked funny, but she liked the way he talked. It sounded sophisticated and she asked him if he were English or something. He laughed and said he was from New Zealand – south of Australia- and New Zealand was settled by the English a long time ago so yes, he supposed he did have sort of an English accent. He also explained that there was a little bird called the 'kiwi' that lived only in New Zealand and so people from there were often called 'Kiwis.'

One afternoon when she came into the trailer to start work, there was a man in a suit sitting at the desk who she thought looked familiar. He looked up from some papers on the desk and smiled. "You must be Vern's daughter. Beth isn't it?

"Yes sir."

"Hello Beth, I'm Mr. Amundsen. I'm a friend of your mom and dad's. I think you might have been to my house for a BBQ a few years ago. Do you remember?"

"Yes sir. I think you have some kids older than me? Like they were in college or something?"

"Yes, that's right. They are grown up now. I guess. You are looking quite grown up yourself."

Beth knew there was something about the man that bothered her mom, but she had learned long ago not to inquire into her Mom's negative views about other grown-ups. *Don't you worry yourself about such matters, Lady Jane* was her usual response. And Beth knew that when the *Lady Jane's* started coming out, it was best to stop what she was doing or otherwise drop the subject. Her Dad was sometimes more forthcoming, but not often and not much. Less risk to asking him as well, but when she did, her dad shrugged and reminded her that her mouth got her in trouble far more often than her behavior. She was proud of herself to remember this idea at this particular moment and simply bit her tongue before she asked if he wasn't the *real* boss. Instead, she simply said, "I have to do laundry now. Is that OK?"

"Sure is Beth, I don't want to keep you from your work. We will visit later. And your mom wants me to help with your homework. Remember to ask me if you ever have any question about social studies, OK?"

The second time Mr. Amundsen showed up, he came with a little guy in a blue suit that was even fancier than the ones Mr. Amundsen wore, and the new guy talked like the bookkeeping lady. All three of them were sitting around the desk and hardly noticed her when she walked in and went down the short hall to start the laundry. Beth got one load started and used the last of the laundry soap to do so. When she went to the closet to get another box, she noticed that it was the last one. Her dad had lectured her about being a good worker and this involved thinking ahead –thinking about ways to do her job better and trying to put herself in the place of her boss –who ever it may be and there were at least two of them out there now so this must be a good time to tell them she would be needing more soap shortly.

When she walked back down the hall, she heard Mr. Amundsen say something about exposure from the out-call tricks. He seemed angry and she paused just around the corner. The little guy with the fancy suit noticed her and slammed his hand down on the desk. The other two jerked around and stared at her. I got very quiet and Beth felt like she was standing there naked. Mr. Amundsen was the fist to speak. "What is it Beth?" He did not look happy.

"Um, we need more soap –laundry soap. Got only one box left and I… I use a lot of it. I just thought… I thought I should tell someone."

She scurried back into the laundry room. Later Mr. Amundsen stopped in to have a friendly chat. "I hope we didn't frighten you earlier Beth. Sometimes we business men get a little excited. Do you have any questions about what you heard?"

Beth decided this another very good time to keep her mouth shut. "No sir, Mr. Amundsen. Just the soap. I mean we will be out of it soon. Soap I mean." She blushed with the realization that she was doing a lousy job of keeping her mouth shut; she was babbling.

Amundsen just looked at her for a long uncomfortable moment. "Well, OK then. Say *Hi* to your parents for me." And he turned and walked out.

When she and Robby finished up and were driving home she asked him if he know what *out call tricks* meant. Robby has no idea, and they decide together that for some reason, this was exactly the sort of thing not to ask their Dad about, and certainly not their mom.

Chapter 42

It had been a nice enough day, until the closing scene in Vegas with Kevin, and the flight had been fine and all, but mostly she was glad to be alone. She needed some time to wrap her head around being a mom again.

She settled in and waited for her dad's call with the details of Rickie's flight but it didn't come. When she finally went to bed around midnight she couldn't sleep. She got up first to clean the place, but it wasn't all that messy after Tonia's visit. As she tried to get to sleep for the second time, it occurred to her that there was nothing for a child to do in her home, so she got up again and wrote out a list of toys, books, and most importantly –the sort of food he liked. Or had liked when she left him in Topeka. Depending on when the flight came, she would do some shopping at Walmart on her way to Sloulin Airport. Or maybe they would go together after she picked him up. Or maybe both. Or maybe she would buy books and toys and bring them home and set them all out like she was well prepared for his coming all along. Then she would go shopping a second time with him and they would team-up to get the sort of food he liked best. That would be fun. She finally fell asleep a little after three and it seemed her cell phone rand only a minute later. It was eight o'clock. "Hi Dad. Were you able to get Ricky a flight?"

"Non-stop? Good. Thanks. Gets here three this afternoon."

pause

"I don't think I need the flight number. It's not that big and airport and there aren't that many flights –from Missouri or anywhere else for that matter. Is Ricky excited?"

pause

"One hundred and fifty bucks extra! Are you kidding me? It costs an extra handling charge for a kid to fly alone. A *handling charge*? For a little kid? That's bull shit. Tell Ricky to ask for extra everything and have him get me a bunch of 'em little bottles of booze."

pause

"I'm kidding Dad."

pause

"I got a lot to do. Love you too. See ya."

After she hung up she realized she hadn't asked about her mom. She considered calling back, but decided against it. With six hours to go, she figured she had plenty of time to do all sorts of shopping first. They could go to McDonalds or Pizza Hut if Ricky was hungry. He used to love both burgers and pizza. This was not likely to have changed in a year.

She finished her first trip thru Walmart in time for a second swing thru *Books on Broadway* for some more books and educational toys, and got to the airport in plenty of time. Sloulin Field International Airport was a single building that handled a dozen or so commercial flights a day –mostly to and from Denver, Minneapolis, and Houston and mostly flew oil people of one sort or another. Small or not, they took security very seriously, but she suspected it was more to do with TSA justifying its tiny workload than any real threat. There were no concourses with the retractable tubes big airports use to pipe passengers into and out of plane; they used rolling staircases and passengers walked across the tarmac in fair weather or foul. Her plans to greet Ricky as he got off the plane went out the window. The other passengers –many of them carrying backpacks with hardhats– filed thru the aisle beside the X-ray machines and she finally saw a steward leading her son by the hand. He was bundled up well and wearing a small back-pack. It was a nice picture. He was a sweet and beautiful child in her eyes; evidently in the eyes of the airline guy too.

Janet knew Ricky to be a pretty outgoing kid so when they finally came thru the door and she knelt to hug him, she was surprised at how quiet he seemed. She realized it had more to do with it having been too long since they had been together than it had to do with shyness. "Hi Pumpkin. How are you? I'm so glad you are here." She smiled up at the steward. "Thank you for taking care of my son for me.   Did he behave himself?" The man smiled back. "He was a perfect gentleman –he charmed the entire crew." He touched Ricky's head. "So long Ricky. Come fly with us again."

"Are you ready to go honey?"

They drove the few blocks to Walmart and had an early dinner at McDonalds. Ricky was quiet until after lunch when they went shopping for food and then the ice finally broke. He had strong feelings on breakfast cereal: *Captain Crunch* but *not* the kind with red things mixed in, fish sticks –*sticks*, not nuggets, *Tater-Tots* of any sort were good, canned corn, but *not* the kind with green and red icky bits, and *PopTarts* had to be the chocolate frosted ones, *not* the one with red gook on top Janet smiled to herself and told him she preferred the ones with strawberry frosting. They decided to buy a box of each, and on second thought, two boxes of each.

By the time they left the store and started the drive to her house, Ricky really opened up. She learned that Grandpa said he needed to take his pajamas, and that was OK, but he had to leave his transformers behind and it was because flying was hard enough for a little boy with out having to worry about luggage and gramdma said he was a very smart little boy but grandma was mean sometimes and grandpa said it was because she was sick and they let him sit by the window and look out but not the window by the little door because he was small and they needed a big strong man to open the door if there was a 'murgency and what's a 'murgency? and the plane went way up and then it went thru the clouds and then they were on top of the clouds and the gave him soda and then he had to go to the bathroom and the bathroom was a little tiny room that smelled funny and it was hard to figure out how to flush the toilet but he did and then it flushed with blue water and that was weird and…

When they got home Ricky dropped his back-pack on the floor and looked around. It didn't take very long. "Why is your house so small Mommy?"

"I live all alone Ricky." She thought maybe he needed a nap and thought about calling her father and asking him. But there were so many questions she needed to ask. Perhaps it was time for her to start sorting these things out for herself.

"Do you need a nap Ricky?"

"No. Where is my bedroom Mommy? I have my own bedroom at grandpas' house."

"You can sleep in my bed and we will go out later and make you a bedroom."

Another trip to Walmart for fabric.

"OK." He climbed into her bed and lay down. He seemed to be asleep within minutes,. *That was easy* she thought to herself.

When he awoke, he had more interest in watching television than the toys and books, so the afternoon passed on to dinnertime to the sound of cartoons. Robby was content and quiet. She opened a can of Tomato soup and made grilled cheese sandwiches. It was her favorite meal when she was a kid and Ricky liked it too. Desert was Pop Tarts topped with ice-cream. Ricky informed her that Gra'ma only let him eat Pop Tarts for breakfast. He thought it was a keen idea to have them with desert too. Even so, he only finished half the PopTart. "Honey, is it time for you to go to bed?"

It was only seven o'clock and she expected an argument, but he climbed down from the table and asked, "Will you read me a story first? The one about dinosaurs."

"Ok. Go brush your teeth and get ready for bed."

"Am I supposed to sleep in your bed again Mommy?"

Another surprise. Was this really the first time he had called her 'Mommy' since she picked him up? Strange she hadn't noticed and how wonderful it sounded now.

"Ya, sure."

"But where will you sleep?"

"I will come to bed later and we can sleep together."

Ricky looked thoughtful for a second, "Grandma sez I'm old enough to sleep in my own room in my own bed." He thought for a moment more, "But I guess it's OK." And he went off to the bathroom. Janet brushed a tear from her eyes with the back of her hand.

The book she had bought that afternoon at the little book store and the one he picked out proved to be a landmine of unpronounceable dinosaur words. *Tyrannosaurus Rex* she got right, but stumbled over *Triceratops* and Ricky corrected her. Then it became a game with them for her to deliberately mangle a word and they would giggle as they tried to work it out together. When she got to *Pterodactyl* it was impossible and she held the book open for him and put her finger under the word. He pushed her hand away so he could see the picture and spoke confidently, "That's a pterodactyl Mommy."

"Goodness you are a smart little boy, Ricky. "Did Grandpa teach you to read? And that's a hard word."

"I can't read yet Mommy, but Grandpa taught me how to say the names. It's fun."

Clearly it was a night for emotion and guilt. She realized she had no idea about what he knew and what he didn't. Furthermore, she had no idea what a boy of his age should know.

They got thru a few more pages: *Iguanodon* and *Velociraptor*, but by the time they got to *Euoplocephalus*, Ricky had mercifully put his head own and was drifting off to sleep. She kissed his cheek. "Good night honey." And waited till she was sure he was asleep. She put on her parka, grabbed her call phone, went outside and called Willy's Place. "Can you put Mel on the phone?"

There was a short delay and she heard an old disco song in the background.

"Mel. This is Janet."

"How was your trip?"

"Las Vegas was fine."

"Kevin had a nice time?"

"No, I think gambling was not going too well. Why do you want to know? Did you give him some money to place a bet for you or something?" Her joke fell flat. "I came back early. Yesterday."

"Are things not going well between you two?"

"No. Yes,. I don't know. Look Mel, what I wanted to call for was I'm not coming in for a while." All the girls took time off when they wanted to. It was not a big deal. They just lost their place in what they called *the rotation* shift-wise.

"I'm confused Janet. I like my friends all to get along."

"It has nothing to do with Kevin. I just have… I'm just not coming in for a while." There was no way in hell she was telling him she had a child –or anything more about her personal life than she had to.

"OK. But let us stay in touch Janet. There is always a place for you here at Willy's. How long do you need?"

"I don't know how long. Maybe for good. I'm just not coming in for a while. That's all I have to say Mel. Good-by"

Ricky was still sound asleep when she came back in. She cleaned up the dishes and opened the dinosaur book again. She wondered if she would feel too silly asking her teacher how to pronounce the dinosaur names. Probably. It reminded her that the science and math tests were all she had left to take. The hated math would have to wait, but maybe she was ready for science. She opened a Pepsi and got out her test-prep book and settled down to study when her cell rang. It was Kevin. She considered ignoring it, and putting on her coat and shoes and going back outside to talk was just too much of a bother. Curious he would call so soon after she spoke to her boss at the strip club –the guy who introduced them. Curiosity got the best of her and she answered quietly. "Hello Kevin. Ricky is asleep so I can't talk."

"That's OK Janet. Can you listen for a minute?"

"Sure." The whole thing with him and their time in Las Vegas seemed suddenly seemed trivial with Ricky asleep across the little efficiency apartment. She gave him a cheerful "What's on your mind?"

"Janet. I want to apologize for the way I was in Las Vegas. You took me by surprise when you told me you had a son."

She made a non-committal sound. He went on. "Can I meet him sometime? I mean my kids are grown up and I don't know how I feel about it all, but I do know I don't want… well, I still want you in my life."

Janet didn't say *You want to keep fucking me and think you can do it for free if you play your cards righ*t, but she thought it. "We will see Kevin . Right now Ricky is my biggest priority."

"Are you going to stay on at Willy's Place?

"Probably not." She was pleased at how pleasant and conversational she was keeping her tone and she was sure she wasn't giving anything away. "I'm not sure what I'm going to do."

"Listen, I need a manager out at the man camp. You might be able to look after your son and my interests at the same time. Probably not make as much as you make at the club, but you know… Ricky –is that his name? well, you could work days and, I don't know how to say it, you could be a mom at night. Is this the OK way to say it?"

She smiled. "Yes, that about says it." It wasn't the worst idea she had ever heard. "I'll have to think about it Kevin. Can we talk about it later?"

"Sure. Maybe we could drive out there sometime when I get back to town. I'm leaving Vegas tomorrow."

"Good night." She turned off her cell and got up to pour a little rum into what was left of her Pepsi. Ricky was just a lump in her bed with a brown mop of hair at one end, but the most beautiful important lump in her world. Could she separate the sleaze of the strip club from Ricky if it allowed her to give him more that she would be able to give him working at McDonalds? How did motherhood fit together with the college girl persona she was working so hard to create. The college girl image was fuzzy. Much more fuzzy with Ricky stirred in. She tried it stirring together with Ricky, a lawyer husband, and the college girl wearing a conservative skirt, white blouse & blazer, high-heals and stern scholarly horn-rimmed glasses. This image worked. It worked until she put Kevin into the role of lawyer husband, then the image fell apart again.

One way or the other, she knew she would never let Ricky go. And this was enough for one night.

Chapter 43

There had been a few nice days in north-western corner of the state. It got well above freezing for four afternoons running. Then a cold front dropped down from the Arctic but did so slowly that the moisture fell out of the sky first as rain and later as snow. As the front continued south, it got cold enough for the rain to freeze once it hit the ground. In other cold climates this would be 'black ice' but in North Dakota it was covered with an inch of snow and slicker than the proverbial snot on a door-knob. Schools were closed and all the police and all the tow truck drivers were called in to work.

Toward the end of his shift, Jeff stepped outside for a little air. The parking lot was slick and he almost fell on his ass, so he took it upon himself to forklift a pallet of bagged sand to the side of the over-head door. He spread a couple of bags around the door to the warehouse. He figured that if the guys had a bag of sand in the back of their trucks, they might have the means of getting themselves moving again if they carelessly parked on an icy patch. The old hands knew better, but there were a lot of young hot-dogs driving around the oil patch. The gravel roads out in the countryside were so rough that black ice was no threat no matter how bad it was, but on the paved main-roads and in town, it was an entirely different matter.

As he was filling out the paperwork for *Sand, bagged, for traction,* his boss checked in on him on the way home for the evening. "I need to you to work an extra shift Jeff. The day guy slid into a telephone pole and messed up his shoulder. Can you cover for him? I think you know the people on the day shift."

Jeff nodded. "No pro'lem."

"If you need a little rest, you can sneak into my office and catch a few zee's"

"Thanks. I'll see how things go."

The boss hesitated a moment. "How you coming with the GED thing?"

"I've passed the Math and Science tests. Leaves social studies and literature. Pretty easy. And writin' - 'at's the hard one, but when I get back on nights, I can get he'p down to the college. Mornings and all –after I finish up here."

"Good. You are back on nights starting now. Shall I put you in for some training next month in Houston?"

"That might be pushing it a tad. Maybe the next month?"

"OK –but let's get'er done. I need you to run things come summer."

Jeff grinned. "Fin'ez frog's 'air."

Other than the need to work two twelve hour shifts back to back, it *was* as fine as frog's hair. It would be good to be going back to class mornings –at least after he got his sleep schedule sorted out. He had done this often enough to know the shift change would just take a few days of feeling like warmed over dog-shit and then he would be fine.

No telling what would happen with Janet. He hadn't heard from her in a while. *No Big* he told himself, but he was a little disappointed. There was also the matter of his roommate telling him that he was pretty sure she was a stripper. *No Big* seemed to be the best way to think about this too.

The night wore on. He put fifteen bags of sand on eleven different trucks. Work on rigs could go on in almost any weather, but tool-pushers –the boss –the guy who lived in a trailer on site and was responsible for making depth- took it easy. Too easy for bones to get broken when men were hurrying and every steel surface on a rig was coated in ice and everything on a rig was steel. Bits kept turning and cuttings kept floating out of the well-bore on a tide of the mud pumped down the drill pipes, but the dozens of little maintenance tasks that needed to get done but could be put off, got put off. Made Jeff's life a little easier. The rigs called for fewer of the fiddly miscellaneous supplies. They always had pipe and they always had mud.

At about the time he would have ordinarily been thinking about heading off to bed he noticed he was hungry and ordered a pizza. He took his GED book out of his bag and took the pizza back to his boss' office, put his feet up, and settled down to a quiet meal and a little study time. The pizza went quickly, the studying was dull, and he was trying not to nod off when his cell phone rang in his shirt pocket. "Mrf –'is'iz Jeff"

"Hi Jeff. This is Janet"

Deep breath. "Well, howdy Janet. Where ya' been?"

"I took a trip. How are you?"

"Fine. Where'd you go?"

"Las Vegas. When can we get together to study?"

"Well kiddo, I'm back on nights now –at least for a while. Ya' want to go back to studying in class ever' morning?"

"I'm not going to be able to come to class anymore. Jeff, I'm taking the science test today and if I pass, I'll only have the math to get thru. And I need to be done by May."

"Well, I have to get thru them…."

Janet made a snap decision and interrupted him, "I want you to come to my place. We can study here."

Jeff sighed. "Are you sure that will be convenient for you?"

The sarcasm was lost on Janet. "Ya. When can you come?"

"Janet dear, we supposed to be he'ping each other. Works out to you spend five mints readin' my writing and then we spend an hour doing your math. And now I'm supposed to come by your house when it suits you? I'm kind'a getting the short end of the stick here."

"Oh." She realized he had a point, but it had been a long time since any man – especially a young man and most especially oil-field worker had spoken to her like that. But she needed him and she needed to stay home with Ricky. He had always been a gentleman: he might have been gay for all she knew. What was it her Daddy always said? *In for a pint, in for a pound.* "What time do you get off?"

"Six." he grunted.

"Tell you what. You come by here and I'll fix you dinner. Then we can study."

Jeff held the phone about a foot away from his face and just stared at for a second before he answered. "Just did shift change. I needs me a days or two to get my sleep all sorted around. Wha'z your address?"

She giggled, "For starters, You *need* –without the *ess* at the end. He or she *needs*. You or I *need* –one person -no *ess* at the end. We are going to get thru this together Jeff."

He paused. Now *this* was new. "Who are you and what have you done with my friend Janet?"

She giggled again and they sorted a time a few days later, as well as her phone number, and address.

Chapter 44

Mike had a mess of left over chicken drumsticks and thighs from last night's roasted chicken dinner. He hated waste and so he started pulling meat from the bones and chopping up for a big pot of corn & chicken chowder. He hadn't gotten very far before he decided it was a bad idea. The time wasted at tearing and chopping cold chicken got to be more irksome than the notion of wasting food. Each bone that he tossed into the trash had a little more meat on it. He decided that from here on, chicken going into the dining trailer would either be on the bone, or it would come into the kitchen trailer boneless and damn the cost.

About half way thru, there was a knock on the door. His hands were dirty so he just shouted. "Come on in." figuring it would be the Kiwi or Robby out of school early and coming to help. It was the rotund black frack hand he met his first night in Williston. "Well howdy Kermit. How's things?"

"Got me a day off and got bored sitting around my bedroom so I thought I'd come by and see how the kitchen worked."

"Happy to see you. Give me a minute and I'll make us some coffee. Or you want a little something else?"

"Coffee would be nice." He watched Mike pull at a drumstick and toss it into the trash. "Did I ever tell we was poor coming up kids?"

Mike shrugged. "I think so –you mentioned a big family from the south and all. Maybe I kind of inferred it."

"*Inferred* That's a good word. I'll have to remember it. Well anyway, my momma would never throw away a chicken bone with the least little bit of meat on it. She'd boil 'em in this big wire basket thing she had in this even bigger pot till weren't nothing but bone left. And my Momma was a great cook. She could make all manner of soups and stews from after the family ate a couple of her famous roasted chickens." Mike stopped and looked down at the leg quarters he still had to get thru, looked into the trash at the bones he has already tossed, and looked back at Kermit. "You're right. I should have thought of it myself." He dried his hands on his apron and turned to get a big pot. "I've already started the chowder –cream and all, but I could simmer the bones in some water and pour the chicken-y goodness thru a colander in before I serve it. Right"

Kermit nodded. "Momma would be proud."

Mike started on the coffee. "So what is new in the world of fracking out in the oil patch? Hope no one else died."

"Nope. Pretty quiet. The weather slowed things down a little, but I had lots of work to do in the lab. This is my first day off since I ran into you t'other night. So what's new here at the man camp?"

"We have new management. The lawyer who owns the place is here a lot and there is an odd little woman manning the front desk. The Kiwi and maintenance guy are still here. The maids are mostly still here. Except for the usual turn-over anyway. There are a couple of high school kids working here too –friends of the lawyer I guess –or kids of a friend of the lawyers or something. The boy helps me out in the kitchen. Nice kid."

Mike poured the coffee and Kermit nodded his thanks. "I'm curious about something. You remember I told you about the guy on our crew who got killed?"

"Um -ya. He was the… shall we just say an *assertive* young man."
"Yep. Well it turned out he was on meth. Or that's the rumor anyway. Dumb thing to do. He would have been fired in a heartbeat come the next drug test, and he was hyper enough to begin with."

Mike was puzzled. "I understand about drug testing and all, But what's with hyper?"

"Oh. Some guys use it to keep going when they have been on the rig too long. Usually older guys but not always. Depends on how the job goes, but you usually pull onto a site and work like a mother for six or eight hours to set up the pipes and pumps and all, then you sit around trying to stay warm and maybe get s few winks while the pressure builds up. Someone is watching the pressure, but that's usually a company man. Someone has to keep the tanks full of sand and chemicals and all, but the rest of the crew has a little down time. Our little buddy has been volunteering to load the tanks *and* run and up down the derrick as necessary. No one does that unless they're crazy. Or doing drugs."

"Yikes. Do you think he was on drugs that afternoon we met? I mean is that why he was such a jerk?"

"No. He was always a jerk. But what the fuck, he was young and making good money. That don't excuse it, but we was all young once't wasn't we? It's only been a few weeks that he was acting this way."

Kermit sipped his coffee and paused before he went on. "The thing is, I think he was getting his drugs from someone here at the man camp. That's better than getting them from someone in our company, but I still don't like it."

"How do you know this? I thought you guys worked so hard that when you were around here, you were either eating or sleeping."

"Ya, that's true, but a couple of times when it was time to leave in the crew truck, he'd head out early and have us pick him up at the trailer with the office on the way out. No explanation. And when we got on site, he'd head straight for the shitter and lock the door for a few minutes." Kermit shrugged. "I may be making something out of nothing, but I don't like the idea of people getting killed because they are on drugs and I don't like the idea of drugs being sold where I live. Or as you put it, where I eat and sleep. Either way, I don't like it."

Mike asked, "Have you been in the office lately?"

"Nope" There's never no need for us to go there. The company handles our rent and meals."

"Well, there is a new… I guess she is the manager –a little woman from Boston who seems to be in the office all the time. But I can't see her as a drug dealer. And the lawyer who owns the place is a decent sort –for a lawyer anyway. He and I had to have us a pissing contest right off, but we get along fine now."

"Oh, that reminds me. You remember the little Asian hooker with the big boobs that fucked Kenny that evening?"

"Ya, first set of boobs I've seen in a long time. Last ones too, for that matter."

Kermit chuckled, "I wasn't paying too much attention to her face. Specially when she had her shirt up, but I think maybe she's living here now. Or someone who looks just like her- with her boobs covered up anyway. And she's doing business too. That don't bother me none though. Helps the young fellows blow off steam."

"If I ever catch up my sleep, I might have a little steam to blow off too. Someday. But probably not." Both men laughed.

Chapter 45

Good news, bad news sort of a day. Janet passed the GED science test leaving only math. She had taken Ricky along because she had overheard Mike chatting with another student who had kids. He urged her to sit down and study with her children. He said it was a good thing for kids to see that studying in hard –even for their parents. Janet thought it would be a good example for Ricky to see his mom doing school work. Besides which, she had nothing else to do with him. It turned out to be a big mistake.

The bad news was that she realized she had a lot to learn about being a mom. Ricky got bored and everything she did to get him to quiet down seemed to wind him up tighter. She knew he was bored but when had he become such a little monster? "Go look at your book" had no effect and a promise of McDonalds for lunch wasn't soon enough. She thought she had been well behaved at his age. Not so much when she was older. After adolescent, it seemed she and her mom were always at each other's throats. She tried to remember how her parents did it when she was Rickie's age, but she was also trying to pass the test.

Finally, she just ignored him and he had a full blown temper tantrum –laying on the floor on his back kicking his heels and screaming. The test was done on a computer and was timed so she couldn't just get up and take him out of the classroom but he was totally disrupting the other students and her own concentration was shot to hell. Finally, the teacher stepped over and simply stood looking down at Ricky. Janet had no idea why it worked, but Ricky stopped and just looked up at the teacher. "Would you like to go see a really big bus?"

Ricky got up with out taking his eyes off the older man. "I guess. Is it really big?"

"Yet it's really really big. It's the bus the college band uses to go places and play music at games out of town. I know where they hide it."

Janet was sure Ricky had no idea what Mike was talking about, and was pretty sure Mike hadn't a lot of experience with kids, but at least Rickie's tantrum was over. "Ask you mom if it's OK to go see the really big bus."

"Can I Mommy?"

Janet looked from Ricky to Mike. "Where is it –the bus?"

"It's just down the hall. It's in the garage where the college keeps extra desks, and Christmas decorations and such. And the Bus. The Williston State College Buffalo's bus."

Janet nodded OK and Ricky asked, "Are there were going to be buffaloes?"

Mike nodded toward the door, "Let's go see. I know the bus is there, maybe a buffalo too."

They walked out of the room and Janet turned back to the computer and tried to wrap her brain around a graph showing the growth rates of primrose –what ever the fuck a primrose was- corn, and cucumber. It looked suspiciously like the graphs Jeff was teaching her to make out of an equation involving X's and Y's, but the more she thought about it, the more it seemed to be a simple matter of finding the highest part of the primrose graph, and looking down at the scale. They grew fastest at fifty degrees, and 50° was B) so she clicked that answer and went on to consider another graph that charted the percentages of a car's weight made out of light-weight materials over a twenty year time frame. It sounded a little like math, but it was really just a matter of reading the question carefully and looking at the words on the horizontal and vertical parts of the graph.

She went thru about twelve questions when Mike and Ricky came back. One of the men in the class –a beefy older guy in the ubiquitous oil-patch baseball cap, hoody, and greasy parka looked up and asked Ricky if he would like to see a big truck with its engine all tore up. Janet was hesitant –he was a big old oilfield worker after all –but at least she didn't remember him from Willy's Place. More permission was granted from Mom, but Ricky had to put his coat on because the truck was in another building where they fixed cars and trucks and off the two of them went. Janet got thru another twenty question. Next it was the woman who Mike had urged to study at the kitchen table with her kids that asked Ricky is he wanted to see where they made the lunches for the student's and maybe see if they might find something to eat. Another fifteen or twenty question got answered.

Rickie's last field trip was to the library with Mike's boss Linda. It was not so much a success as the other ones, but sufficient for Janet to finish the test. She passed. Just barely, but she passed.

As she was gathering up her stuff and buttoning up Rickie's coat, she smiled thanks at the other students who had helped with Ricky. It occurred to her she had been – if not bitchy- at least stand-offish with these people and yet four of then has stepped up to help out. Was it because he was a cute kid, or because they were pulling for her on the test? Mike was standing at the door as she left. "Congrats on the test. Just math last to go now?"

"Yep. That's it and then I can enroll in college."

"Listen Janet, I've never been a parent and I can only imagine how difficult it must be, but we can not have another scene like this today." Janet just nodded. "And I hope you noticed how many of these folks jumped in to help out. They are good people and pulling for you. Maybe you should…." He let the thought trail off.

She looked down and whispered, "I understand." More for her to think about: parenting as well as how to be a good student. Was this part of being a college girl?

Her promise of McDonalds had not been forgotten. She was tempted to tell him his behavior was so horrible that there were to be no hamburgers for him for a long time. But it all seemed to have blown over and so she let it go. Ricky told her about the bus and the trucks and the huge bar they pulled down on to make French fries out of potatoes. He got to try it, but he was too small to pull it down so they helped him and he could do it then. But it was really cool anyway. The man with the truck told him a bunch of stuff about trucks and motors that he didn't understand, but it was pretty cool too. He didn't think much of the library –just books and people sitting around reading them and the lady made him be very quiet.

When they got home, she immediately Googled child care and found an even dozen day-care businesses with phone numbers. The first number had been disconnected. The second was not taking any more children at the time, the third number rang, but there was no answer. The forth number was a recording explaining that it was nap-time and no calls would be answered until after two, the fifth and sixth were not taking on more children nor was the seventh, but this one would be happy to put her on a waiting list. Janet asked how long the list was, and the woman said there were 23 names ahead of her. Janet thanked her but said not to bother. The eighth number was disconnected and the ninth was a recording explaining that they were not taking more children at the time.

The tenth call gave her some small hope. The woman who answered seemed pleasant, but said she was full up. Out of exasperation, Janet asked what advice she might have for a working mother. The voice on the phone was sympathetic, but explained that even in North Dakota daycare in a woman's home highly regulated and getting a license was a long drawn out and expensive process. There were a lot of working mom's out in the oil patch so it was really a seller's market. She knew of one daycare –she wouldn't say which, that only took children of professional people "Doctors and lawyers you know. Not oil field workers, because, you know, even the good ones, sometimes have to work long hours and the kids get left for far longer than was allowed." The woman told Janet a confusing story about how she heard of one kid whose father dropped him off on a Monday morning didn't come back. Late Wednesday evening, a woman came by for the kid and said she was the father's girl friend. The little boy seemed to know the girlfriend who explained that the mom was in jail –probably for drugs or something. "With two little kids of her own –God Bless 'em- what else could she do? The little boy had been there for almost three days by then." Turned out the mom was in jail –probably for drugs- and dad was… well, the girlfriend just shrugged. It was all so sad that the woman let the four year old boy go home with the girlfriend. The next day the police came. By the time it was over, she had lost her license, had to pay a lawyer about three thousand dollars and everyone –even the judge- agreed she had done the Christian and charitable thing, but she should have called Child Protective Services right away and further more, she should have known to have done so. The woman explaining it all to Janet asked if she knew anything about the CPS dormitory for misplaced kids? It was over in Minot? Janet didn't know.

"Horrible place. Scares the stuffing out of the title ones. Two hour drive and it takes forever for people to get their kids back. But that's just the way things has gotten ever since the fracking an' all started."

Janet shuddered. No way she would ever let Ricky get taken off to Minot. "Oh dear. Well thank you for explaining this all to me. Maybe I can ask a friend to help me. You know all informal like."

"There you go. Best not to let the authorities know nothing. That's the way we likes to do things in North Dakota. But I got'a go and see what my kids is up to. If I don't they will paint the cat or some-damn thing. Good luck to you honey."

Janet called the last two numbers and got the same 'full-up' response. It wasn't quite two o'clock, but she tried the one that didn't answer the phone till after nap-time and got no answer again. She gave up and ate the hamburger Ricky had left on the table.

Kevin said he was coming by at three to take her out to his man-camp and talk to her about working there for him. After the elation of having passed the test, she had decided to call and cancel. She had enough money in the bank –and more in the Mason jar in the back of the broken dresser drawer. But hadn't he mentioned something about her being able to take Ricky to work with her? And she thought he should be starting Kindergarten next year. Suddenly Kevin 's offer looked a little better –with or without sex-strings. But then again, she didn't feel it was time to introduce him and Ricky just yet. Soon, but not yet.

She called Tonia and –wonder of wonders- her friend answered on the third ring.
"Hi girl. How's tricks?"

"Hi Tonia. I'm fine. How's ticks your end?"

"Turning lots of them, thank you for asking."

"Tonia, I need a big favor."

"Anything for you girlfriend."

"Ricky is living with me now. I need a babysitter. I have to go see about a job and I can't take him with me and I can't find a day-care place that has any openings. We are supposed to go there this afternoon. Can you come by for a couple of hours?"

"Ya sure. So he's here in Williston? Can I meet him? That's dumb –I guess I can meet him if I'm babysitting, can't I? Aren't you working down at Willy's Place anymore? What's the new job?

"OK. Let me see. Yes, I picked him up at the airport a couple of days ago. Yes, you can meet him this afternoon. And no, I'm not working there –at least for a while. My mom is sick and my dad needed to send him here so he can look after my mom."

"Bummer."

"Oh, and the job is working at a man camp –kind of a managing thing I guess. I told you about that lawyer? He wants me to run the front desk or something and he says I can have Ricky there with me."

"Oh cool. Is this the same guy back when? How is it going with him?"

Hard to say. We went to Las Vegas together. We had fun for a little while, but I think he got tired of me –or he lost too much money at the tables, or I got tired of him. All up in the air. He says he wants to keep things going, but things have changed. Ricky and all."

"Hold on a second, What's the man camp you are going to work at?"

"It's the Bakken Lodge up north of town..."

"Tonia squeeled. "Honey –Tom and I are living there now. Doing lots of business too. Why don't you bring Ricky by and I'll look after him here?"

"Um, I don't know Tonia. I kind'a don't want to introduce Ricky to Kevin yet. Please Tonia, Can't you come by here. Ricky is used to things here. I took him with me to class this morning and he was a little shit. I think maybe too much has been changing and I don't want to mix him up anymore."

"Sweetie, are you worried about him staying here with Tom and me doing my thing?"

It hadn't occurred to Janet that Tonia might be turning tricks in her own home, but it damn sure did when Tonia asked. "No Tonia, that's not it at all. I just don't want to spring Ricky on my lawyer or vice-versa. And I don't want for Ricky to have another tantrum. Please Tonia. Come by here. I'll owe you so much."

Tonia was a little late and Kevin was a little early, but it worked out. Janet was waiting by the door when she heard him drive up. She kissed Ricky, "You be a good boy now Ricky." She blew a kiss at Tonia and left. Kevin had gotten out and opened the door for her and leaned to kiss her as she was getting in his car. She stopped and smiled. It was a nice kiss. Janet had no idea what it meant to her. Evidently it meant a great deal to him. "Can't I come in and meet your son? We are not in a big hurry?"

"No. Some other time. He's taking his nap." A good lie –an effective one anyway. Kevin shrugged casually, smiled, got behind the wheel and they made their way out of the little sub-division where Janet rented her little studio apartment.

Chapter 46

Vern's kids got the man camp exactly twenty two minutes after the last bell rang at Williston High School Beth drove two blocks and picked Robbie up at his middle school. Robby had managed to eat only two of the three bologna sandwiches his mom packed for his lunch but it was a close thing. He inhaled the third one as Beth herded the Toyota up Highway 2 to where the gravel road turn-off to the man-camp. "Eat much you little twerp?"

Robby swallowed. "Pound sand. Just because you are always trying to loose weight, don't mean no one else can eat. Sheese"

"I don't care if you eat, but you might try chewing a little once in a while. And chew with you mouth shut."

She pulled into the short road leading downhill to the office trailer. Robby wadded up his lunch sandwich and tossed it into the back seat. "Drop me off here. I got'ta check the water plant."

Beth pulled up beside the big white Butler building and stopped. "Listen you little creep, don't leave your crummy trash in the back of my car."

"It's Mom's car, not yours." but he reached over the seat and grabbed the wad before he go out.

Beth drove thru the washboard a little too fast and parked a little downhill from the office trailer while Robby walked to the door of the water-treatment building. As he was digging in his jean's pocket for the key to the padlock on the door he noticed the front bumper a car parked on the side of the building away from the drive. He unlocked the door and curiosity got the better of him. It was only a few steps around the corner and he saw a woman sitting in the driver's seat with the door open. She was about his parent's age. There was a rifle across her lap. He stopped. "Oh! Planning to do a little hunting? I thought antelope season was over."

The woman looked at him for a moment, then shook her head. "Nope, just waiting for someone. Going to go do some target shooting."

"Well, have a nice day" and Robby walked back to the door into the plant to tend to his chores inside. He had just started checking the chlorine levels when the door shut behind him. He figured it was the wind.

Kevin pulled up to the office next to Beth's Mom's Toyota and got out of his car and came around to Janet's side to open the door but by then she was already out and standing by the side of the car wondering what he was doing. It took a second for her to realize he was doing the gentleman thing. She smiled and started to thank him when his car's rear window exploded inward behind him. A half second later there a sharp crack that might have come from up hill. Kevin turned around and stared at the missing glass. Janet started to speak, "Is someone sho…" and a loud bang rang out behind her. As she turned there was the sound of a second crack. By now she was sure it was coming from up the hill. There was a deep hole in the fender of the car just behind the front wheel a few inches from her knees. Both Janet and He realized it was gunfire and both ran around the car –Janet to the front and Kevin to the rear. There was a third crack. Janet stumbled, hit her shoulder on the hood of the car, and slipped to the ground. Then both of the front side windows disappeared in a shower of safety glass pebbles, and there was a forth crack an instant later.

Kevin had gotten the driver's side door open and flung himself across the seat, fumbled his keys into the ignition and got the car started while stretched out on the front seat. Another bang –this from somewhere behind him and another crack. He twisted around just enough to get his foot on the gas, used his left hand to yank the gear shift into reverse and floored it.

The car shot across the parking lot, slowed a little as it bounced over a pile of hard snow that had been plowed to the edge of the parking lot, and tore across the prairie. The driver's side door still open and his right foot sticking out a few inches.

Janet found herself sitting in the snow -alone and exposed at the edge of the parking lot. The wall of the office trailer behind her, a narrow gap to her right between the trailer and more parked cars. To her left was the hillside from where the shots seemed to be coming. But what was in front of her was the sight of Kevin's car bouncing and swerving across the frozen stubble. She thought she saw his head pop up above the dash-board for just an instant and disappear again. When it was about one hundred yard away, it seemed to rear up and stop suddenly. She realized it had backed into a shallow ditch at full speed. The front wheels were suspended a foot or so of the ground and the underside of the car was visible. There were three more cracks in rapid succession and steam began to pour from the grill.

Several things occurred to her at once; First she realized that she was completely exposed to the shooter. Second, the shooting was at Kevin not her. Third, she realized he was an utter coward, and finally, it all struck her as funny and she fell on her side laughing hysterically.

When her laughter diminished to sporadic giggling, she got up and walked slowly up the wooden steps to the office. There was no one at the desk but she heard pop music coming from a tinny little radio down the hall. She thought someone had to do something when there was shooting, but what ever it might have been, she knew she wasn't up to it. So she walked down the hall to the music. It was a crowded little laundry room with a girl in blue jeans and *Hard Rock* tee shirt with her back to Janet.

The woman was pulling white sheets out of a dryer.   "Excuse, are you in charge?"

The woman turned around and Janet saw it was a young woman –maybe sixteen or so. "Um, no. Isn't Mr. Spencer out there?"

"No." Giggling erupted again and it took Janet a moment to suppress it.

""Um… no one and there has been a shooting. We need to tell someone."

The girl just stood there with a white wad of laundry in her arms. "Oh 'm Gawd. Are you OK? Is anyone hurt." Janet giggled again. She couldn't help herself. The girl smirked, "Ok. That's not funny. Mr. Spencer will be back soon and you can play your little joke on him. And Mr. Amundsen is going to be here soon. You can tell him your joke too. I've got work to do." She dumped the laundry on a table against the wall and turned back to the dryer.

The giggling became breathless sobbing. "I came with your Mr. Amundsen – they shot at him too -he might be hurt -he's out in the field -is there someone we can call -maybe the police –on my God –the guy with the gun is still out there." She dropped to the floor and crawled into a little space beside last washing machine and wedged herself in. She put her face in her hands and tried to get control of herself. "Please. Please call someone."

The young woman was clearly not convinced, "I'll see if I can get someone." and she left the room. Janet remembered her cell phone and dialed 911. She got the *Service Not Available at This Time* message and lost control of her crying again. She thought she heard the girl talking to someone about maybe coming quickly, but wasn't sure. Why in God's name couldn't she stop giggling. It was better than crying, but crying at least made sense. And shouldn't someone go see about Kevin?

She heard a door open and more words from the girl. Something about *maybe drugs*, and *I don't know* and *call Mr. Amundsen*. Footsteps came down the short hall and Janet looked up and was astonished to see her teacher in a stained white apron. "Oh thank God. Someone was shooting at Kevin and me out in the parking lot and I fell down and he drove off and drove in a ditch and that little bitch doesn't believe me."

The girl had followed Mike but now gasped, turned, and stomped back out. Mike leaned down and held his hand out to Janet. "We will sort this out Janet. Now come out of there and take a breath."

She let herself be pulled out and up to her feet. She started giggling again. "Why are you here teacher? You look like a cook." The giggling became a sob before she got a hold of herself again.

"Well, I *am* the cook –afternoons anyway." He gave her his goofy teacher look –the one he gave her the first day in class. "Now, tell me what happened. No one is shooting at us now."

He lead her down the hall, past the desk, where the girl was sitting with a really pissed look on her face. "Beth, why don't you see if you can go find Spencer and your brother?" He took Janet to the little office just beyond and sat her in a chair in the corner, sat himself behind the desk and picked up the phone on the desk and dialed 911. While waiting for an answer, he remarked, "Now might be a very good time for a shot of brandy. How you feeling?" Before she could answer, he spoke on the phone. "This is Mike Williams, I'm out at the Bakken Lodge Man camp. There has been a shooting. Can you send someone out to help?"

He listened for a moment. "I don't think anyone has been hurt, but it's all rather confusing." He started opening and closing drawers in the desk.

"Ok if I put you on the speaker? I have something else to tend to right now."
The speakerphone crackled, "We have someone on the way out there. Please stay on the
line."

"Good. Thank you. We are in the office trailer by the entry." He put the phone
down on the desk and opened a bottom drawer. "Oh good." he said, "The woman that
used this office left us a little something something." and he set a small half full bottle of
peppermint schnapps on the desk. "But she took a powder so I don't think she'll mind.
Can you manage without a glass? I know you are all lady-like and everything, but…."

Janet almost giggled but not from hysteria this time. She took a long swig from
the bottle, gasped, wiped her lips with the back of her hand, and finished off the liqueur
in another pull. "Thank you. This helps. Um, Kevin drove off when the shooting
happened. He wrecked out in the field. Maybe someone should…   what if the shooter
is still out there?"

"Maybe we'll just sit tight till the police get here. Any chance it was an accident
–you know, and hunter way off in the distance shooting at an antelope or some thing?"

"No way." She counted on her fingers. "There were at least four or five shots.
They hit the car. Broken windows and everything. Maybe more after he drove off."

"Where were you when he drove off?"

Janet thought for a few seconds. "I was just sitting there. I mean I tried to get
behind the car but I fell. And he drove off while I was sitting on my ass in the snow."

The front door to the trailer opened and Spencer came in and stopped the snow
from his boots. Mike got up and went out to the desk in the living room. Janet followed
slowly. "Hi Spence. Been some excitement. Did you hear anything about ten fifteen
minutes ago? Maybe like gun fire?"

"Gun… bless me, no. I was around back with me' head under a trailer thawing
out some pipes."

Janet went to a window facing the prairie and peaked out. "Look out there –in
the field. It's Kevin's car in a ditch. And… oh my God, and it's on fire. Someone has to
do something."

Both Mike & Spence looked out. Spence spoke first. "That's just steam I think.
But something is going on –that's for sure." He turned to the girl from the laundry room.
"Beth, where's you brother Robby?"

"I just dropped him off at the water plant when we were coming in."

Janet asked, "Where is the water plant? Is it that building up the hill?"
Everyone turned to her. No one spoke and she whispered. "I think that's maybe where
the shots were coming from. When was that?"

Beth's eyes flashed at Janet, "Listen you…." She caught herself. "Robby
would never shoot at anyone." Then it dawned on the girl, "Oh my God. What's
happened to Robby?"

She moved toward the door but Mike stepped in her way. "Hold on Beth. Let's
calm down and wait for the police."

Beth started to cry and Janet reached out tentatively to hug her. The younger
woman fell into Janet's arms and they both started to cry on one another's shoulders.

Mike and Spencer just looked at one another.

Chapter 47

Kevin crawled thru the snow & field stubble on his hands and knees till he couldn't feel his fingers. He had followed the shallow ditch where his car crashed and stood up and felt a dull ache in his ankle. His hands were too cold and numb to do more than pull up his sodden pant cuffs and check it out. No blood but it was swollen. He remembered the car door slamming on his ankle when he crashed into the ditch. It suddenly occurred to him that someone had been shooting at him and ducked back down. He walked a little further down the ditch crouched over and with his hands in his armpits trying to warm them. He felt like a fool, so he risked a quick look around. To the north were three squat farm silo things. He turned to the east and then the south: nothing but prairie. Somewhere to the west was the man camp but all he could see was the roof of the water treatment building. He figured this was where the shooting had come from. His dad had been a hunter and had tired to get him interested, but it hadn't taken. He liked the gun part and did well but not the hanging out in the woods early on cold winter mornings. part. Even so, he remembered enough the gun training to be pretty sure he was far enough from the building that it would take a hell of a shot to get him. And they would have to be on the roof anyway. The shots fired at him when he got out of his car in the parking lot all missed, so maybe the shooter wasn't that good a shot. Unless the shooter was just trying to scare him. He tried to put himself in the mind of the shooter and it suddenly occurred to him that the only person who hated him enough to shoot at him, was that bitch Sara Mahon. Would she come walking across the prairie with a rife looking for him or would she drive off before the police came? And if she did run off, would she try again another time. He would have to think about that later. For the moment, he needed to get out of the open and he needed to get someone to get him out of the damn field and probably to a doctor. He pulled out his cell phone and started to dial 911 with stuff fingers, but stopped on the second 1. Too many questions would need to be answered. He needed time to think things out more clearly. He called his office praying Beulah was still there. She answered, "Amundsen Law Offices."

"Beulah, there has been an accident, You need to come get me. I'm at…"

"Oh my Gawd. Have you called the police?"

"Listen to me Beulah, I am hurt and don't have time to fiddle with the police. I'm out by the man-camp, but…"

"Can't someone help you there?"

"Listen to me Beulah." He shouted. " I'm not there. I'm in a field north of there. I'm hurt. Please do not argue. Get in your car and drive north on Highway 2. Turn right at Highway 6 . Can you do that Beulah?"

"She was not used to being shouted at and answered in a meek "Yes."

He lowered his voice. "Do you know north and south and where Highway 6 is?"

Another meek "Yes."

"Good. After you have turned right on the dirt road, call me on my cell phone and I'll tell you exactly where to find me. Got it?"

"Yes"

"Please hurry. I'll explain it all when you get here."

He put the phone back in his pocket and limped up a gradual rise from the ditch to the three silo things. When he got there he looked over his shoulder. From where he was standing the entire butler building was visible. If the shooter was there, he had been in plain sight for most of his walk –sharp-shooter or not. He quickly ducked behind the closest of the cylindrical bins. He edged around the first one and looked out toward the road where he expected Beulah to be coming.

He reviewed his situation. For starters, he was cold, wet, and in pain. But he was still walking around. Next, someone had been shooting at him. Damn sure the police would have a lot of questions, but he didn't know who or why or what. He had a suspicion, but any lawyer worth a shit could deal with the ambiguity and turn it to his advantage. But if he was right, and it was Sara Mahon, he had an ongoing problem. He needed to find out if it was –or even could have been- the bitch. The obvious task at hand was to talk to Mel. He had carefully avoided knowing any more about the cook and what ever he had done to get his money back. Ignorance might be a good starting point, but not in the long run.

He had learned from Mel. Phones –cell phones in particular, were problematic for sensitive situations, but he had no choice and he dialed the strip club's number. Mel answered, "Willy's Place"

"Good afternoon. We have a situation." He was proud of himself for having remembered not to use his name then he realized the police could… what did the call it on TV? *Pull his lugs* and know about every call he made. Mel hadn't spoken. "Can you meet me at the hospital sometime this evening?" Something with a siren was coming up County Road Six –clearly the police, so there was no point in over-doing the clever double-talk. "There has been a shooting."

Kevin wasn't sure if it was the word *hospital* or *shooting* that did the trick, but Mel surprised him by agreeing immediately. "Certainly councilor. Mercy Medical Canter?"

"Yes. The Emergency Room." And he hung up.

He spent the next few minutes having imaginary conversations with the police:

Mr. Amundsen, why did you not call the police immediately?

"I guess I was in shock."

"Mr. Amundsen, why would anyone want to shoot at you?

"I have no idea. I'm just an accountant and lawyer. I do taxes and investments."

Mr. Amundsen, why did you call your secretary come get you rather than wait for an ambulance?

"I knew she would get here sooner and I didn't think I was hurt that badly. I guess I was in shock."

Mr. Amundsen, why did you call the manager of a strip club before you called the police?

This one was tricky. "I had an appointment with the manager later that day and I was going to be late." He knew it was little weak, best to stick with it. I guess I was in shock."

By the time he saw Beulah's old Buick coming down the road, he was confident he would come out of it all in good shape. He was still cold, wet, and in pain, but his legal ass was covered.

Chapter 48

Right after Vern turned onto County 6, a Williston cop car tore around him with siren screaming and lights flashing. Beth's call had been a mixture of hysteria and her adolescent attempt to be calm and mature. It was a confusing account of gun shots and Robby. Whatever the hell was going on, Vern figured he wasn't alone in responding to something serious so he put his foot in it and followed in the cop's wake. When they hit 70, he felt the rear end get squirrelly because of the washboard. Occurred to him that he hadn't driven that fast since he was seventeen or so. Funny where the mind goes in tense situations. He eased off the gas, but still pulled up at the man-camp office trailer as the cop was getting out. There was s sheriff's car parked there too, and it occurred to Vern that he didn't know if he was still in the city, or out in McKinsey County.

It seemed that the party was in the trailer so he followed the officer in and glanced around at the people standing in the crowded office. There was a blond sheriff's deputy in brown uniform that looked familiar. There was also, a twenty something Williston cop in a blue uniform, a guy in a cook's apron, a little guy sitting behind the desk and not saying anything, pretty woman in blue-jeans and tight sweater with her arm across Beth's shoulder. "I'm here Bethie. It's going to be all right." He hadn't called her 'Bethie' in years and had no idea if it was going to be all right, but…

"Oh Daddy, I don't know what's going on." She nodded at the pretty woman. "She says someone was shooting at them out in the parking lot and said the shots were coming from where Robby was and I knew Robby would never shoot anyone, but now Robby is missing and they won't let me go look for him and no one is doing anything."

The cop waded in, "Now hold on here." He turned to Vern, "You are the Dad?" The cop was holding a notepad and started writing.

Vern ignored him and turned back to Beth. "Was Robby up checking the water plant?"

"Ya, I dropped him off when we got here."

"Sit tight sweetheart. I'll go see what's going on."

The cop looked up from his note taking. "Nope, no one is going anywhere till I get this sorted out."

Vern glanced at the young pecker-head. "Fuck you." and Beth gasped. She had never heard her father talk like that. He walked past the guy and out the door while the guy was sputtering about 'an investigation' and 'obstruction of justice.' When he got outside the sheriff's deputy followed him out.

"You mind if I join you, Vern?"

Vern glanced at the guy in surprise as he started toward the Butler building out by the road. ""Oh –I know you. We do the Son's of Norway thing, right. Forgot your name."

"Sven. I think our wives do some of the cooking together."

It came back to Vern. "And didn't you used to date my sister Veronica?"

"Yep. She was more interested in the football players though." Vern was in a hurry and the deputy had to hustle to keep up. "It's not clear who has authority here, city or county, but I think that police youngster is a little out of his depth. I got here just a few minutes ago and have just a little more information." He gestured off across the prairie. "You see that car out yonder? The young woman with the cleavage came here with some guy. She says bullets started hitting the car and he took off without her. He made it as far as the ditch there. She scampered into the trailer and tried to get someone to do something. Evidently your daughter was skeptical –at least at first. The guy in the apron is the camp cook. Or a teacher. Or both. Not sure about the little fellow behind the desk. Works here I think."

When they got to the water treatment building, the door was open. Vern called out. "Robby, are you there?" Nothing. The two men looked at each other.

The deputy unsnapped the strap on his automatic's holster. "You mind if I go in first?"

Vern just nodded. He realized that Sven was just trying to protect him. He hoped it was to protect him from danger, rather than protect him from the sight of his son lying dead inside. Clearly this deputy was one of the good ones. It took the guy only a few seconds to glance around the tanks and pipes. "Nothing here. Come on in."

Vern had to look for his son in spite of himself. Then he glanced at the gauges and levels. He found the logbook right where it belonged. "Look here. Robby has entered the data in the book. Dated it today. Whatever happened, he did his job –before it happened."

The deputy nodded and went back outside. When Vern came out, the deputy held up a padlock. "Found this off to the side. Does it belong on the door?" Vern nodded. "Is your son a careless sort? No offense."

Vern shook his head. "Less than most kids I guess, but he did the date entry all careful like. I don't know why the door wasn't locked."

"Vern, I have to show you something else. He nodded toward the side of the building away from the road. He gestured to something on the ground –something shiny and brass. "Thirty ought-six I think. Deer ammo looks like." He gestured again, "There and there too. S'pect more of them fell into the snow all hot and melted down into the snow. I'll see if I can't get our policeman to dig around and find them all. Keep him occupied." He squatted down. "My grandpa was full-blood Mandan Indian. He could have looked at the ground here and tell you what the shooter looked like and what the shooter had for lunch too -if the stories about Grampa were even a little true. But he was also a drunk. I can't make anything out of it. Looks like footprints in frozen ground to me."

Vern almost chuckled, but not quite. He nodded off to the car with its nose sticking out of the ditch. "Shall we?" and they started off across the stubble together. It took longer to get there than it did to get to the Butler building. They saw tire tracks swerving thru the snow where the wind had not scoured the snow down to frozen dirt. Pretty clearly the driver was not doing a very good job of going in a straight line. There was no one there. The sheriff counted out loud as he pointed at bullet holes: one each in the front and rear fender, back seat passenger's side window, and the windshield. He looked at Vern, "Do you smell radiator?"

"Yep"

The deputy bent down and looked at the engine. "I don't see anything, but I bet a careful exam would find some holes in the radiator or maybe engine block."

Vern had gotten around to the driver's side. "Here are some tracks. I guess they are tracks. This looks like a hand-print, but I'm not sure what's going on."

The deputy joined him, "Looks to me like the driver crawled off on hands and knees. See any blood?"

"Nope. I am pretty sure I know whose car this is -who the fellow is. It's my lawyer. Name's Kevin Amundsen. The pretty woman is his latest squeeze. He owns the man-camp. I invested in the water treatment plant. That's why my son was checking on things. My daughter Beth does laundry and makes beds after school. Sven, what in God's name has happened to my son?"

"I have no idea, but I have to be honest with you, kidnapping is what comes to mind. Why the shooting as a prelude, I don't know. Kidnappers don't want to draw attention to them selves. Shooting at people draws lots of attention. I think we need to find your lawyer guy and see what he has to say about things."

Vern nodded off to the east. "Do we follow the tracks now and see where they take us? I mean didn't the woman say he drove off. Without her no less. Truth to tell, the guy is a good lawyer I guess, but kind'a a putz otherwise, at least around women."

"I think I ought to tell you to take your daughter home and wait for a call."

"No. Let's see where he went. I don't see no blood."

They set off again. The ditch sheltered the snow from the wind and so there were tracks to follow. A few hundred yards along the confused tracks changed into a man's foot prints. They followed them a little further until there was a single step on the side of the ditch and the tracks disappeared on dry frozen ground. "Back there is where he started walking and here, he climbed out of the ditch and went… I don't know where he went. Let's go see what we find over by 'em grain bins."

Vern started but stopped. "Nope. You go. I want to get back to my daughter. I'll wait for you there. I want to chat with Kevin's… his girlfriend."

When Vern got back to the office, another cop had shown up -but it seemed that things were not going any better than when he had left ten minutes later. His daughter had gone into pout mode.   The girlfriend was sitting next to Beth and just looked pissed. The guy in the apron was doing most of the talking. "Look sergeant, none of us were there except the young woman, and she has already told you everything she can possibly tell you."

Vern jumped in. "The sheriff deputy and I looked around up at the building by the road -where they think the shots came from. We found brass. Then we went to the car out in the field. Bullet holes and shattered windows. No sign of the driver."

The cop looked at him. "You messed up my crime scene. Thanks Who are you?"

"I'm the father of…"

"Get his name and address Officer Smyth."

The woman sitting next to Beth stood up. "I'm sick of this. I need to get back to my son." She turned to Vern. "Could you give me a ride back to town?"

The older cop interrupted again, "You need to answer a few more questions. You can't leave." Vern nodded.

The guy in the apron spoke again. "Are you arresting her officer?"

"I am detaining her for questioning."

The guy spoke again, "ARE YOU ARRESTING HER?"

"No."

"Are you arresting ANY of us officer?"

Vern figured things had gone on far enough and tried to make nice. "Officer…"

"It's sergeant."

So much for making nice. This guy was either a total ass, or as badly way out of his depth as the younger cop. Vern looked at the lieutenant with a cold level gaze, "There is a sheriff's deputy out in the field looking around and looking for Amundsen. He can answer any of your questions about *YOUR crime scene*. Come on Beth. We need to get home." He turned to the woman sitting next to Beth. "I'd be happy to give you a lift. You ready to go?"

Both women got up and went to the door.

"You can't leave."

The guy in the apron spoke again as Vern moved to follow his daughter. "You decided to arrest them after all Sergeant?" Vern kept going and decided he owed the apron guy at a beer.

It was cozy in his pickup –Beth next to him and the woman sat beyond and stared out the window. Beth was looking at the Butler building as the drove out, "Oh daddy, He has to be there. I dropped him off there. It's my fault. I was all snotty to him."

"It will be OK Beth. Why don't you introduce us."

The woman seemed to wake up. "I'm sorry. My name is Janet. I am… I was Kevin's girlfriend. I don't know. He was bringing me out here because he wanted me to work for him here, but he drove off. He fucking drove off and left me sitting on my ass."

Janet's language made Vern and Beth glance at each other. Vern knew that Beth knew that this sort of language was not acceptable in their family, but under the circumstances… He shook his head and Beth understood.

"Nice to meet you Janet. I'm Vern. I 'spect you've met Beth? It looks like it all hangs on our friend the councilor and until we either find him or t'other shoe drops, there's not much any of us can do."

Vern made a left turn onto Highway 2. "Janet, was anything bothering Amundsen?"

"No. He was pretty happy lately. There *was* something bothering him, but it all got better a couple of weeks ago. He took me to Vegas and everything. But then I had to come back because my dad needed to send Ricky my son up here 'cause my Mom was sick and I want to get home and make sure Ricky's OK."

Vern immediately thought of having delivered a check to Amundsen when he bought the water treatment plant. Much more to be learned here, but best to get home and sit by the phone –if it was a kidnapping, but he damn sure wasn't going to let Beth be the one to tell her mom about it all. "You OK if we take Janet home first, Beth." Beth was back in pout mode. "Maybe you can get Janet's phone number?"

And she came out of pout mode and went into melodrama mode. "OMG –I left my back-pack in the laundry room and I have a book report due tomorrow."

Once again, Vern had to suppress laughter that might have verged on hysterical. "I think it will be OK Beth. I can write your teacher a note." He handed her the little notebook he always carried in his shirt pocket. "Do the phone numbers here. Where do you live Janet?"

They dropped Janet off at a house surprisingly close to their home. Vern was not looking forward to telling his wife that Robby was missing. It turned out that she already knew about it.

Chapter 49

When Janet got home to her little garden apartment, Ricky was playing with the dinosaurs she had bought him a few days earlier. Tonia was on the phone. She hugged Ricky and just managed to hold it together. As she listened to him explain the little models, her attention was drawn slowly to Tonia's side of the conversation.

"I'm half Japanese and I have great boobs 'cause I'm half Italian too. What do you like Tony?"

pause

"Ooo. I like that too Toney." She glanced at Janet and did the finger down her throat thing and rolled her eyes. "Wait just a minute hun." Tonia held the phone against her thigh and spoke to Janet. "Ricky was a dear. It OK for me to go now? I have a date."

Janet nodded. Tonia put the phone to her ear again. "Can do sweety. What's your address?"

Ricky squirmed a little in Janet's lap.

"Got it. Let's make sure we understand each other, it's $200 for the date when I get there. Then we will see where things go. OK?"

"OK Tony. I'm looking forward to meeting you. We will have us some fun. See you in about twenty minutes." She hung up and bounced across the room and hugged Janet. "Ricky was such a dear. We had some fun, and I swear-to-God, this was the only call I've had all afternoon. He ate some PopTarts. You remember that night we got all silly and ate Pop Tarts?"

Janet always envied Tonia's enthusiasm and street smarts. Worried her a little too, but she was too wrung out to go into it.

"How did it go out at the man-camp?"

She almost broke down and told Tonia about the shooting and the fuck-stick cop, but found herself saying, "It was OK. I don't know yet. Not sure I want the job and… well, I just don't know." She went over and sat on the edge of her bed where Ricky had been playing. "Are you hungry sweety?"

She let him climb down from her lap. "No."

She looked from Ricky to Tonia with a questioning look.

Tonia shrugged. "Maybe we had too many PopTarts. I'm sorry sweety, I just couldn't say *NO* your kid."

"No worries." They hugged and Tonia took off. When Janet closed the door behind her she sighed, dropped her head, and her shoulders sagged. It would be so good to break down and have herself a good cry but for Ricky. Instead she went to the kitchen cabinet where she kept a small supply of booze. The peppermint schnapps she had at the man camp seemed to have worn off. A little bourbon, some cheap brandy, and most of a bottle of Jägermeister. *Where the fuck did she get the* Jägermeister? *And did she and Tonia drink all the Irish Cream?* No matter, the bourbon would do the job. She figured that after the shopping she had done with Ricky, she had enough food on hand to not to need to leave the house for days and days if Ricky could stand it. Suited her just fine.

She poured some bourbon into a glass and sat at her little kitchen table. She took one sip and jumped up to get ice and see if she didn't have some mixer. Bourbon and diet cola would have to do and she sat down again. Another longer sip and then she drained the glass. *Holy fuck. This is not the way I drink.* She decided she was starving and jumped up again. Weenies and beans sounded wonderful and she had plenty of both. She got a can of baked beans going on the stove and was chopping the weenies when it occurred to her the bourbon wasn't doing the job. She made another drink and went to sit next to Ricky. "Wouldn't you like some weenies and beans Ricky?"

"OK" He was absorbed in his dinosaurs. "Mommy, can I get some more dinosaurs. I don't have a Ti-a-saurus Rex. Ti-a-saurus Rex is the coolest dinosaur. I have one back home. Do you have a boyfriend Mommy?"

"Oh! Sort'a. Why do you ask Ricky?"

"Sometimes Grandpa and I do things without Gramma. Grandpa says a boy has to do man stuff sometimes. Can I do man stuff here sometime Mommy?"

Evidently Janet was still strapped into the emotional roller-coaster, but given the excitement of being shot at that afternoon, this was almost anti-climactic. She would have to deal with it later. She wasn't sure if it was Ricky or the bourbon finally kicking in, but she was beginning to feel warm and comfortable in her own skin for the first time in what seemed like forever.

And then there was a knock on the door. Her first thought was that it might have been that poor guy whose son was missing. He was a nice guy and she felt for him. She didn't want to think about how she would feel if it were Ricky. Then it occurred to her that it might have been the pecker-head cop with more dumb-ass question and she sure-as-shit didn't want to deal with him. But if it was the cop, it would do no good to ignore him, so she got up and opened the door without her usual peek thru the little peep-hole. It was Jeff. Two things flashed thru her head: *Christ he was big.* and *We were supposed to be studying tonight.*

"Hey Janet. How ya'll doing tonight"

She put her hand to her mouth and stared at him. Then she started giggling. Then she hiccupped. Then she started crying. "I forgot." she croaked and she slumped against him crying quietly and shaking. Jeff had no choice but to put his arms around her, pick her up and gently move her inside. He shut the door with his foot as he set her back down. If it all wasn't weird enough, there was a little blond boy was standing in the middle of the room staring at him.

"Are you my Mommy's boyfriend.?"

"I'm your Mommy's study buddy. I'm Jeff. How d'ya do little guy."

"What's a study buddy?"

Janet was collecting herself but she did not move out of Jeff's embrace. She answered in a fairly calm voice. "Jeff and I study together Ricky. Jeff is my friend."

"Do you like dinosaurs?"

Nothing else he could do but go with it –what-ever *it* was. "I love dinosaurs. Is your name Ricky?"

"Yes. I'm almost five. Grandpa says I'm always s'posed to hand-shake when I meet somebody."

Jeff understood the boy's problem. "Your grandpa is sure'nuf right." He started to move Janet to his left side so he could give Ricky his right hand when Janet took a deep breath, straightened up, and backed away.

Jeff dropped to one knee and held out his hand to the boy. "Pleased as a pig in… Pleased to meet you Ricky. Ya'll can call me Jeff."

"You talk funny.

"That's because I'm from the great state of Lo'sianna. We all talk this way down that away. Do you know where Lo'sianna is?"

"No. I live in Kansas."

Janet had wiped her eyes and gotten most of her composure back. "We are about to have dinner Ricky. Go wash your hands." Ricky ran off and Janet turned back to Jeff. "Thank you. I had a *real* bad day. I'll explain it all later. OK? I just want things to be as normal as I can make them for Ricky."

He shrugged a little hopelessly. "Sure enough." Nothing else he could do as far as he could see. Jeff wasn't sure if Janet was embarrassed about it all or not. She seemed a little spacey –whatever was going on, he was sure it was better then her ice-princess saphisto-bitch attitude . She did however pour him an admirably tall cocktail without his even asking. Nor was she bashful about refreshing her own glass.

Dinner turned out to be a little disappointing though. Tiny little portion of weenies and beans served on mismatched plates and Ricky whined because he couldn't eat off his *Super Bear* plate but he didn't eat much. Conversation was mostly between Ricky and Jeff who got Ricky happy again by insisting that all the best dinosaurs came from Lo'sianna. He had Ricky giggling with made-up dinosaur names like the purple-a-saurus that ate only grapes and the stupid-a-saurus rex that was even bigger than the tyrannosaurus rex, but so dumb it fell over all the time. He tried to get a raise out of Janet by offering to make dinner next time and told them about gumbo with shrimp and these little tiny dinosaurs with pinchey hands and antennas and flippy tails that swam backwards and were called crawdads. Ricky decided he had to eat one just as soon as possible. Janet just smiled vacantly. Desert was PopTarts.

As Janet cleared the dinner table, he glanced at his cell-phone, It was only a little after eight. It seemed clear that there was not going to be doing any math this evening –certainly not writing- but just what he was supposed to do now? He figured maybe that tonight at least, he was just a dinner guest and it might be time to leave and let Janet and the lad to themselves. He was looking around for his coat when Janet sat back down and told Ricky to get ready for bed. Maybe he should wait a bit and see. The boy slid off his chair and toddled off to the bathroom as slowly as he possibly could. The pajamas took even longer and Janet seemed not to notice or care. She seemed to be miles away and Jeff could think of nothing to say so they both just sat at the little kitchen table watching the boy's protracted stalling.

When Ricky had stalled as much as he could, he crawled up in Janet's lap and put his arms around her neck. "Good night Mommy."

"Good night sweetheart."

Ricky crawled down and walked over to Jeff. He reached up and pulled Jeff's head down to his level. He kissed him on the cheek, "Good night Mr. Jeff. 'Member, you said we could eat tiny dinosaurs. OK?"

"Sure thing Ricky. Sleep tight kiddo."

He giggled. "Mommy, he called me kiddo."

Janet and the boy went behind a curtain thing hung from the ceiling. Jeff heard good nights from both of them and some whispering that he thought was probably stalling on Ricky's part. Janet came back to the little dining table and slumped back onto her chair.

Jeff looked at Janet. "Sweet kid. You should be very proud."

Janet shrugged. "I'm not a very good mother. I have a lot to learn."

"I don't know nary a thing about being a mother, nor a parent neither, but strikes me you are doing fine."

" *Don't know nary a thing* is a double negative, and not…. oh fuck it. Jeff, I need to talk to someone. I need to talk to you. Been a bitch of a day."

Jeff listened for a long time. He came to understand Janet a little and admire her. He understood that another man in her life had let her down. Hard. He also understood he was not on her radar as anything but a safe and comfortable neuter. He realized that Ricky was her everything and he understood this very well. He had kind of fallen for the kid himself. Finally, he realized that the essay he had made up about her was not inaccurate.

They wound up in bed together after she put a sleeping Ricky in a bundle of blankets and pillows on the love seat by the front door. He knew that sex was an option, but there was no sex. He held her and she cried a little. As he drifted off, his last thought was that this might have been the most memorable nights he had ever spent with a woman. He felt a tenderness toward her and Ricky he had never felt before.

Chapter 50

The staff in the Williston Mercy Medical Emergency Room had seen it all: in large measure young men doing stupid things, or getting drunk and doing even stupider things, or hard working men in the wrong place at the wrong time when something went wrong out on the road or out in the field on a rig. Certainly there were the heart-breakers –soccer moms with a mini-van full of kids loosing an argument with a big truck, but mostly young men and if they had anything in common, it was their macho toughness. They seemed to think mangled limbs could be stitched back up and be as good as new in a day or two. Stupid, but tough.

The walk-in patient –or the limp-in patient more accurately, was quite the opposite. He wore a suit and tie –this alone was rare except among the hospital's oldest doctors. The guy spoke to the nurses politely and deferentially, and this was also rare. He had only a minor ankle injury, but insisted on an X-Ray that he was willing to pay for. But what was most curious was that he apparently had infinite patience. He didn't appear to be in much pain, but insisted he needed to be pushed around everywhere in a wheel-chair. He had a premium insurance plan to match his tailored suit and wanted the full gamut of tests. The attending tried to convince him his ankle didn't need an ultra-sound, but the guy insisted and if it came to that, he would pay for it himself.

After he had been there for a short time waiting for a slot in the CAT scan the guy had a visitor. The visitor was a hairy little guy –also in a suit, but a forest green suit with a pale lavender tie. He came to the nursing station and asked about seeing his good friend Kevin Amundsen. After the young nurse at a computer looked up at him -and not very far up, she told him that Mr. Amundsen was not available, he politely insisted it was important he met with the councilor 'for a pressing legal matter.'

"Oh. Mr, Amundsen is down in x-ray. I think."

"What floor is that on?"

"Fourth"

"Thank you so very much, You are most kind." It occurred to the nurse that is was a day for very polite people in suits.

It took him a few minutes for him to find Amundsen sitting in a wheelchair in a waiting area adjacent to one of the x-ray rooms. He pushed Amundsen's wheelchair closer to one of the chairs in the far corner of the room. He sat down and leaned close to him. "Councilor, I am a busy man. Certainly sorry to see you in the hospital and all, but what is so important that you couldn't explain it on the phone?"

"Someone was taking shots at me out at the man camp. Came damn close too. Now tell me what the fuck your associate did to that Mahon bitch.?"

"I thought we discussed this. I understand she was alive when Mr. Smith last saw her. Beyond that, I know nothing. Furthermore, communicating with Mr. Smith is now exceedingly problematic. Now tell me exactly what happened."

"This afternoon, I drove up there and when I got out of the car, the car windows started exploding. I think it was a rifle –maybe up by the entry road, but I don't know. I took off and fucked up my ankle when I drove into a ditch. Listen, there is no one who might hate me enough to try to kill me except Mahon."

Mell nodded. "Mr. Smith is quite thorough in these matters. If he does not choose a more decisive conclusion to his work, he does so only when he is reasonably certain it is not necessary. He takes steps to be certain it will not be necessary. Perhaps he was wrong, or perhaps the woman was –or is now- a little… off? You hired her if I am not mistaken? You would know better than anybody, certainly better than I do."

Amundsen was not pleased. "Look, get in touch with Mr. Smith one way or the other. I'm going to have to talk to the police soon. We both know you don't need the police spending any more time than necessary up at the camp don't we?"

The little guy leaned back in his seat. Obviously the lawyer was getting up on his hind legs –certainly much more so than earlier in their association. He was learning. He also had a point about keeping police presence to minimum at the man-camp. But Mel had no idea what to do. He looked at the other man and simply shrugged.

Amundsen took out his cell phone. "I have to call the police don't I?"

"Yes. You obviously don't have any idea who was shooting at you, but if you do not report being a target, it will raise more questions than otherwise. I think you are too shaken up to make the connection between this shooting and the fact that an employee disappeared after embezzling funds from your business."

"No shit Sherlock"

Mel smiled. "Sarcasm councilor? It doesn't suit you."

As soon as the scary little guy left, Amundsen dialed 911 on his cell phone. He knew everything was recorded, so he played the frightened citizen, but he did so with his clearest articulation. "Hello. I don't have an emergency, I don't want to tie up the emergency thing, but I don't know the regular non-emergency number. Can you give it to me? Or have someone call me?"

The dispatcher assured him that he was not tying up the line at the moment and asked for his name and what he needed. "Amundsen. Kevin Amundsen. I think someone was shooting –maybe shooting at me. It's all rather confusing. It made me have a wreck. I'm in the hospital now. I think I should report it to someone. Or something."

"Was anyone hurt in the accident?"

"No. Just me. I got a ride to the hospital and they are taking care of me now."

Was there damage to any property?"

"Well, my car."

"Was there another vehicle involved or damaged?"

"No. Just my car. I drove into a ditch."

The dispatcher heard stories like this every day. The guy on the phone didn't sound drunk, and nor did things seem any too urgent. He glanced at his calendar. It was Thursday, coming on evening. If it were Friday, he wouldn't think twice about wasting an officer's time by sending him out to do an accident report. Thursdays, however, were a push. He did know two big oil-field service companies that had done their shift changes earlier in the week. By now a lot of their workers would have caught up on their sleep enough to be ready to raise a little hell and keep the police busy. He made his decision. "We can send out an officer tomorrow morning. Or early next week, if you like, or you can come to the police station and file a report. For your insurance company and all."

"Thank you. I'll do that. Is there any time limit on my making a report?"

"No sir. Wait till you are feeling better. Have a good evening sir."

Kevin felt it couldn't have gone better if he had written the whole exchange as a script.

Chapter 51

By about ten o'clock that night, Vern and his daughter Beth had worked out an efficient routine. They would stop at every gas station and business with a cash register facing the road. There were few towns, and those that there were rarely had any business anywhere but the main street –few of them had much more than a main street as it was. Beth hopped out and took a picture of Robby and asked anyone she found if they had seen her little brother. After the first few times they did it together, Vern realized Beth was better at it than he was. Under different circumstances, he would have been proud of her. No more affected teenager with an attitude. She was like her mother –she was on a mission and nothing was going to get in her way. She was also a cute young woman. Vern simply stayed in the pickup on the phone with his employees and marking up assorted road maps of the county, North Dakota, and Montana as well as Canada.

They were almost to the Canadian border when his cell phone rang. Beth was in charge of the phone while he drove and she said, "It's Mom. Do I put it on speaker?"

"Sure."

Sherrie did not bother with the niceties, "Come home. Come home now."

He slowed down just enough to make a screeching U-turn and floored it back toward Williston. "We are on the way honey. Be about 20 minutes. What's up?"

Sherrie's voice crackled inaudibly and Vern noticed he was accelerating past 85 mph. He got a grip on himself, took a deep breath, and got off the gas. Beth was glancing back and forth between her father and the speedometer. When they were back down to fifty-five, Beth spoke up, "We didn't hear you Mom. What did you say?"

"I got a call from Robby. He is OK, but he has definitely been kidnapped. I want Beth…   I want you both back here."

"Call the police Sherrie. You want to ask for Sergeant…." He pulled out his pocket notebook and was fumbling with one hand while he drove.

"Do you mean Sergeant Otis, Daddy?"

"Ya. That's it. Then call Deputy Bohler. You know –Sven from church. Or leave a massage. See if he can't come by."

When they got home there were two Williston Police cars parked in the driveway and a third parked out front. It irritated Vern of that he had to park across the street from his own house and he told himself he needed to adjust his attitude. He needed all the help he could get to get his son back and the Williston Police and McKinsey County Sheriff's department were his best bet.

Inside he found two cops sitting at the kitchen table with Sherrie. One –drinking coffee- was the short sergeant with the crew-cut he met out at the man camp. The other one was new. A little older, and grey hair & bushy mustache. He also had lieutenant bars on his collar. This was the guy taking notes and Vern figured he was in charge. Sherrie was also writing on a yellow legal pad and only glanced up before going back to her writing. The sergeant got up and nodded at Vern to the living room. There were two more men –not wearing uniforms- in the living room huddled over the family phone at the far end of the couch. They were setting up a recording device of some sort. It did not appear to be going well and they were referring to a loose-leaf notebook spread out by the phone on the end table.

"Look sergeant, maybe we got off on a bad foot out at the man-camp this afternoon. I'd like…"

The cop interrupted him, "Don't worry about it. Only to be expected when a parent's worried about a child. We now know it was a kidnapping. Earlier we were just thinking about the shooting."

That's bull-shit thought Vern, but he said nothing.

The crew-cut gestured to the two guys with the recorder. "We are setting up a wha'chu call a 'trap' on your phone. Glad to see you still have a land-line. Makes it easier." Vern glanced at the two cops trying to sort out what the instructions were telling them. *That is self-evidently not easier –at least for these two pencil necks.* The other guy went on. "Your wife took the call and we have her writing it all down –word for word as best she can remember. It was your son on the phone and he said he's OK. The kidnapper is a woman, but it seems he wasn't supposed to say this and your wife thinks he got slapped or something. We are having the phone company figuring out where the call came from. Not as easy as it is on the TV shows, but we ought to have an answer early tomorrow."

Beth wondered in. Vern had forgotten all about her. "Honey, why don't you get ready for bed."

"There is no way I'm going to be able to go to sleep Daddy"

"I know honey." It was past her bedtime and it hadn't been any easier for her than for Vern or Sherrie. She was clearly exhausted. "But get ready just the same. We will all see what's what when your mom is done." He dropped into the couch. He was pretty wrung out himself. "Any coffee left?"

"I'll see." and the cop went into the kitchen. Vern sat listening to the older cop prompting his wife as to the ransom call and the two tech looking guy's confused discussion as to the phone and recorder.   It crossed his mind to get Robby to help them. This was the sort of thing his son was real good at. Then he realized how confused his thinking had become. He felt helpless.

The lieutenant and his wife came into the living room. Sherrie handed him a cup of coffee and sat down beside him. The older cop introduced himself. "How do you do Mr. Furness. I'm Leutenant Sam Burrows. Williston PD." The guy sat in one of the matching wing-back chairs opposite Vern and Sherrie. The sergeant leaned in the doorway to the kitchen. Everyone seemed to ignore the two guys fiddling with the recorder at the far end of the couch and they seemed preoccupied with the phone and loose-leaf notebook.

The lieutenant was clearly in charge now, "Maybe we should talk about the phone call your wife got." He looked down at his notes. "It was Robby on the phone. He said he was OK. It seemed he was reading from a script. You wife says he said 'You are to get together two hundred fifty thousand dollars and I will be OK.' Your wife then said something about not having that much money. Your son started to say something like 'The lady….' and there was a loud pop of some sort and your wife wasn't able to understand anything. It seems likely that your son may have inadvertently gone off script and got his face slapped. After a moment, he came back on the phone. Your wife said he said only 'Get it.' and then there was more miscellaneous sound and we're guessing the phone was taken from him and hung up."

The officer paused and felt around for the right words. "It seems to make sense that the shooter is also the kidnapper. That is good conjecture. What is less conjecture and mere guess is that the shooting was the plan and the kidnapping was an improvisation. This makes it difficult for the kidnapper and he –or *she*, has to make it up as he or she goes along. This makes it harder for us too."

Vern took Sherrie's hand. The cop went on. "What can you tell me about Amundsen?"

"He is my lawyer and I've invested in his man camp –indirectly.   I forgot all about him. Has he turned up?

"Yes. He is OK. He's in Mercy Med with injury to his ankle. Not a gun shot injury, but an injury from crashing his car when he drove across the prairie trying to put as much distance between himself and the shooter. I have been out to the hospital to interview Amundsen. He claims he has no idea what's going on."

Sherrie snorted derisively. The cop glanced at her and nodded, "I share your wife's… skepticism. There is much more to be learned in this direction." I plan to interview the girlfriend in the morning. I understand she was real shaken up when the sergeant interviewed her this afternoon out at the man-camp."

"I'm a little embarrassed, but none of us…" Vern shrugged and glanced at the sergeant standing in the doorway to the kitchen.

The guy spoke up. "It was a difficult time for everyone. No worries."

"Did I miss something here? asked Sherrie.

Vern answered. "Oh, ya. Something else I forgot. Kevin was there with his girlfriend, and when the shooting started, he took off. He left her… I guess he left her sort of a sitting duck and took off across the field in his car. I dropped her off on the way home." Vern paused. 'So what's the plan?"

"We have an APB out. But mostly we have to wait for the other shoe to drop. The FBI have been notified, but Robby is too old for what they call a 'tender age', but if it turns out that the ransom call came from out of state, it becomes and interstate issue and they will jump on it. If it even looks the least little bit like it came from out of state, I promise you that within minutes of our hearing from the phone company –and with cell phones, it may be several phone companies –I will be on the FBI like a duck on a June-bug. If there is any indication it comes from Canada, we get the Mounties involved too."

"I've got a bunch of my employees out stopping at every gas station and fast-food place within a hundred miles."

The lieutenant remembered and nodded. "That's right. You wife mentioned it." He shrugged. "Can't hurt. This is no time be time to be territorial. Speaking of which, there is also the sheriff's office. They are part of our All Points Bulletin. I understand you know Sven Bohler? He's a good man. But don't none of us have much experience in kidnapping.

Vern looked at Sherrie. "What do you think Sweetheart, shall I call my guys in? Let then get some sleep. We can get organized and head out again tomorrow."

The officer reminded them, "By tomorrow we should have a direction for them to look. The more eyes we have out there, the better. The FBI might take a different view, but till they show up…" He shrugged.

The phone guys seemed to be ready. One of them pulled out his cell phone and dialed. When the house phone rang everyone jumped and Sherrie yelped. "Just checking guys." he said sheepishly.

The lieutenant scowled at him. "God damn it Kamarowitz. Think once in a great long while. Does it occur to you that the phone ringing in a kidnap situation might be a little fraught?"

"Sorry" The guy turned to the recorder and fiddled with something. They all heard *God damn it Kamarowitz. Think once…* before he hit another button. "Yep. It's working. Sorry Mrs. Furness."

All the cops left. Beth went to bed. Vern kicked a footstool over to the front of the couch and stretched out. Sherrie got a blanket and curled up at his side with her head on his shoulder. Vern started making phone calls calling his guys in. Sherrie had fallen asleep by the time he was done. It took him much longer to nod off.

Chapter 52

Jeff woke up well before first light –a little later than usual. He figured it was from the psychic energy it had taken to lay next to a beautiful woman all night and *not* have sex with her. Just the same, he was sure it was the right things to have done. He was pleased with himself. When he untangled himself from her still inert body next to him and rolled over, he found Ricky in his 'jamies standing at the edge of the bed just looking at him with a half-asleep vacant look. He whispered, "Goo' morn' kiddo."

Ricky's face lit up, "What's *kiddo*?"

"Kiddo means… I guess it means an endearment for kid –like in a little kid."

"What's *'dearment*?"

A little early for vocabulary, but he took his best shot. "An *en*dearment means I like you. Iz' like when ya' mom calls you *honey* and such. But men don't call each other such like. And 'cause you a young-en, I call you 'kiddo' as kind'a manly endearment "

The kid giggled. It occurred to him that it remained to be seen what version of 'Janet' Janet would be when she woke up, but he had certainly done well with the younger part of this little family. "Do you know how to make coffee Ricky?"

The boy shook his head. "Can I have Pop Tarts for Breakfast?"

Jeff remembered the sad little meal of weenie and beans from the night before. "Well, let's see what we can find in the kitchen. And ya' think you old 'nuff to know how to make coffee?"

Ricky thought for a moment. "Is making coffee manly?"

"Manly! Coffee? Mercy, why, what a question! I'm here to tell you that making coffee is just about the most manly'est thing ever was. But it's hard. You might be too little."

"No I'm not. You can teach me."

"Well, I'm not sure. You think you can pay attention right close?

"Yes."

"You recon you can remember all manner of important steps an' procedures?"

"Ya. What's *'cedures*?"

"Procedures are things you have to do just right and in order. All right kiddo. Let's see what we can do. I recon your momma'l be right happy if she was to have a nice cup of coffee waiting for her when she wakes up. Extra special nice if it was you what made it."

Jeff pulled on his blue jeans and stopped off in the bathroom before he started tip-toeing thru the cupboards looking for coffee and filters. He pulled a chair up to the counter so Ricky could reach the sink and sat himself down in the other kitchen chair.

It took him about ten minutes to direct Ricky who did everything himself but Jeff had to sit on his hands when he wanted to step in and do it himself. It involved a lot of *Use both hands*, and there was a minor puddle on the counter, but Ricky got the coffee maker underway. He smiled to himself when he realized that if only he were able to spend the night a time or two more, he had no doubt he could get Ricky to nail it. In some small way, it came down to how much Janet liked waking up to coffee. He hoped he hadn't over done things with Ricky in her eyes.

"Go see if your momma's awake. Ask her if she wants some nice fresh hot coffee."

Her voice came from behind the fabric wall, "I am and I do." Janet appeared in tee shirt and sweat pants. Her hair was a mess bit she looked awful good to Jeff. And it was pretty clear she was a little chilly. *Mercy* he thought to himself. I am one *hell* of a nice guy to have laid next to that last night and been all sensitive 'n polite.

Ricky had taken a coffee cup out and was about to pour the coffee. "You had better let me pour my own cup Ricky."

"But I made it, I want to pour it for you Mommy."

"Hold on there kiddo. 'At pots pretty big and plum hot. You've did the important part, best to let your Momma pour it the way she likes it."

Jeff decides to play it by ear —no big deal to sleep with a woman and not have sex with her —he did it all the time. They sat at the table drinking Ricky's coffee while he ate cereal. Other than mentioning that they hadn't gotten a lot of studying done, he didn't comment on the future —their future- and he damn sure was hoping there was to be some. The morning was comfortable. Not a lot of it, he had to get to work and it struck him that going off to work fit perfectly with the *no big deal* act.

He put on his shoes and found his coat. "I'z all very nice 'n ever'thing here, but I has to get to work."

As he was putting on his coat, Ricky jumped down from the table and hugged his leg. "You said we can eat little tiny dinosaurs, -'member?"

Jeff patted his head, "Sure thing kiddo."

Janet went to the door with him, reached up, and kissed his cheek. "We can study some other time. Thank you Jeff."

He about lost it then and there. *Study? STUDY?* Well, sure, a little study would be fine, but surely there was promise in that kiss, chaste thought it was. As he walked to his car, he realized it was going to be a long damn day.

When Janet shut the door behind Jeff she shut out the rest of the world. Here she was safe and warm and her son was there with her. Jeff had been a comfortable and comforting intrusion, but an intrusion none the less. The horror of the previous day was long ago and far away. She thought about the poor man who gave her a ride home and whose son was missing. What would she do if it was Ricky? She couldn't bear to think about it. Nothing she could do about the man's son. This morning she had nothing to do and nowhere to go. Maybe she would try to study some math, or do something with Ricky. She had been thinking about painting a couple of walls by her bed. Maybe Ricky would enjoy helping. Or enjoy not getting in the way too much. But no. She would have to go out and buy paint and she didn't want any part of the world. Not for a little while anyway.

For a little while did not work out. A little after Jeff left, there was a knock at the door. She jumped and was seriously considering not answering it but Ricky was on his way to open the door. She just managed to grab him and sit him back down at the breakfast table. A loud authoritative voice came thru the door. "Ms. Howard, it's Lieutenant Burrows of the Williston police. I have some questions."

She wasn't sure what the asshole cop from yesterday name was, but if it was the same guy, she wanted nothing to do with him. She hooked the chain on the door and opened it. It was a different guy. Fat. Older. Short gray hair, gray mustache, and gray eyebrows. His eyebrows were nearly as busy as his 'stache. He wore glasses and looked almost like someone's grandfather. His uniform might have been fancier –more metal doodads- but she wasn't sure. She lied, "My son is asleep. Can you cone back later?"

"No I'm not Mommy." His high voice carried perfectly. Nothing to do but let the guy come in.

When he came in he immediately looked around her little home like he owned the place. He even looked behind the curtain surrounding her bed. It didn't take long, but nor did he miss anything. The grandfather image went out the window. She sat at the table and gathered Ricky into her lap.

He sat down across from them and opened a notebook. "It seems pretty clear that this has been a kidnapping. Also pretty clear that your friend Amundsen is not a suspect, but a big question mark. How well do you know him?"

"We have dated. I don't know much about his business."

He nodded. "I notice you haven't asked about what happened to him?"

She shrugged, "He drove off and left me sitting on my ass with someone shooting. I kind'a don't care."

"You told officers yesterday that you didn't see the shooter?"

She shook her head. He pressed, "No idea who it was?" She shook her head again. "No idea why someone would start taking shots at you?"

"No."

"Do you think the shots were pointed at you or at Amundsen?"

"I don't know. When he drove off it didn't seem like anyone was shooting at me anymore."

"You heard more shots, but didn't see where they went?"

"Ya. I mean I didn't see where they went."

"But you think the shots were coming from up the hill?"

"Maybe. I really don't know. Haven't you guys done some kind of crime scene thing? The kid's dad said something about that. Or something."

"What is you occupation Ms. Howard?"

Ricky was getting restless and she used the distraction to think before she answered. "I'm unemployed."

She thought there was a trace of a smirk on the cop's face. "A pretty woman like you unemployed in Williston? Seems odd."

She just shrugged and hugged Ricky.

"Seems very odd indeed. How long have you been in Williston.?"

"A few months"

Have you had a job since you have been in Williston?"

"Yes."

"There we go. Where did you work?"

Her friend Tonia turning tricks out at the man-camp crossed her mind. Janet hadn't done anything like that.   She had sex with Amundsen and he had given her money, but it wasn't the same thing. Not really. Then she remembered her teacher standing up to the other asshole cop the day before and tried it herself. "Are we done here?"

"No I have a few more questions."

"Let me pit it differently. We are done. Leave."

Ricky stopped wiggling and looked at his mom in little kid surprise.

"Don't you want to help the Farness family get there son back?"

She put Ricky down, stood up, and moved to the door. She didn't say a word – just stared at the cop. She opened the door and just stood there holding the door knob in one hand and Ricky's hand in her other.

The guy shrugged and walked out. She had to restrain herself from slamming the door after him.

Chapter 53

Despite having had a crappy night's sleep on the living room couch, Vern felt on top of things. Helpless, but ready to do whatever it took. His usual morning involved mostly getting off to work; Sherrie was in charge of the house and getting the kids off to school so he usually had himself a pretty casual morning watching all the household excitement. Not this morning. As he waited for Sherrie to wake up, he made a mental list: more pictures of Robby, perhaps a poster of some sort –Sherrie had some skills in this direction. She had run up some nice fliers on her computer for the church's rummage sale and whatnot.

He figured he had some time to get the printing done. His company was doing only one job that had a time-certain clause in the contract. It was a well-site pad that had to be finished. He figured his two best guys –a dump truck and loader driver could finish out in a few hours. If he didn't hear form them by late-morning, he'd call them. That left three other jobs they would not be showing up for. He owed the site-supervisors explanations; two were more or less local guns and he was sure they would be understanding. The third was kind'a a dick from New York. Nothing to do, but to do it. There was one bid he had to get out, but he stopped himself. Robby was more important. He could afford to loose a job from time to time.

The guys would be calling in when they were ready to hit the road once again. He'd have them come by the house and load up with pictures and posters and what-not.

There was also the matter of dealing with the police. He simply did not feel comfortable relying on them. He could only hope they would keep him informed. Particularly about the source of the ransom call and possible involvement of the FBI. He decided to call the deputy. Of all the various law people he spoke to in the last… –God, was it really only fifteen hours ago? Seemed a hell of a lot longer. But anyway, Sheriff Deputy Sven was the one whose opinion he really valued. He added that call to his list, but it would wait till he heard from the Williston police. Lots of waiting he had to do.

There was, however, one thing he did not want to do and could not wait. He had to call his father. If it came to it, his dad was the only possible way he could come up with the money. Given the last conversation they had, it was going to be tricky. His dad Evert liked Robby –at least as much as he liked any of his grand kids. His brother and the two nephews were in Minneapolis and stayed there. His sister's kids were pretty young. Heaven only knew how things had sorted themselves out since she walked in on him with… -what else could he call a naked young woman- the hooker.

He got off the couch and went to the big window looking over the back yard. It was just light to the east and it looked very cold to Vern. Sherrie woke up. "Any word?" she asked.

"Not a peep. How do you feel?"

"How am I supposed to feel?"

"I know honey. I meant how did you sleep?"

He knew it had to be coming. Sherrie had been a rock, but she was used up. "Oh God Vern. How can this be happening to us?" He went back to the couch and gathered her into his arms and she sobbed, "We are just an ordinary family, and Robby is so… Robby is so…. he's just Robby."

Vern feels himself start to puddle up. It would do no one any good if he started crying. Fortunately, Sherrie got a hold of herself and wiped her eyes. Vern didn't think she didn't let it out enough, but it would wait for another time. "You know you have to call your father don't you?"

"Ya, and I want to do it from the office. I don't want to risk missing a call from the kidnapper. Is OK? If the woman calls –if Robby calls, tell them… tell the kidnapper… tell who ever we will pay and are working on getting the money" He doesn't mention the few other small pieces of business he wants to tend to before coming home again.

"Can you handle the guys calling in on my cell phone? I'll make more copies of Robby's pix. And if anyone else calls about business, just tell we are closed. Or all taking the day off. Or whatever you have to tell them."

I'll make coffee. You want to make a poster about Robby? Something like 'Missing Child' with his picture and phone numbers and all."

Sherrie sat at her computer in the corner of the kitchen while Vern poured water onto the coffee maker. Beth tiptoed into the kitchen in her PJ'ies. "Didn't you guys go to sleep last night?"

"Morning honey. We kind'a fell asleep on the couch."

"What about Robby?"

"No word yet."

"Dad, do I have to go to school today? Are we going out again?"

"The police are involved now and my guys are going to be going out again later today. The FBI might be helping soon. I've got to go to work –just for a little while, and your Mom's going to be here… organizing things."

"I want to help find Robby."

"I know Beth, but there is not much any of us can do. We just have to wait. You don't have to go to school, but it might take your mind off things if you went. I'll leave it up to you."

Sherrie was evidently listening in as she tapped at the computer. "I think you need to go to school Beth."

Vern and Beth looked at one another. He expected the girl's well practiced eyes-to-heaven look. He was surprised when it didn't come. "OK Mom." and she went off to get ready for school.

Sherrie called, "Come have a look at this." as the printer started whirring.

Vern leaned over her shoulder. "Do you think we should have the police phone number as well as ours?" Sherrie said nothing and turned back to her keyboard, typed, and hit print a second time.

With both the little poster and Robby's 8x10 picture school picture in hand, he thought about breakfast and decided he wasn't hungry. "Sherrie, do you think the copier in my office is good enough?"

"My God Vern, it's a broken down piece of... Spend a dime for you son for God's sake. Go to the damn printers and get it done right."

Hell of a morning for emotion. Vern knew it was worry that made Sherrie talk like this. "I meant should I wait till nine o'clock when they open, or get it done sooner at the shop?"

"Oh... Ya… The Fed Ex store opens up at eight. Do it there." Sherrie started to tear up again. "I'm sorry Vern. Go. Do what you have to do. I'll hold down the fort."

He hadn't been back to the shop yesterday afternoon and whomever had locked up forgot to turn the heat off in his office. Ordinarily against the rules, but he was grateful for the warmth when he got to his desk. Fact was that someone had taken it upon themselves to turn off the lights and lock the door spoke to the quality of people ha had working for him. No small thing for seven guys to spend an evening driving around the countryside asking about a missing kid.

He settled into his desk and got about half way thru a list of people he would need to call when he realized he was stalling. His dad –a farmer all his life –or a farmer till he started getting oil royalty checks anyway- had probably been up for hours. And if he wasn't, tough. It would impress the old guy with the urgency if he had to get out of bed and walk down the hall to answer the phone. He'd be angry, but he always seemed to be angry lately anyway.

Vern dialed. His dad answered after the third ring. He was probably at the kitchen table close to the only other phone in the old sprawling farmhouse. "Who's it?"

"It's Vern Dad."

"What the sam hell you calling for at this hour?"

Vern glanced at the clock on the wall –it was only a little before seven. "Robby's been kidnapped dad. I need two hundred and fifty thousand dollars, and I need it quickly." He congratulated himself for yanking the band-aid off so quickly.

"Tell me what happened Vern."

Clearly he had his dad's attention. He hadn't heard this gentle tone of voice from him since well before he decided to join the navy and leave the farm. "Robby is working at a man-camp north of town yesterday afternoon. He is looking after a water treatment plant." He started to say that Beth worked there too and had dropped him off there etc, but decided to leave that part of the story out for the time being. "There was shooting –not a Robby, but right out the door of the building where he was. When the shooting stopped and things calmed down, Robby was missing. Sherrie got a phone call last night. It was Robby. He was OK, but said the kidnapper wanted the money. The police are involved, and maybe the FBI, but Sherrie and I are going ahead and getting ready if the police can't get him back."

Vern paused to catch his breath. His dad spoke –in an even gentler tone. "Tain't sure they's is that much cash money in ever' bank in the entire town of Williston, nor McKinsey County come to it. But I'll see what my banker can do. Where do you be with a phone?"

Vern gave him his cell phone number and explained that Sherrie might be answering because she was coordinating things. They also didn't want to tie up the house phone when the kidnapper called.

The old guy grunted assent and hung up abruptly. Vern sighed. He felt some small optimism and went thru the list of calls he had to make. Got thru to most of the people he needed. The guys who were in charge of grading roads, construction excavations, and –this time of year- drill-pads, seemed to keep farmer's hours. He had to leave word for only one and when his phone rang a few minutes later, he expected it to be the guy calling him back. It was Robby.

"Hi Dad." The kid didn't sound good.

"Where are you Robby?"

"I don't know. She makes me stay in the trunk of this car. It's cold."

There was a rustling sound and a woman voice came on the line. "How you coming getting my money back Furness?"

"What? I don't have the money. I'm tying to get it, but it's not that easy. The banks aren't even open yet."

"Get it from Amundsen." And she hung up.

Chapter 54

Mike woke up a couple of hours before first light, and stumbled about half way thru the coffee-making process before he remembered the excitement of the previous day. There was no one he could ask -not for a few hours anyway, but as he got breakfast ready he hoped the kid was OK. He was momentarily ashamed of the thought that he would likely be without a helper that afternoon if things weren't OK. He had come to enjoy the kid's company. He simply was a nice kid and a pretty good worker.

It was just barely light light by the time he got to class. Williston was about 15 miles from the Canadian border and winter time and it was still colder than hell. Attendance was good –not great, but he figured that most of those who showed up had at least a 50 / 50 chance of getting thru the GED tests. He noticed Janet wasn't there. Not an altogether bad thing: she was a pretty girl but a demanding student. Better for the big Cajun to help her. He started with math as usual, sorted out some confusion with negative numbers for one of his students, one who he figured was probably was not going to make it, but he admired her persistence. He guessed class simply gave her something to do and get out of the house. By abut ten o'clock he figured it was late enough to see if he could find out about Robby.

He started with a call to the Kiwi. "Hi Spence. What have you heard about yesterday's excitement? Has the lad shown up?"

"Nae. Not as far as I know."

"You think you could dig up his home number? He did the paperwork for FICA and all didn't he? Or if not, see if his sister listed their home number."

"Give me half a tick." The New Zealander found the number. "Be sure to call me and tell me how t'ings run."

When the Furness family phone rang shortly after nine, a relay clicked in Williston and a recording started in the FBI Residence Agency in Minot. Beth had finally decided to go to school so Sherrie was alone. Her heart rate shot up and her throat tightened. She tired to collect herself before she picked it up. "He…" Her throat closed. She swallowed. "Hello."

"Hi. Is this Mrs. Furness?"

Mike heard a whispered "Yes."

"Hi. This is Mike Williams. I'm the cook out at the man camp. Robby has been helping me out in the kitchen. I don't want to disturb you, but I'm hoping all is well." He stopped, but there was no answer. "Or if not, how I might be able to help."

"Robby is still missing." Her answer was flat –without affect or expression.

"Um. Look. I serve close to 100 men breakfast and dinner. They fan out across the state. Perhaps if there was some way I could get them to help? To keep an eye out for him." He was regretting calling.

Sherrie relaxed. "Of course. Yes. Robby has mentioned you. You have been helping him with his schoolwork, haven't you?"

"Yep. He is a smart kid."

"We have printed up some flyers. I don't have many left, but if I printed another original, you could make copies?"

"That would be great. Happy to do it. Shall I come by your house this afternoon?"

She gave him her address and they agreed he would be there about twelve thirty. She noticed that the big old-fashioned reel-to-reel tape recorder the police left next to the phone had been running but stopped when she hug up.

The relay clicked off and the server recording the phone call in Minot also stopped recording. Their email client sent an IM to each of the three agents in the office, but only the most junior agent was there to read it. The other two agents had left for Williston right after the phone company called early that morning with the notification that the ransom call came from Montana and the suspected kidnapping became interstate. It was now justifiably within the FBI's purvey.

The junior agent listened to it twice and carefully noted the details. He decided to wait till the other guys checked in when they got onsite in Williston. There should have been a recording there as well. He would, however, send timely notifications to the local PD's. He pulled out the General Order Manual to GO 309.5 (Handling Kidnapping and Extortion Cases, effective date September 13, 1991 Part I. Section A.3,f-g. thru Section B.2.e(2)-(3) It wasn't quite what he was looking for. He knew not to waste time, so he flipped back and forth till he found GO 308.13: (Use of a Civilian in Tactical Operations) which seemed to fit. He logged it and emailed both the Williston Police and McKinsey County Sheriff's Department an update and a brief narrative re. Mike Williams –the camp cook. He was proud of his terse and businesslike note and referenced GO 308.13, (Use of Civilian etc.), but mis-typed it as GO 308.31 (Detain Person of Interest).

The situation in the Williston Police dispatcher's deck was similar. The night dispatcher was an old hand and could handle multiple calls about drunken oil-field workers then dispatch as many as twelve police cruisers from bars to strip clubs, to apartments, and to single family homes, (where anywhere from five to ten guys lived), all around the town. He made it look easy. The regular morning person wasn't so good, but there was usually less going on anyway. So the captain puller her off the deck and had her try to make sense of the thick manual that came with the fancy new phone system that was supposed to record and trace things like ransom calls. This left the third string dispatcher to receive the email from the Minot FBI RA. He was a consciences young man and promptly pulled down the manual and looked up GO 308.31. He then issues a DETAIN order for Mike Williams the camp cook at the Bakken Lodge.

One car was up at Walmart and radioed back that he was close and on the way.

Another car, the first guy that had shown up the day before at the man-camp, was about done being a 'presence' as the high school student's parking lot filled up so he radioed back that he was on the way too. He told the dispatcher that he thought knew the guy.

The second officer got there as the first one was coming out of the office trailer. "The guy inside says that cook teaches class down at the college mornings. You want to follow me down there?"

They notified the dispatcher where they were going and drove off with sirens quiet. Williston State College was spread all over the prairie on the east side of town. None of the buildings had ivy or looked particularly collegiate for that matter. It took the two young cops some time to find the registrar's office and even longer to find someone who had a faculty phone book. The Mike Williams guy wasn't in the book. The traffic back and forth between both of them and the dispatcher got a little busy. They had the dispatcher call the man camp and try to get better information as to where the cook might have been. They used the time to drive slowly around the campus. Their lights were on, but sirens quiet.

As they drove by the *Train ND* building, a few of Mike's students noticed. They used the cops as a good occasion to rest their brains. Mike wondered over. "Seems a little early for drunks, doesn't it?   I hope it's not someone got hurt. Anyone see an ambulance?"

A third officer –another comparative young guy- had shown up but he hadn't gotten quite the whole story. He was well aware of the G.O. for DETAIN, but had gotten the idea that the DETAIN target was playing games and –by God- no one played games with the Williston Police. When they heard back from the dispatcher as to where the 'cook' was 'teaching,' all three cars parked by the front door of the building. The third guy, the last one to show up had no authority, but he said they needed to proceed under GO 8.02 Paragraph Section 1, Paragraph B, *Barricaded Suspect Incident*. His was one of those brains that could memorize vast amounts of stuff and not understand any of it. The other two guys were less confident, so they followed his lead. Besides which, they had never had the chance to take out their guns. Mike is working on a related rate problems with some of his advanced students: a tricky one involving a mixture of 20% solutions mixed with 50% solutions to arrive at a 30% solution when he was arrested at gun point and led off in handcuffs.

Young Officer Smyth realized the teacher was the same guy wearing the apron out at the man-camp the day before, Made no sense to him, but sorting it all out was someone else's problem.

Chapter 55

Senior FBI Agent Francis O'Connell had a good old rapport with the good old local tech-manager at the phone exchange in Minot, so he got the call at home when he was half way thru his morning prayers. He was told that the call to phone number such-and-such, at exactly such a time, originated at a cell tower in Montana. O'Connell ran thru rest of the Rosary quickly. He dressed and called Agent Green who was also at home. It was a brief call. "Word came down. The kidnapping in Williston is now interstate. I'll pick you up in twenty minutes."

The two hour drive from Minot to Williston was uneventful. The sun-rise was spectacular as it sometimes was on North Dakota winter mornings, but it was behind them as the drove west. The sun crept over the horizon and its light came in under the high over-cast, but the rest of the day was undoubtedly going to be gray. They stopped about forty minutes west of Minot in Stanley for coffee. O'Connell had coffee. Green bought organic carrot juice. Despite her health food obsession, O'Connell thought Agent Green was good company –for a woman. No interest in sports let alone any conversation about hunting or fishing, but she asked intelligent questions and listened carefully to the answers. Furthermore, she didn't mind it when he drove. He had worked with one other young woman who took it as in insult when he took the wheel. But young Agent Green took such things in stride. He hated to be in a car when he wasn't driving. There was one occasion when they were driving back from Fargo and he was flat-out exhausted. He asked her to drive and that was no big deal either. He surprised himself by actually falling asleep. He took this as another good omen for their association.

He had been coming to Williston for years. It seemed the edge of town was further out every time he made the drive. Gas stations and fast food franchises, but more services yards full of trucks, and Butler buildings for oil-field services were growing where only wheat and rapeseed had grown in years past.

The procedure for getting into the police squad room went a little faster than usual because Lieutenant Burrows was waiting for them. Didn't hurt that they were FBI. O'Connell introduced his Junior Agent to the Lieutenant. To his credit, the local cop took the tall young woman in stride without seeming to notice her gender. As they made their way to the briefing room they were joined by Sergeant Otis. He was not so tactful. He looked her up and down carefully. He had to look up because she was taller than the ex-marine.

After everyone got coffee from the pot in the back of the room –all except Agent Green- they settled and Burrows started things. "The officer who was first on scene is not here now. He is pretty much fresh out of the academy and doesn't have much to offer, but he'll be along shortly. He's out on patrol now." He paused. "This has obviously this gone interstate?"

Agent Greene answered. "Yes, the call came from a cell tower just over the border in Montana. Not absolutely sure, but close enough. We've been on the road for a couple of hours now. Anything new this end?"

Burrows answered, "Yes. The father of the kid got another call in his office this just a little bit ago. What with all the phones people have now, we hadn't put a recorder or tracer on that one. Appears pure chance that he was there when the call came, but the Mom figures there are three or four phones in the family one way or other. Anyway, we planned to head out to the family place and meet him there and get details. When he called me, I asked him to take a moment to write down every word he could remember."

Agent O'Connell set down his coffee cup. "Where do you guys usually set up your sok?" He noticed the blank looks from the Williston police. "Sorry, SOCC. The Synchronized Operations Command Center. Where we set up shop to communicate with the police, sheriff's department, highway patrol etc. Get everybody all playing from the same rule-book. Could be here or at the family home. If we do it there, the procedure is not to have and black and whites out front. Might scare the perp off."

Green spoke again. "But if the suspect has already crossed at least one state line, it's unlikely that he is spying on the house. I presume the place is kind out in the open? Be hard for someone to be lurking around with out the neighbors noticing and getting all up in arms?"

Sgt. Otis and Lt. Burrows looked at each other. Clearly this was going to be the FBI's dog and pony show. Otis answered. "It's a suburban house on the east side of town with big lawns and such. Be hard to hide."

Burrows added, "Oh, and it's a she –the kidnapped that is. And one other thing. I spoke to the lawyer's girlfriend this morning. She hadn't anything to offer. She's younger than he is. Pretty enough. I'll let you draw your own conclusions about her if you interrogate her. But like I say –I don't think she has much to contribute."

Agent Green wore her hair in a tight bun at the back of her head and no makeup. The little sergeant has been staring at the woman and trying to imagine her with make-up. He had about decided that she would be beautiful if she wore some. He also decided it was time for him to put in his two cents worth. "Perhaps we could rely on Agent Green's womanly insights as to what the kidnapped might do?" The comment was innocuous enough, perhaps even on-point, but there was a trace of a smirk on his face.

The agent –to her credit- just let it slide. "I'd be happy to offer my opinions when I'm better informed." She smiled and started the little sergeant down. "Or perhaps I could be a comfort to the family –particularly the boy's mother." She turned to the police lieutenant, "Is it just possible that I might have more success talking to the girlfriend as well?"

O'Connell choked on his coffee. God Bless her, he liked this tall slender young woman.

As they were all either recovering from having their ears pinned back or trying not to smile at their discomfort, a pudgy young officer came into the room hesitantly still wearing his watch cap and coat. Burrows figured it was time to do a little in-house moral building and at the same time, smooth over the tension Otis created. "May I introduce Officer Smyth. Young Smyth was the first on the scene yesterday. He did a fine job of controlling the situation."

The rookie smiled. "Thank you lieutenant." He looked at the FBI agents. "We also got your person of interest down in holding." He looked back at the local guys, "It was the cook from yesterday! Go figure!"

O'Connell and Green looked at each other and then they looked at Burrows who explained. "We got your BOLO this morning.. For Mike Williams? The cook out there?"

"Something must have popped while we were on the road. Is he an accomplice?

"Beats me. It's your detain order.

O'Connel was about to suggest Green look into it, but she already had her cell phone out. "Hi Ralph. You issued a BOLO this morning? Sent it to the Williston PD?" She listened for quite a while. "Hold on a minute Ralph." She looked at O'Connell.

"There was a call to the Furness home. Ralph said it was a guy offering to help with fliers and getting the word out. He worked with the boy. Evidently at the man camp. Ralph said he issued a Use of Civilian in Tactical Operations notice. He will be sending you a compressed file of the recording."

Otis looked at Smyth. "What order did you get?"

The young cop wasn't looking happy anymore. "We got a Detain Order. I don't remember the order number. The other guy said it was a Suspect Barricaded Situation. We arrested him. He is in holding."

"Oh shit." exclaimed the Sergeant. "The guy was an ass. Not very cooperative, but not a suspect. We have to figure this out. Where is the recording?"

Burrows told the officer to run down to dispatching and get it. "Hurry man. And when you get back, be ready to tell us why you did the Barricaded Suspect thing." The guy took off at a waddling run.

While they waited. O'Connell looked at Green. "You want to start the IBER or should I?"

"You are senior. It has to have your signature."

"True, but if you are IC and I am FC, we can both sign it."

"You just hate writing, don't you?"

"I got no problem with writing. It's the damn computer I hate."

Otis piped up. "You guys want to let us in on the alphabet soup?"

The FBI glanced at each other. Green spoke first. "Is this per our TOP?"

"Ya, but we will need to issue a CCN first"

Both Green and O'Connell were pleased with their inside joke. The senior agent took it upon himself to sort if out. "IC and FC are Incident Commander and Field Commander. In theory the IC is higher in the chain of command, but it's depends on how big the field is. IBER is Incident Based Event Report –a right pain in the ass for all concerned, but sometimes it's good to be able to go back and learn things. TOP is Tactical Operations Plan. CCN is Central Complaint Number. We *will* need one of these, but they come from the regional office."

And then there is the socks thing. Some kind of commend center?"

"Yep, we will need to pin down one of these too. Let's just leave it here for the time being."

They looked up as Officer Smyth came huffing back onto the room. "They can't figure out how to decompress the audio file. They are going to try to get the Minot guy to type a manu... mana… type it up and email it. But the email said general order…" he looked at his notebook. "GO 308.31. They looked it up and it was a *Detain Order* for sure. But the Minot office typed *Use of a Civilian in Tactical Operations* and that's a different GO. it's…" He looked at his notebook again, "GO 308.31"

No one in the room said anything. They had all heard this story before -in one way or another. Smyth went on. "We did the *Barricaded Suspect* thing because we thought the guy was playing games. I mean one day he's a cook and the next day he's a college teacher? And Taylor said that's what we were supposed to do."

Burrows sighed. "I'll have a chat with Taylor and his sergeant."

Otis bristled, "I'm his sergeant. His ass is mine."

Burrows thought he might have guessed this. Otis' squad followed his lead.
There was a place for pecker-heads on the police force, but not many. He spoke to
Smyth. "You had best scurry upstairs and let the guy out. Pronto. And if you can find a
way to make sure he doesn't sue us for false arrest, you might could be able to have a
career in law enforcement."

"Lieutenant, I was just doing…" He caught the high winy tone of his own voice,
decided silence was the better plan, and hurried off.

O'Connell stood. "It seems to me it's time to head out. A single car to the
Furness place, I think?"

Lt. Burrows agreed. "Lets take your car –it's unmarked isn't it."

Chapter 56

After the crazy woman let him out of the water treatment building and forced
him to get into the trunk of her car at the point of her rifle, he was in shock for the first
hour or so. But an 'hour or so' was hard to judge locked in the trunk of a car. Then he
remembered a silly old re-run on TV about how a skinny Batman in a dorky costume got
trapped in a truck and was able to know exactly where he was by memorizing the turns
and counting the distance between turns in seconds. He tried but got confused. There
was also the mater of the first aimless hour or so driving over bumpy roads.

It hadn't occurred the him that he would be hurt. He was sure his dad and the
police would save him. He imagined himself as the star witness in the woman's trial that
put her in jail and he was the heroic young man everybody admired. He also
remembered having had to read KIDAPPED by some English guy in seventh grade. He
liked the story –parts of it anyway- but it was a story about a kid his own age who was on
a ship from a long time ago. He couldn't find anything useful in his own predicament.

He spent the next three or four hours imagining his family missing him and how
cool it would be when he was returned to them. He planned various ways he might get
the jump on the woman and take the rifle from her. He would then deliver her to the
police station and be a hero. But what if she got off a shot and he was wounded –but not
fatally- and then delivered her to the police before he went off to the hospital. Now
THAT would be extra heroic. His mom and dad would be so proud –even his geeky sister
would cry. Then he amended the story to where *he* had to drive. Better that way.

He felt around in the dark and found an emergency kit in a stiff plastic bag thing
shaped like a little suitcase. It had jumper cables, and a spray can of some sort, and a
little first aid kit and some other stuff he wasn't sure what it was. Nothing useful
occurred to him –nothing he could do to get the drop on the crazy lady. In the crevice
under the kit he found a blanket. It stank, but he was getting cold, so he wrapped it
around himself as best as he could, put everything back in the emergency kit and used it
as a pillow.

The car stopped suddenly and a few seconds later the trunk opened. It was still
full daylight out. He was sure it had been hours and hours and well after dark. As his
eyes adjusted to the bright daylight, she demanded he give her his cell phone.

187

"I don't have one."

"You are lying." and she brought the muzzle of the rifle down and pointed it at his chest.

"We aren't allowed to have then in school and my dad says kids need to study, not talk on the phone." He thought he was being pretty cool, just the right amount of snark.

She stepped back. "Get out."

He climbed out and looked around. A gravel county road and nothing else to see but prairie and the top of a drilling rig off in the distance. Clearly it had not been hours and hours.

"Turn out your pockets and give me your coat."

He had a house-key and a key to his dad's shop on a Green Bay Packers key-chain but the front door had never been locked that he could remember and he had never had occasion to use the other key. He had a few coins in his jeans pocket and a pencil in his shirt pocket. Most of the stuff he carried was in his school backpack he left in his mom's car when his sister dropped him off at the water plant. She felt around in his coat with one hand keeping the rifle pointed at him with the other. "OK. Get back in the trunk." There was nothing else for him to do by climb back in.

He dozed off and awoke to a strange red glow. It took him a moment to realize the tail lights were on and leaking light into the car's trunk. Must have finally been after dark. They were on a gravel road –had been most of the day- when had car stopped again and he heard the engine shut off. The trunk opened and she stood over him looking down into the trunk. It was pitch black out and there was not a sound.

"What were you doing in that building?"

"It's a water treatment plant. I look after it for my dad."

"Who is your dad?"

"He's Vern Furness."

She was taking notes in the light of the trunk lid, the rifle over the crook of her elbow.

"So what? Who is Vern Furness?"

"He owns the water treatment plant. He's a friend of the guy who owns the man-camp."

This got a raise out of her. He had no idea what it meant, but the look of hatred that crossed her face was the scariest thing he had ever seen. "Give me your phone number."

He gave it to her. She wrote it down and slammed the trunk once again.

Nothing happened for a few minutes. He hugged the blanket about himself more tightly to recover what little warmth that he had but had been lost with the trunk open. He thought he might have heard her voice, but wasn't sure. He heard her foot steps on the gravel, the car door open and close. The car started up and they drove off again.

He dozed and shivered for some indeterminate time. He woke when they stopped. He was barely aware but it seemed to him they had been driving on pavement for a while. He heard her footsteps and the sound of the cap being taken off the gas tank followed by the surprising loud sound gasoline being pumped into the tank. No other sounds. He considered screaming for help but remembered his dad always bought his gas at a self service place and used a credit card. Whatever time it was, and he had no idea anymore, he decided there was probably no one around but the woman. He shouted, "I got'ta pee."

"Hold it a little longer." was all she said. The nozzle was removed and they took off again. The need to empty his bladder grew unbearable and he considered peeing in the trunk, but there seemed to be no good way to do so without ending up laying in it. He felt them turn onto a gravel road and drove for a little while. They stopped and she opened the trunk –the rifle in her hands. "Go over there." she gestured to an old abandoned farm truck beside the road. "I'm a good shot. There's plenty of moonlight so don't try to run away."

It was hard to climb out of the truck. He couldn't stand up, but he was so desperate to pee that he hobbled over to the truck like an old man. He fumbled with his zipper and almost didn't make it.

"Aren't you about done yet?"

"No mam." He wondered if it was necessary to be polite to someone kidnapping him with a rifle.

"Get back in the truck."

"I'm hungry."

"Tough. Tell me all your family's phone numbers."

The words, "Fuck you." were out of his mouth before he thought. The rifle muzzle came to his chest and pushed him to the very back of the trunk. He started to cry. It took him a few minutes to choke out the only other phone number he knew besides the house phone –his dad's cell phone.

"Where do your parents work?"

"My mom doesn't work and my dad owns Farness Civil."

"Where is his office?"

"Across the street from the airport. I don't know the address."

The trunk lid came down and they drove off again. He wiped his face and wished he had a handkerchief to blow his nose. He grandpa always told him to always carry one but he thought a handkerchief was the height of dorkyness. Now he felt like a complete dork. When she pushed the rifle barrel at him, he should have done something smart and quick and gotten a hold of the gun. He imagined all the possible ways it might have gone if he were not a dork –if he were a hero. He dozed and shivered. There were a few more stops –none of more than a minute or two. At one stop, he heard the rumbling roar of gas flaring off at a well site. He wondered if it was the one where his dad let him drive the loader. It would be an important clue when the police rescued him.

The last stop was the longest one before the trunk opened. The rifle on her right arm and a smart shapeless bundle in her left arm. "Get out." She gestured to a grain bin in the car's headlights. "Get in there."

"I'm hungry."

"I don't care."

There was a little door at ground level. His grandfather has a row of these things on his farm. He had played in them when his cousins came to visit. They played various games when they were little and took turns imprisoning one another inside. He knew better than anyone there was no way out if the latch was closed from the outside.

As he crawled thru the door, she said "This is about over kid." Her voice was almost kind. "Here's a sleeping bag." She tossed the bag in after him and shut the hatch. He heard the latch drop. There were six inches of fragrant silage on the ground. It made good bedding and he fell asleep in the sleeping bag shortly after the glow of her headlights disappeared from the vents below the cone of the roof.

Chapter 57

Sherrie was utterly wrung out and running on nervous energy.   The police had called and asked if it would be OK for them to come by with two FBI agents. She mentioned that Vern was not there, but was expected back shortly. They agreed that ten o'clock would be fine. She dug the big coffee urn –the one she used at church meetings and Son's of Norway functions. She considered making biscuits when it occurred to her that sandwiches might be a better choice. Breakfast or lunch? The decision was beyond her. Why couldn't she make so simple a decision? She caught herself just shy of sobbing and went to work doing both. She felt better and almost giggled when the notion of the police struggling with the same decision as to what to eat. Just the same, she jumped when the doorbell rang.

It was quite a crowd at the door: Two men in Williston Police uniforms she was pretty sure were there the night before. There was also, a tall young woman, and a middle aged man -stout, florid complexion, and sparse gray hair- both in conservative Jbusiness suits. She welcomed them all in and as she was shutting the door, she noticed Vern's pickup pull into the driveway as an unmarked sedan was pulling away. The younger of the two policemen –the short one with the crew-cut- asked her if there might be room in the garage for the one cruiser that remained. "Best not to advertise our presence, Mrs. Furness. You understand."

She nodded at the guy and he went outside again. The older guy in the suit introduced himself. "Mrs. Furness, I'm FBI Agent Francis O'Connell. Just call me Frank. This is Agent Lori Greene." Vern came in and the guy repeated the introductions. He continues. "I propose we all gather and compare notes. No telling what small thing might pop up and be useful."

Sherrie gestured to the dining room across the front entry way from the kitchen. "I've made coffee and breakfast. Shall we all sit at the dining table?"

The men all got coffee except Vern and the woman FBI agent who sat at the table and unfolded a lap-top. O'Connell –the older FBI guy sat himself at the head of the table in Vern's usual place. He set a micro-recorder on the table and turned it on. "Anyone object to a recording?" He looked around as the police and Vern sat down. "Good. Like I say, you never know what small detail might prove helpful and this let's us hold on to them pesky little things." Sherrie was the last to sit at the chair closest to the kitchen and at Vern's side.

Vern kicked things off. "I'd like the get Deputy Bohler out here. He and I were the first to go up and look around the building at the man camp. The one where Robby was. He might have some idea as to what went on."

O'Connell and Lieutenant Burrows looked at one another. Burrows took a conciliatory tone, "This is not county jurisdiction. City and federal. We might could use county deputies for ground work, but not now."

Vern bristled. "I guess I don't much care about your views as to jurisdiction. You said yourself any little detail. This is my house and if I want him here, he will be here. You all can leave if you find this a problem." Sherrie touched his arm and he took a deep breath. "I'm sorry –you understand this has been… well, you know."

Sergeant Otis had his cell phone out. "I'll call the sheriff's department."

Vern shook his head. "I've got his card with his cell phone. I'll call him direct."

O'Connell picked up the little cassette recorder. "I suppose we can wait a few minutes for him to get here. Any objections?" No one said anything and he pushed a button on the device.

The lady agent -what was her name? -Greene?, asked if there was something in the oven. "Oops!" Sherrie jumped up to check on the biscuits. They were just past perfect when she pulled them out and set them on the stove-top. The woman agent left her laptop and followed her into he kitchen. She had the pancake turner in hand as Sherrie set the hot baking sheet on the counter, "Let me help you with that." and she started easing the biscuits off of the baking sheet. "Do you use real buttermilk?"

Sherrie knew damn well what the woman was doing, but was grateful for the gesture. "Nope, I just use the box mix. My family can't tell the difference. You been with the FBI long?"

"Just a couple of years. My mom makes biscuits with lard and buttermilk, but when I have time to bake, I use the mix too."

"I'm going to make sandwiches too, but decided breakfast might be nice. My husband gets up real early and likes a hot breakfast, especially this time of the year, but we both forgot this morning. Then I make the kid's sack lunches. Robby eats all his and then some, but my daughter, not so much. She's just sixteen and concerned about her figure. Oh dear! I forgot to make Beth's lunch today too. Well, I guess she can buy herself a little something. She gets an allowance. She eats like a bird as it is." Sherrie realized she was babbling, but didn't care. "So what do you think. Should I make sandwiches or order a pizza later. Vern says Williston has the most pizza places per-capita of any city in the world –even Italy- I don't know but what he is right. Young oil field workers and all."

The other woman thought about it for a minute. "Let's start with the biscuits. See where it goes. Do you serve them out of a basket with a big napkin like my mom, or just pile them up on a plate with butter and honey like I do?"

Sherrie handed her a big platter and went to the fridge for butter and jam. The women did the plates and silverware together. The men got busy. There was a single one left when there was a knock at the door. Sherrie was up so she answered the knock and welcomed Deputy Sven Bohler in. "Nice to see you Sherrie.   Sorry it has to be in such circumstances."

Sherrie shook Sven's hand and realized she would rather have given him a hug. "How's… how's your wife?. *Damn it*, Sven's wife was a friend and she knew her name as plain as day. What did the kids call it?. A *brain-fart* ?

More introductions, more coffee, and Sherrie went into Vern's home office for an extra chair for the new arrival. There was room enough around the table for everyone and their notebooks, the recorder, and lap-top computer as well as coffee cups. The table was a wedding gift from an old friend of Vern's dad. The guy was from the old country and did woodwork between planting and harvesting. It was a massive home-made thing appropriate for a Norwegian buffet. The old guy called it a 'groaning board' and Sherrie loved the ugly thing despite the fact that it neither fit with her décor, nor did it quite fit in her dining room. *Why in heaven's name,* she asked herself, *was she thinking about a stupid table just now?*

When Sherrie got seated, the FBI guy started. "Mr. Furness, let's get down to it. I understand you heard from the kidnapper again this morning.?"

Vern took his little notebook out of his shirt pocket. "Ya, the police asked me to write it down as carefully as I could. I was alone in the shop when a call came in on the regular line. There was no one else there so I answered it. It was a woman's voice. Short conversation. She said, 'Is this Vern Furness?' I said 'Yes.' and she said 'When will you have the money?" I said 'We are working on it and it will take some time and I'm not sure I can get it.' She said "Get if from Amundsen' and hung up. That's all there was to it."

"What can you tell us about her voice?"

"I don't know. Average voice, not young, not old. Maybe a little deeper than average."

"No accent?"

"No –I didn't notice one anyway."

"Mr. Furness, I'm from Saint Luis and have a different accent from people around here. Do you notice my accent?" Vern nodded. "But you didn't notice her accent?"

"No"

O'Connell looked at Green. "So we might conclude the woman is from around here, or not too far off anyway."

Green nodded. "Or at least eliminate Texas or Boston and such. But the big takeaway is this Amundsen person, right?"

The police lieutenant chimed in. "This was the lawyer who we think was being shot at in the first place." He looked at Sergeant Otis. "Has anyone spoken to the guy yet?"

"I don't know. Don't think so. I'll get right on it." The sergeant pulled out his cell phone and went into the hallway to make a call.

Deputy Bohler spoke for the first time. "This is where I might be of some help.

Vern and I checked out the building where the lad was and found spent brass. We then went looking for the driver of the car poking up out of a drainage ditch across the field. There were what appeared to be bullet holes in the fenders –front and back- as well as shattered windows all around, but no one there. We followed the tracks a ways. It appeared the guy was crawling on hands and knees –probably trying to take cover from the shots. About 200 feet away, he evidently got up and walked and about 100 feet further on, he climbed out of the ditch and walked toward three grain bins. Then his tracks disappeared.” He looked at Vern. “Did I mention that there was a hole dug beside one of ‘em bins? I was curious and looked inside. There weren’t nothing but a big old bolt dropped thru the hasp. Looked like someone was camping there. A sleeping bag, lawn chair, some books and other stuff. No idea what the hole was for. If they dug it up when the ground was frozen, it had to be a lot of work to steal at some silage or oats or rapeseeds or whatever.

The FBI agents and lieutenant were taking notes. Agent Green asked, “There was also a woman involved in the shooting. Do you know anything about one Janet Howard Mr. Furness?”

“No. I drove her home that afternoon –my gosh, was it only yesterday? But anyway, she was pretty shook up and just wanted to get home to her little boy.” He thought a moment. “Come to think of it, Amundsen mentioned he had a new girlfriend and she was… I gather he thought she was very… attractive.”

“Amundsen is divorced and has become a horn-dog.” Sherrie made her disgust clear.

Vern agreed. “A messy divorce. Cost him a lot of money. That’s why Robby was in the building. Amundsen needed an investor and so I…” He looked at Sherrie, “…*we* bought the water treatment plant from him as an investment and Robby was in charge of maintaining it.”

O’Connell looked down at his notes. “Robby is thirteen years old. Seems a tad young to be taking care of a big piece of equipment?”

Sherrie defended her son. “Robby is pretty mature for his age.”

“And he has grown up helping me maintain heavy equipment. No big deal to follow the manual about some pumps and tanks and such like.” Vern added.

Otis had been talking quietly in the next room and returned to the meeting. “The lawyer evidently did report an accident. But it was listed as a car wreck. He drove into a ditch. He is supposed to make a complete report for insurance. At his convenience. The dispatcher said he was getting patched up in the hospital when he called.”

The lieutenant smacks the table in disgust. “It looks like we screwed up again. Someone has *got* to run this guy down and have a long chat with him.”

O’Connell shook his head. “The guy’s a lawyer, right? It’s second nature to lawyers to answer police questions without saying anything useful. I want to talk to him myself. The FBI has some ways to ask questions that lawyerly types can’t wiggle out of. Damn curious though.”

Green looked at the senior cop, “Maybe I could chat with the girlfriend as well. She might be more forthcoming with a woman?”

The deputy said he wanted to check out the grain bins again. The meeting broke up. Everyone agreed to meet back at the house as soon as possible. When everyone left Vern and Sherrie alone and they were very alone. Their home felt very cold and silent. It had never felt this way before.

Chapter 58

All things considered, Kevin Amundsen was pretty pleased with how things seemed to be working out. His ankle still hurt, but no big. They wrapped it in ace-bandages at the hospital and gave him crutches. He didn't really need them, but hobbled into his office the next morning anyway. It was a nice touch –made his erratic actions – or more accurately, his lack of appropriate actions the day before seem more believable.

Someone had taken shots at him and that was worrisome, but he had reviewed some stuff about security on-line and felt that with a little luck and by varying his routine, staying in town, and keeping his curtains drawn everywhere, the police would run the bitch to ground sooner or later. More worrisome was the police or the FBI looking too closely into his dealing with Mel. That appeared to be a diminishing possibility.

The first thing he did when he got to his office that morning was to pull out the insurance policy on his car. Nothing about putting it in a ditch because someone was shooting at you, but nor was it an 'act-of-God' so he figured he was in pretty good shape. Just a matter of crossing the T's and dotting the I's. No hurry. Driving a loaner –or a series of loners, made him less of a target as well and the reading he had done said this was the sort of thing he needed to do.

He would, however, have to make an official report to the police and get a copy of the report to the insurance company. He could honestly say he was completely ignorant of the source of the shooting –well informed conjecture not with-standing. If the police somehow linked him to the woman –and if it indeed was her and not some drunken oil-field worker- there was no way they could link him to Mel's 'recovery expert'. Best not to know anything about what the scary little guy did to get the money out of the Mahon woman.

Best to know even less about what was going on out at the man camp with the woman Mel had suggested as a temporary manager. Janet came to mind when he thought about the day to day management of the man camp. THIS was what was bothering him – this was the annoying little thing just below the surface. He had taken off and left her. He thought he had heard at least two police cars drive up while he was hiding behind the grain bin and waiting for his secretary to come and get him, so he was sure Janet got home somehow. He would have to figure out how to fix that little faux-pas, but all in good time.

His secretary Beulah was doing the mothering thing about his ankle. She brought him coffee without being asked even once, and left the door to his inner office so he could 'Jes' holler if'n ya'll need anythin' honey'.

He actually started to do some real work –first he had done since the man-camp's finances got hinkey. It was for a land owner who was being asked to give an oil company permission to drive over his land to get to a drill-site on another farmer's land. The easement would save the oil company a pile of money not to have to build a county

194

approved road with engineering, so many hundred feet of right away, so many inches of this kind of gravel and so many more inches of that kind of gravel on top of that and ditches of a given width and depth. If the county maintained their own damn permanent roads as well as the oil folks were required to build temporary roads, there would be a lot less work for suspension and front-end alignment mechanics in the area. Probably a few less accidents -fatal or otherwise too. Amundsen's job was to figure out how much to charge the oil company so it was just barely worth while to pay the farmer rather than build another road. The farmer wasn't doing very damn much with his farm road anyway, but no point leaving money on the table.

He hadn't paid that much attention to the time –other than to be able to bill the farmer for his hours, and was surprised when he heard Beulah talking to someone in his outer office and he noticed it was noon. She stuck her head in looking a little awed. Not her usually bored look at all. "Mr. Amundsen, the FBI is here and would like a little of your time."

So much for having a nice day. He got up and remembered to reach for his crutches just as a black suit moved past Beulah. "Mr. Amundsen, how d'ya do. I'm Agent O'Connell of the Minot Field office. Can I have a few minutes of your time?" The crutches made their handshake theatrically awkward in what seemed to Amundsen to be just the right measure.

"Certainly. Please sit down."

"So I understand you had a little excitement yesterday?"

"I'm not entirely sure what happened yesterday. What to the police think?"

O'Connell knew this game. The lawyer was answering questions with questions of his own. Or maybe he was just curious about what had to be a strange situation for anyone. "Any idea who might have been shooting at you?"

"Nope."

That was a throw away question. They both knew it. "You knew that Vern Farness' son is missing?" *This* got a reaction. He clearly didn't know.

"What are you talking about?"

"The boy was in that building where the water treatment plant is. This is where the shooting came from. The police found brass on the ground outside the door. Then he was missing. There have been two ransom calls. Both from a woman. The one this morning mentioned you." The lawyer slumped back in his chair. THe agent thought either he was a damn good actor, or it was news to him. Now was the time to go for the throat. "Mr. Amundsen, what is your involvement in this matter?"

"I have no fucking... I was the one being shot at. You think I..." he shrugged and collected himself. "I was mentioned?"

The agent pulled out his little notebook. Mr. Farness said he couldn't raise the ransom. The woman said –and I quote from what Mr. Furness said 'Get it from Amundsen.' and she hung up.

His own kids crossed his mind. Vern Furness was as close to a friend as he had lately. There were happier times with his wife when the Furness family came for BBQ and the kids had a dip in his pool in the backyard –one of a very few in Williston. He considered his own exposure. He considered just how clever this old guy might be. He stirred it all together for a few seconds and made his decision.

"There was a woman who managed my man-camp. She disappeared and it seems she embezzled a lot of money from me. I am still trying to unravel what happened. Bills and invoices and all."

"What was her name?"

"Sara Mahon. I must have her social security number and previous address somewhere. Probably out at the man-camp office."

"Thank you. But why would she steal from you and then come back and shoot at you? This makes no sense. You would expect her to get as far away as possible, wouldn't you?"

"I misspoke when I said the man-camp was mine. I am the general partner as well as an investor. One of the other investors hired a detective agency of some sort. I believe he called it a *recovery expert*. I understand some of the money has been recovered. Perhaps she is unhappy about this. Or perhaps she is simply crazy."

It was O'Connell's turn to think. There was far more to this story than she was *unhappy* or *crazy*. But it was something to get started on –the sort of thing the FBI did very well. Worth a gentle push anyway. "What is the name of your recovery specialist?"

"Not my hire. No idea, but I'll ask my partner for the name."

Time to stop. O'Connell knew it was better to leave the door open with lawyers than to push too hard. "Can you get me the information on this Sara Mahon?"

"Beulah, can you find the employee files for out at the man camp for me?"

They chatted about Williston's growth and the price of crude oil while Beulah opened and closed file drawers looking for employee files. It appeared not to be going well for her.

Chapter 59

Officer Smyth was having a bad day all around. A little confusion around the cook slash teacher and then the excitement of arresting the guy. Then it all fell to shit just when he went upstairs all set to impress his training officer. Back down stairs again with his tail tucked between his legs to let the guy out again.

Even releasing the guy had not gone well. The guy was polite when they brought him out of holding, but it was a frosty cold politeness. The guy was pissed –not the least grateful for being let out. Smyth and the teacher / cook stood on one side of the property counter just outside the holding area. There was a fat sergeant behind the counter who took his own damn time finding a big manila envelope holding the guys belt, shoe-laces, cell phone, keys, billfold, and some small change. The clerk made it clear he had much better things to do than return detainee's property. He left both Officer Smyth and the guy standing there while he worked on a crossword puzzle. Finally, he glanced up and pushed a clipboard at him and said "Sign here" and went back to his newspaper.

The guy said a single word, "No."

Officer Smyth was starting to feel for the guy. He was embarrassed by the attitude of one of his fellow officers. The fat ass didn't even look up from his paper. "Then you don't get your shit back."

Smyth thought he had never seen a human being so very very angry and so very very quiet. He had seen angry men -drunk men –stupid men before, arrested some of them himself, but they were loud and belligerent. This guy was different. Frighteningly so. The guy looked at Smyth. "There is nothing I can do Mr. Williams. You can go now."

The guy didn't say a word, he just turned around and walked off down the hall toward the EXIT sign. Smyth went upstairs to the bull-pen to think a moment and find a desk where he could take notes. He was learning taking notes might be a very good thing for his career, particularly when some other pecker-head suggests they arrest someone at gunpoint. He gathered his thoughts and called Lieutenant Burrows. As he waited for an answer, he thought *Damn it, don't none of this mess is my fault.*

"Burrows."

"Officer Smythe here sir.   We released Mr. Williams, but he refused to sign the property receipt and so we still have all his stuff."

"Fuck. Where is he now?

"Walking home I guess." Smyth thought about making a joke of the guy holding up his pants with one hand because they wouldn't give him back his belt. He quickly decided against it.

"Oh for the love of… Go find him. Drive him wherever he wants to go. Do NOT handcuff him. Do NOT put him in the back seat. Your job now –your only job- is to do anything and everything the teacher needs or wants. I will sort it out with the property guy."

"Should I drive him back to his car?"

"If that's what he wants. You will offer to drive him all over the state too if that's what he wants."

It took him only about ten minutes to find the guy walking north on Forth Avenue. It did look like he was holding up his pants with one hand. He pulled past him and got out of his car. The guy stopped in his tracks, looked at him and slowly raised his hands. Smyth couldn't tell if he was being a smart-ass or really thought he might get shot. The guy's expression was completely blank. His pants slowly fell to his knees. The guy ignored them.

"Mr. Williams, I'm sorry for everything that has happened to you. It all started when the FBI screwed up a message. I just got off the phone with my boss. He says I am to be your chauffer –all day if you like. I can't do anything about your property, but anything else I can do…." Smyth noticed that cars were backed up going both ways on the street. Even in Williston, a police car and a guy with his hands in the air and his pants half down was not a common sight. Maybe late at night after drunken shift-change antics, but not in the morning "And you can put your hands down sir."

Williams dropped his arms, pulled his pants back up, and sighed. "You were just doing what you were told to do, right?"

"Yes sir."

"How long you been a cop?"

"Not quite six months."

Williams nodded and almost smiled. Almost. "All right officer Smyth. First stop is the home of the kidnapped boy." He reached for his cell phone and realized it was not in his pocket. "You know what time it is? Doesn't matter. I'm late. You know where they live?"

"Yes sir." There wasn't one word spoken for the drive to the east side of town and the Furness house. Smyth pulled in the driveway and Williams got out without a word. He came out a few minutes later with a bundle of papers. Things seemed to have thawed a little. "Your boss was in there. Burrows is his name? He said to tell you I could get my stuff back anytime. I told him that I would let my lawyer recover my property." Williams didn't even try to suppress a smile. "He was NOT happy."

"Mr. Williams, I…" he didn't know what to say.

"Don't worry about it. The problem isn't with you. It's your department's policies and procedures. Anyway, next stop is back at the school. You are going to have a little chat with my boss. If indeed she still is my boss –that is to say if I still have a job."

"Happy to do this Mr. Williams."

They walked in together and Williams introduced him to a middle aged woman who Smyth thought might have been his 6th grade English teacher. Williams then leaned against a table while Smyth explained how the FBI had intercepted a call from a phone tap and issued one order, but then used the wrong general order code and so they arrested him by mistake. He was pretty sure no one followed his ramble so he simply stressed that Mr. Williams was in no way a suspect and, in fact, was helping the police in a difficult matter.   Smyth thought he did pretty well.

The teacher woman said, "Oh my. What is the difficult matter? Is our Mr. Williams in any danger?"

Williams answered. "Someone's been kidnapped. A young boy. He is someone who…"

Smyth interrupted him. "Best not to say more Mr. Williams. Things are still pretty confusing."

Williams nodded. "As evidenced by my arrest, I suppose." He turned to his boss. "It occurs to me that Officer Smyth's boss might come out tomorrow and do a little PR on behalf of the Williston Police Department for the students?" He turned back to Smyth. "You think we could manage this Officer?"

He was still between a rock and hard place. A reasonable request, but Smyth was hesitant to commit his boss to such a thing. Then he realized the guy was just messing with him. A little. "I'll certainly see what I can do mam."

Williams then asked to be driven to the old Frontiersman's Office Building on Fifth Street and Second Avenue. As Williams got out he said, "You mind coming in with me Officer?"

Smyth had no choice but to get out, lock his cruiser, and follow. No idea where they were going or why, but he had a bad feeling. Sure enough, it was a lawyer's office and a nice lady with the southern accent showed them into the fancy inner office with out a second thought. This might have been predictable, but what wasn't predictable was the presence of the FBI agent was in the conference room that morning. The image of the fat German guard from the old TV show about the WWII POW camp came to Smyth's mind. *I know nothing. Noooothing.* He decided this was the perfect attitude for someone at his pay grade to take.

The teacher -by now Smyth thought the notion of the guy just being a cook didn't fit- apologized for the interruption. He nodded politely when he was introduced to the FBI agent and then the teacher introduced Smyth to the lawyer sitting at the desk. Smyth thought it was nice to be included, but worried just what he was being included in. He didn't have to wait long.

The FBI agent said he was just leaving, but would like to have a word with Williams at his convenience as he was getting up to leave.

Williams glanced at him. "Wait just a moment Mr. O'Connell." He turned to the guy behind the desk. "May I hire you in a matter of false arrest Mr. Amundsen?" Smyth tried to make himself as small as possible.

"Certainly. But might we not discuss this at a later time?"

Williams nodded with exaggerated decorum. "It is clear that getting the young Furness boy back to his loving family is our highest priority, but I while we have both the FBI here –who I understand issued the order for my arrest- and the arresting officer, it occurs we might just touch on some of the niggling little procedures. For example, those necessary for me to recover my belt from… the rotund individual in charge of personal items in the jail. And a few other issues besides.

The FBI agent started to explain that it was a harmless mistake when the teacher shrugged and snorted a single word, "Harmless?". His pants fell down again. He said nothing more - just stared at the agent who decided to stop talking.

"Perhaps it might be a good time for young officer Smyth to drive me home where I can get a belt." Unless you have question for the officer Mr. Amundsen?"

Amundsen didn't even try to suppress a smile. "I think I'll ask the good FBI agent a few questions about the originating order, and we will wait to another time to see what the arresting officer has to say. Now off you go."

Williams pulled his pants back up and left with Smyth following. He had learned about double talk. This teacher guy could get more threat and just all-around scariness into polite quiet conversation that he would have thought possible. And as for the lawyer, he didn't ever what to face this guy on a witness stand.

Chapter 60

Robby had never been up past midnight but once. It was last New Years Eve when his dad's brother and family came for a visit from Minnesota. The parents all stayed up and talked and somehow forgot to tell the kids to go to bed. Robby just made it to midnight, but gladly crawled into bed and was asleep two minutes into the new year. Nor had he ever slept during the day since he was a very little kid and his mom made him take naps. He hated being sent to his room to "go take a nap" and hit on the idea of hiding toys, (cars and trucks usually) under his bed so he could play with them quietly rather than sleeping. When he was three or four years old his Mom gave up the battle of making him take a nap. So when he woke up in the silo, he had no idea what time it was, and panicked. Was it the next morning? The day after the crazy lady made him get in the trunk of her car? There was light coming in between the ceiling and the walls of the grain bin and he knew that it was dark out when she had opened the trunk and demanded phone numbers from him. Was it morning or afternoon? Or had he slept thru one day and one night and it was now a day later?   Not knowing was the worst part. He cried for a little while before he convinced himself he was being a big baby.

There was the sound of distant rumbling. He thought it might have been the wind, but it was different -very steady –not like the gusty wind he was used to. Then he remembered the sound a natural gas flare made from the time he was helping his dad out at a drill pad. It was a pipe that came out of the ground and went straight up about fifteen feet. There was a huge roaring flame flaring off natural gas from the top of the pipe. There was a three of four foot dirt dike about twenty feet out from the pipe. Even standing beyond the dike, he could feel the heat from the flair.

He was also hungry. He was often hungry, but this was different hunger. And cold, but the sleeping bag was almost thick enough. He thought that if he had something to eat, he might not have been so cold. He thought of the TV show about he guy who was able to make the most astounding contraptions to rescue himself and spent the next little while reviewing the tricks the guy did to get himself out of difficult situations. Kept his mind off the empty stomach, but nothing came to mind. The thing hanging down in the back of his throat was all swollen up. He dad took him dear hunting down in South Dakota's Black Hills a couple of times. They left their motel before dark when it was even colder that it was in North Dakota. His dad told him that a person can get dried out even in the cold and when that thing got swollen up, it meant he was dried out. There was another word he dad used, but 'dried out' was what it meant. He dad shared a thermos of hot tea with him that day. He was not to tell his mom about the tea though. *Just our little secret.* It had something to do with his mom's religion.

Then Robby thought about one Saturday when he was a little kid. He had a school friend over to play and they all sat down to lunch. They said grace and his friend said his family said a different grace and they only said it at dinner. His mom asked his friend about his families' beliefs. He said they were Baptists. Robby then announced "We are Lutherans, but Mom and her family are morons." His dad was drinking lemonade and laughed so hard the lemonade sprayed all over the table. His mom was not happy. He wasn't in trouble, but his dad took him aside and explained the difference between morons and Mormons. They also talked about how his mom didn't drink coffee or tea or beer and only had an occasional glass of wine. She would make coffee for his dad but not drink it herself. So the hot sweet tea they drank when out in the Black Hills of a cold late autumn day was a special memory. He would have liked some now.

After a while he crawled out of the sleeping bag and kicked the straw from the ground against one wall of the bin and made himself a thicker cushion to lie on. He got back in the sleeping bag and immediately got out again and made a thicker pile at the head for a pillow. While he was up, he peed. It was almost brown. When he crawled back in the bag, he realized he was missing school. It wasn't his fault and missing school was a good thing, but he would rather be in school -even on spelling-test day. He imagined what his teachers might be saying about why Robbie Furness wasn't in class today. He's be kind of hero. The other kids would think he was... he wasn't sure what they would think, but it would be cool. He drifted back to fitful sleep thinking about what his classmate Mia Magnatta would think when she heard he had been kidnapped

Chapter 61

No word from Robby or the kidnapper by late afternoon, but the number of phone calls going every direction provided more that enough diversion. Either by default or design, Sherrie had come to be the message center for all of the law enforcement crowd. Vern felt himself resenting what he saw as an effort more to fill out forms and follow procedures that it was an effort to actually find his son. But it was clear that Sherrie was filling the role and was… if not happy, she was feeling less helpless. An altogether good thing. His people –God love them- had started at mid-morning calling in for assignments as to which direction to go off asking about Robby.

Vern made a point of holding up their second meeting until Sven got there. He listened politely to both the Williston Police and FBI explain -once again and with labored patience like they were talking to a dim-witted child- that it was not a County Sheriff's issue. Vern nodded politely, but he felt his blood raising. He simply said, "Thank you. I will keep what you say in mind, but I want him here just the same. We will wait." He smiled and said no more.

When the deputy had gotten there a few minutes later, Sven was the only one to make a point of thanking Sherrie for the plate of sandwiches she has put out on the table, but it may have just been because he was the only one who knew the Furness family before things hit the fan. Still and all, Vern thought this gesture was telling.

The tall FBI lady got things started. She had nothing material to report from the conversation with Janet about the shooting, but she stressed that she and the woman had had a good enough rapport that the agent had a vivid impression of the lawyer guy. Other than tactfully suggesting her impression would not contradict Sherrie's negative views of the guy, she said little.

The FBI guy had rather more to report. The lawyer's mention of the embezzler, the Sara Mahon woman, had started a flurry of action in Minnesota. There were agents from the Minneapolis office waiting outside her home but there had been no answer when they knocked on her door. The conclusion was obvious: the woman was a good suspect. Her motive was –at least in part- revenge for having the money she had embezzled 'recovered'. There was some ambiguity as to how it had been recovered and the lawyer wasn't saying, but the FBI was sure this was the best direction to go. The problem was that it was no in particular direction. The process to get search warrant had been started, but was not expected for an hour or two. In the meantime, a BOLO –Be On the LookOut- for her Lexus had been issued to every police department and county sheriff's department, and the highway patrols of both North Dakota and Montana.

Deputy Bohler had a little something to add as well. He had driven back to the grain bins where he had lost the lawyer's tracks the day before. "Let me bring the FBI

201

team up to speed on this." Vern admired the tact Sven used in speaking to the FBI. "Yesterday I was looking for the driver of the car in the ditch –the one with bullet holes- and followed his tracks to a couple three grain bins at the end of a little farm road. I lost the tracks, but noticed a hole dug in the ground to the side of one of them. There was a big bolt thru the hasp of a little hatch in the side of the door, so I took a quick peek inside. Weren't no one there, but it looked like someone had been camping in there. There was a lawn chair and a sleeping bag and some books and some cereal boxes and such. Struck me as queer, but since I was looking for the driver, I didn't waste my time. I lost the tracks a short ways down the farm road and sort'a forgot about it."

The little police sergeant finally had something to say. "Likely some oil field worker camped in the grain bin for a spell till he got his first paycheck and could pay rent in one of our more… economical motels. Don't mean much else."

The deputy nodded. "There's more. The sleeping bag was missing this morning. It was there the day before. And one more thing. I didn't notice it yesterday, but the hole was dug out from the *inside* –like someone had been trapped and had to dig them selves out."

"What are you suggesting Deputy?" O'Connell asked.

"It may just all be coincidence, but it do seem queer."

Sherrie came in from the kitchen with more sandwiches. "Vern, I forgot, your dad called. He said the bankers will have the money –the two hun…" she choked, "… two hundred thousand dollars will be ready by four o'clock. He is down at the bank ready to sign the paperwork and get the money."

Green looked at O'Connell pointedly. O'Connell said, "We will take custody on the money after the bankers provide it."

Vern shook his head. "The fuck you will."   Sherrie put her hand on his arm and he leaned back in his chair and folded his arms.

O'Connell went on. "I understand your reticence. But we only want to record the serial numbers. There are however, things we can do when the kidnapper tries to get the money. It's your money –or I gather it's your Dad's, but this is when she –if it is indeed the Mahon woman- is the most exposed. –the best time to nab them is when the kidnapper goes after the ransom.

Vern was not impressed. "When is the best time to get my son back?"

O'Connell shrugged. "That's harder to say. If the kidnapper is in custody, we have some leverage."

There seemed to be nothing else to say. After a long moment, O'Connell turned to Green. They started a discussion about contacts to be logged and reports to be filed. Sven caught Vern's eye and nodded toward the front door. Vern nodded, got up and went into the kitchen while Sven muttered something about needing to check in with his dispatcher. They met on the front porch a moment later. Vern had two cups of coffee. "You ever see my home shop?"

"I don't believe I have."

"It's this way." and he started across the crusty snow on the front lawn to the big garage on the side of the house. A rare clear day with a glaring winter sun had warmed up outside and the shop was a colder inside than out. Vern set his coffee cup on the fender of a small front-end loader and lit a kerosene heater on the floor. He straightened up and pointed to an exposed cluster of pipes on the machine's firewall. "I was teaching Robby how to bleed hydraulic systems… I guess it was the night before last. Seems a long damn time ago."

Sven didn't have anything to say. Vern pulled the driver's seat from some piece of machinery over to beside the kerosene space heater. He kicked an empty five gallon bucket of engine de-greaser to the other side of the heater and sat down and leaned his back against a workbench cluttered with tools and greasy parts. Sven took the un-mounted driver's seat and stretched his legs out in front of him. Both men made themselves reasonably comfortable. The sipped their coffee silently as the kerosene burned a dull red between them.

"So Sven, what's on your mind?"

"Done a little research Vern. FBI has all this data. No other way to say it, odds are not good. The fact that he was still alive, after what? four hours after you reckon he was abducted from the water plant when you got the call from him?" Vern's mouth went dry and he only nodded. "Being alive that long and he had already beat the odds. It ain't just the FBI. Don't no one do much better. "Em big-city east coast police departments don't do any better. Not even in Europe. Let the FBI do whatever they want to do to the money, but keep it close. Give it to the kidnapper anyway she wants it. Don't do nothing fancy. Don't try to trick her, and don't let the FBI try to spring a trap. What they *are* good at is getting the money back. I know that ain't your big concern, but your best bet is to just go along with the kidnapper."

"Thanks Sven. I had kind'a been thinking along them same lines myself."

"That's the bad news. The good news, and it ain't so much good news is just some noodeling I've been doing. See how this sounds. Someone –maybe this Mahon woman- wanted to kill your lawyer and then Robby got in the way. They –she- had to do something –something without no planning. She has no choice but to drive around with your son. Lots and lots of empty country around here, but that is still tricky for her, so she wants to park him somewhere. Feasable so far?"

Vern nodded. "Ya, I think the FBI and Williston cops have gotten this far."

"OK. This is where I go off the reservation. So the reason she took some shots at Amundsen was because of the money she stole and they recovered –they stole it back from her -and they weren't nice about it. Someone stuck her in that grain bin while they sweated the money out of her. Don't know how long it might'a took –banks and computers and passwords and all, but it might'a been a few days. Wouldn't have been pleasant. Finally, when they –and I have no idea who they might'a been but they were not nice people –when they got all the money they wanted, they gave her a shovel and had themselves a few hours head start before she dug herself out. So flash forward. She has Robby and needs to park him while you get the money together. She remembers her own time in a grain bin. She's driving around and around –mostly back roads so she swings by the bin to grab the sleeping bag. This is some small good news anyway -she is taking care of him -just a little anyway. Least wise if my theory is right."

Vern got up and started pacing. "Make sense to me."

"Vern, don't no one know where Robby is, but I'm betting he's in a grain bin somewhere out on the prairie somewhere within a few hours drive." He shrugged. "Pretty thin, but it's as good an idea as anything they have come up with sitting around your dining room table."

"So what do we do now? There must be a thousand grain bins all over the countryside?"

"So how many of your guys work for you are out there asking questions?"

"Had five guys in three teams out last night –heading north, south, east, and west. Beth and I went north. We just got to Canada and headed back when Sherrie called about the first phone call."

"What about today?"

"Four have checked in with Sherrie today."

"Well, that's about four more'n the FBI and police have working the problem."

Sven smoothed his mustache while he thought. Vern went on. "There's also the cook out at the man-camp came by to get a stack of flyers to give the men out at the camp come dinner time. Think Sherrie said he wanted a hundred –I guess he feeds that many folks. I don't know."

"Well, that's something, but they're spinning their wheels. We need to get them… get every damn one looking in ever' damn grain bin, or silo, or farm outbuilding within a hundred miles. Vern, I think we need to build our case before we try to get the boys in blue to buy in. How well do you get along with the Amundsen guy?"

"Well, we used to see him and his wife at Sons of Norway gatherings all the time. But after the divorce, his wife moved away, and then, not so much. He is my lawyer. And he hit a cash crunch and got me to buy the water treatment plant to get him by. I guess he made me a good deal. But Sherrie is right, he ain't no upstanding family man any more. I don't know for sure, but I'm guessing that pretty girl who was in the car when the shooting started was…" He shrugged and groped for the right word. "… well… exactly the kind of woman Sherrie would object to."

"You don't know anything about the Mahon woman, the embezzlement, or what they are calling the 'recovery'?"

"Other than it explains his cash crunch, not a thing."

"Recon he'd be honest with you if you were to run our theory by him?"

Vern shrugged again. "If the recovery was out of line –legal wise- I suspect maybe not. What to they say, 'Off the record'? Maybe."

"What do you say to go ask him –man to man- without the FBI or police, or even me there?"

"Sounds like a plan."

"I'm gon'na see what I can get the sheriff's department to do about searching farms and all.

Chapter 62

By late afternoon, Amundson had reassured himself that he was still more or the less in the clear. He hadn't lied and he genuinely knew noting about Mr. Smith's methods of recovering embezzled funds. No doubt they were brutal, but the woman was still alive. Unfortunately. As he reviewed the conversation he had with both the FBI and the camp cook –evidently his latest client- he was more worried about loosing the cook than he was worried about the police. The cook was doing a good job in the kitchen. A lot cheaper than the previous guy too.

He figured he had done two hours of work for the farmer thus far and wasted another hour on the FBI. Pitty he couldn't send them a bill. Might be a good time to go visit Mel at the strip club. Their conversation the day before in the hospital was not satisfactory. He wasn't enthused about admitting he was rattled and concerned about the police poking around, but better to get out from under the little guy's subtle threats than to feel foolish for a short time.

There was something else nagging at him. Rent on his office and apartment? Been a squeeker, but he was current. Credit cards? More minimum payments and interest charges that he would have liked, but that situation was correcting itself. Mel had made him hire a woman he knew to sit at the desk in the man-camp's office. She was working out but he was now reviewing and paying all the bills. He wasn't entirely comfortable with her, but Mel seemed to be happy. Not a small consideration. It was a temporary situation anyway. Alimony? Also been late, but he brought it current before he went to Vegas with...

Janet?   Janet!

That was it. He still needed to fix this situation. Instinct took over and he began devising his argument. He had driven off and left her to draw fire away from her. He was thinking only of her, and was injured doing so. He would have called earlier, but the pain and drugs put him in a bad state. Simple matter to get –stay- on her good side. Who knew, she might also make a good front desk person. For that matter, given the horny young clientele of the man camp, she might make a great point woman –regardless of any organization or bookkeeping skills she might have. Solve his previous problem with the woman Mel had insisted he hire too. There were things going on at the camp he wasn't sure he liked. Better than the Mahon bitch, but still worrisome.

Yep, Janet was the top of his To-Do list. He tidied up his desk and was pondering a gift –flowers? Better a nice bottle of wine: they might sit and drink it together ant that might lead to sex. He ought to swing my Mel's place first and see if she was working and if not, he felt justified in breaking her rule about not coming to her home.

He got half way across his inner office before he remembered to go back for the crutches. As he gathered them from behind his desk, he heard the outer office door opened and Beulah's drawl. "Well, howdy Mr. Vern. How's ever' little thing with your family?"

Amundsen was grateful she remembered Vern's name and that he had a family, but what a horrible thing to ask a man whose son had been kidnapped. She had no way to know, but there was nothing for him to do but get Vern into his office before Beulah said anything else –stupid or otherwise. "Hey Vern, come on in."

The handshake cum crutches thing worked well again. "Sorry Vern. Beulah didn't know." Vern just shook his head. Have a seat. Need a beer?" Vern shook his head again. "I'm sorry about your son. He was a nice kid." Fuck. He was worse than Beulah. "*IS* a nice kid. I'm sorry Vern. Anything new?"

"No. The FBI are sitting on the Mahon woman's house in Minnesota I guess. She is the best suspect and they are looking for her car. Other wise, zip." Kevin hobbled behind his desk, sat with a quiet groan, and put on his best thoughtful lawyer look and waited for the other man to get started.

"Look Kevin, I have a theory I want to run by you. Just between you and I. The FBI and police are… well, I ain't entirely sure what the fuck they are doing but it seems to have little to do with actually finding Robby. They aare mostly filling out papers. Anyway, I just want to ask you if you think something is feasible."

"Absolutely Vern." Amundsen knew damn well that this earth moving contractor in jeans and a worn flannel shirt had recently been able to raise two hundred thousand dollars, and then a cool quarter of a million in a few days later from his dad in less than twenty four hours. Not an uncommon thing around Williston, but it never paid to underestimate this sort of men and their insights. He figured Vern knew he was on the ragged edge of something he didn't want to police to know about, and Vern would keep it to himself. But it was his kid that was missing and he was equally sure Vern would throw him to the wolves in a heartbeat if it would save his son.   "What's your theory."

"The recovery expert you hired to get your money back locked the embezzler in a grain bin while he did things with banks and so forth. Probably illegal things. I don't care. But if Mahon is both who was shooting at you and the person who took Robby, she might need to park him somewhere safe. Somewhere like a grain bin where she was locked up. Just conjecture, but do you know anything that contradicts this possibility?"

Amundsen thought about his own kids –grown and more in their mom's camp than on his side since the divorce, but sill and all, his kids. "Vern, I genuinely do not know what the guy did to get my money out of the woman, but he was a right weird 'n scary little guy. What is more, he was recommended –actually hired- by another of my investors in the man-camp who was also a frightening guy. I am trying to get in touch with the expert now, but it seems these things take a while."

Vern started to bristle and say something. Kevin raised his hand. "Swear-to-God Vern. This is not lawyer talk. I'm out of my own depth here. I don't know and I can't bring pressure to bear on the guy who knows –if indeed even he knows. I will say this though, it sounds reasonable. I'm guessing we are talking about them grain bins up north of the man-camp?"

Vern nodded. Amundsen sat back in his chair. "Ironic. When the shooting started I took off over the prairie and wound up there. Had no idea that was where she had been. You sure about it?"

"The sheriff deputy –you might know him. Sven Bohler?"

"*Y*a, good man I think."

"Well, he followed your tracks and found what the police are sure is just some field hand's campsite. It was Sven that came up with the notion that we ought to be looking for Robby in such a place."

"How can I help. Vern?"

"You have time to drive around and poke around in farm buildings?" Amundsen gestured at the crutches leaning against the corner of his desk. "Well, we have my guys and your cook thinks he might get some help from the guys at the man-camp. We got plenty."

Kevin thought about it. He quickly realized he had no exposure from a dozen people poking around silos and grain bins. For that matter, it would look good if he had been helping out when and if the stink wafted his way again. "How about I man the phones? There must be a thousand silos within a hundred miles of here. Can't have people crossing each other's paths –looking in the same place twice and all."

"Thanks Kevin. Fetch your cell phone over to the house. Sherrie is kind'a the switch-board operator for this whole circus. She would appreciate the help."

"I got a couple of errands to run. Might see what maps I can scare up. When do you want me there?"

"We are trying to get the police to think the way we do and then we will might be getting help from the cooks talking to the guys at the man camp, and so I think tomorrow will be about when things start happening."

"I'll be there."

Vern got up. "Thanks. By the way. That pretty young woman you were with yesterday?"

Amundsen paused as he was getting up. "Yes?"

"You might want to look into patching things up with her. You were on her shit list yesterday when I drove her home."

Amundsen smiled in spite of himself. "She is the errand I had in mind." He almost thought to brag about what a hot little piece of ass she was; but decided this was not the time.

"Don't let the FBI worry you when you get there. They are… danged if I know what they are doing. Ignore them." Vern made a mental note to have a word with Sherrie when he got home to have her ignore her feelings for the lawyer as well. They shook hands and he left for home.

Amundsen decided he didn't have the time to waste buying chocolates or flowers. There was a passable bottle of Pinot Noir in the bottom of the little refrigerator behind Beulah's desk. It would do. He didn't think Janet's taste in wine was all that sophisticated. He practiced as he drove to her house. He was pretty satisfied with what he wanted to say about what had happened the day before when he left Janet behind. *Concerned only about you... -wanted to draw fire off of you. –unconscious for a time – the pain –then the police came -not thinking straight –the drugs they gave me.*

It didn't work. She opened the door when he knocked and glanced at his crutches but said nothing. He got out, "Thank goodness you…" and she shut the door again. It was going to need more than a bottle of wine and some nice words, but now was clearly not the time.

Chapter 63

When Beth got home from school, she didn't need to ask if Robby was OK.

There were strangers sitting around the dining-room table to the right off the entry hall. They were on cell phones and one –a lady, was working at a laptop. Her mom was in the kitchen and just looked sad and tired.

"Oh Mom, you have to call Ms. Hansen." Her mom's eyes flashed, but she didn't say anything. Beth realized she had better explain and do it quickly. "Um, I was thinking about something and didn't understand the question.

"Ms. Hansen is your science teacher, right?"

"Ya. She said I have an attitude but it's not fair, Mom. I was just thinking about Robby, and didn't know something about some stupid rocks or something. Hansen just hates 'cause I'm a cheerleader, and in drama club and everything." Beth knew she wasn't out of the woods yet. "Mom, I just miss Robby so much."

"For starters young lady, you will address her as *MS* Hansen." Sherrie moved to her daughter and hugged her. "Oh honey. All right. Find me her number and I'll call her."

That was easier than Beth had any right to hope for. She had friends –not the friends her parents approved of, but the cool kids. These kid's parents had to call teachers all the time, but this sort of thing never happened in the Furness family- at least till now.

She went to her bedroom and dropped her book bag on her desk and draped her coat on the back of her Hello Kitty desk chair. Her dad had taught her to just get started on her homework first thing when she got home from school He said she and Robby should sit down, pull out their books, find paper & pencil and what ever else they needed, and 'Plan Your Work.' Her dad was always saying things like that. Once the homework was all set up to begin –not necessarily actually begun, but all set to begin- it was OK to go into the kitchen for a snack. Beth got out her math book and put it on the bottom of the pile with Science and English on top. How *this* was a plan, but then she realized she had no idea what her homework was. She always had math to do and usually a few questions in science, but she had no idea what the assignments were. Everything happened to her. It just wasn't fair. She threw herself face-down on her bed and hugged one of her stuffed animals.

She really was thinking about Robby when old lady Hansen called on her. She hadn't even raised her hand or anything. She remembered this one spring day when Robby was in third grade and she was in fifth. The winter had been longer and harder winter than usual and the first warm day Beth wanted to walk home from school instead of taking the bus. Robby overheard and he wanted to come too. Beth didn't want him, but her mom made it a condition of permission. So the little twerp tagged along behind. It had been her plan to walk with some sixth grade girls and make friends, but the sixth grade girls had some middle school friends that started making fun of her. Then two seventh grade boys caught up with them and teasing the little fifth grade girl and it got even nastier. Beth was soon in tears and this was all it took for one of the boys to go overboard and shove her. She was knocked on her butt and as she was sitting there in shock, she saw her little brother streak head-first into the older boy's gut. They both went down and the other boy joined the melee. Robby came out of it with a black eye, torn dirty clothes, and was strangely pleased with himself. When they got home, their mom was upset and all set to call the police. She held off till Vern got home. Her mom explained it first and Vern turned to Beth for a first hand explanation. Beth found herself telling the story like Robby was a hero and she was proud of him. Her dad tried not to show it, but Beth was pretty sure he was proud too.

She lay there thinking about her brother –his good moments and her snotty moments. They seemed to run about equal in number. She had always thought of herself as a better than average kid. She knew her parents were stricter than average so she *had* to be better than average. But as she lay on her bed hugging her stuffed teddy, it was hard to think of herself as anything other than a snotty little brat.

Beth's bedroom faced the street so she heard her dad's truck drive up. She also noticed she was starving. Enough with feeling sorry for herself and more than enough worrying about homework. She went into the kitchen to make herself a snack and make herself small so she could listen to what was going on in the dining room. She got in on the end of something about someone's car that was missing. She peeked into the dining room. The stranger who was explaining that bolos –what ever they were, was a middle aged guy in a dark suit. He had red hair and his face was so red, it looked to Beth like he had been holding his breath. He kept saying the bolos took time to work and her dad needed to be patient.

There were two guys in police uniforms: a little guy in a crew cut and an older guy with gray hair. The older one had more decorations on his uniform. They weren't saying anything. The woman at the laptop was the most interesting. She was on the opposite side of the table and faced into the kitchen where Beth was standing. She wasn't saying anything either.

The older cop in the uniform cleared his throat. "It occurs to me we have too many cooks in the soup. We have police, county sheriffs, and the highway patrol out looking for the black Lexus, and…" He turned pointedly to her father. "We have what? -five or ten of your employees out beating the bush too, right?"

She saw her dad in profile, and saw him lock his jaw give a curt nod. She knew the signs, and decided she had already been skating on thin ice with her mom so she backed back into the kitchen out of sight. If her dad was going to blow, she was going to be out of sight. She could still hear everything.

The old cop went on. "I'm thinking that if the Mahon woman gets a whiff of all the people out there, she will get nervous. If she gets nervous…"

The red voice interrupted, "No telling what might happen, but it may not be good."

Her mom's voice. "So you think we should call all our employees in?"

The red voice again. "Yes, Mrs. Furness. I think the risk is not justified by the results."

"And tell me abut *your* fucking results O'Connell" This was her dad? He never spoke like this. Never! As much as anything, this frightened her. If her dad… she couldn't finish the thought.

Her mom's quiet voice, "Vern. Honey.", and then her *PAY ATTENTION* voice.

"Mr. O'Connell, please forgive my husband. But we are no closer to finding our son than we were a day ago. You mentioned a search warrant for the woman's home?"

The young woman's voice, "Hasn't come thru yet."

Beth heard a chair slide across the floor. If it was either of her parents, if it was her dad, and he was coming into the kitchen, she really wanted to be somewhere else. Anywhere else, but her bedroom was too far away. There was not enough time to do anything but try to look busy with the PB & J. Her luck held. Her father's voice. "Deputy Bohler and I were talking. He has a notion. I guess you guys call it a theory. I went to have a man to man with Amundsen. We go back a long way together and I think I got a straight answer from him –at least as straight an answer as a lawyer ever gives a body."

He paused and Beth risked a peek. He was standing at the window with his back to the room. Everyone was looking at him. Everyone but the young woman who looked directly at her gave her a slight nod, and looked down again. Beth wondered if maybe she had an ally in the dining room.

Her dad went on. "We do not know how, but the guy that Amundsen hired to get his money back –and he didn't actually hire the guy- turns out another investor of his hired the guy- but anyway, it seems that who ever did it may have done it in some pretty nasty ways. Bohler has also discovered what he thought –what we all thought, was a camp-site in a grain bin just north of the man-camp. But the sleeping bag that was there yesterday, was gone this morning. If we put ourselves in the mind of the kidnapper, and if the Mahon woman *is* the kidnapper, and if she was locked up in the grain bin while they got Amundsen's money back from her, *and if* she is driving around with Robby, it stands to reason that she would want to ditch him somewhere. The countryside is scattered with grain bins and silos. Stands to reason that Robby might be stuck in a grain bin somewhere. Let's hope he is in the sleeping bag. We can also hope he has food and water. I know a thing or two about cold and hunger myself. Thirst is a funny thing in the cold too. It can sneak up on you."

Both gray hair and red hair spoke at once: "Good theory" and "Makes sense."

Her dad's voice –and his tone was back to normal, "Ok. Here is what we are going to do. Sherrie and I will call in all our guys –call it a day. We will then organize a search of ever' damn grain bin, silo, elevator, empty farm building for a hundred miles around."

Red hair's voice: "I don't think that's necessarily a good idea."

Her dad's voice: "I don't care what you think." Now THIS was her dad.

The young woman's voice. "Um. Excuse me. We just got word from Minneapolis. They got the search warrant and the black Lexus is in the garage."

A new voice –must have been the guy in the crew-cut. "Beautiful. We have been looking for a car that is in the next state. I'll call off the bolo."

The woman again: "There is another car registered at the same address. An older Buick. Registered in the name of Shauna Mahon, aged twenty three."

Red hair: "Her daughter, maybe. Away at college?"

The new voice: "Give me the description and I'll issue a new bolo."

There was the sound of chairs being pushed away from the table. Beth grabbed her PB & J and darted into the living room. She had time for one bite when the young woman came into the room and sat down beside her on the couch. "You must be Beth?"

Beth nodded.

"I'm agent Green, but you can call me Lori." They shook hands. Beth hoped there wasn't jelly on her fingers. "How you holding up?"

Beth shrugged and swallowed. "My dad is a really nice guy. He's just worried about Robby."

"I know sweetie. We all know how worried your parents are. You too, I'm sure."

"What's bolo?"

"Be on the look out. Used to be called an all points bulletin –an APB."

"Will you be able to find Robby? My dad…" Beth wasn't sure how to deal with her father's anger. He got angry at her –more and more lately, but she had to admit she was often snotty. But she had never heard her dad talk like he had in the dining room just then. And if he was scared… but her dad was never scared. "Miss Green, there was this one time when Robby was trying to fix my CD player and broke it worse and I was so mean to him. I want to tell him I'm sorry." She started crying, "He was trying to help and I was so mean. You have to find him so I can tell I'm sorry."

Agent Green felt woefully out of her depth but just then Sherrie came in and sat on the couch beside her daughter. "Honey, we are all doing everything that can be done to bring Robby home." Sherrie looked at Green for something.
It took the agent a second or two to react.

"It's not just the victim who is victimized in kidnappings is it?" It was the realization that if the boy was not found, his sister would never be the same that made her speak. She also realized it was also a monumentally stupid thing to say.

Chapter 64

Mike had been working to get away from the need to order thirty pizzas from the Pizza Palace in town. But tonight is was a justified. He planned to drop by the place one of these days and introduce himself to the woman who was always happy to hear from him. No wonder when he ordered five hundred dollars of food at a crack. He had an idea she was pretty and maybe his age, but he had no good reason to think so. He also wanted to see what he could learn from a kitchen that could put out a stack of pizza boxes about four feet tall with an hour's notice. The guys liked pizza well enough. It was expensive, but his boss the lawyer had to know why he had to do so. Hell, depending on how things turned out, the lawyer might be able to get the pecker-heads at the WPD to pay for it. While the young guys would happily eat pizza three meals a day, there were enough older guys trying to watch their diets that he made a huge bowl of salad, poured a couple of gallon sized cans of broccoli into one big pot and an equal amount of chili beans in another pot. It would have to do. As it was, there was only just enough time to heat up the healthy stuff before he carried it over to the dining trailer. Damn, but he missed the kid's help -over and above the fact that he simply liked Robby and the kid didn't deserve being kidnapped and all.

He forgot the flyers Mrs. Furness gave and made a trip back to the kitchen for them. Not a big deal. Getting dinner set up took five or six trips back and forth anyway, but he had hoped to say his piece before the men had filled their plates with food and got engrossed in whatever was on one of the three big-screen TV's bolted to the walls of the dining trailer.

One of the guys had a beer bottle sitting on the table next to his plate of pizza. Bringing beer or liquor into the dining trailer was against the rules, but Mike had far better things to do than enforce hopeless rules. He asked the guy, "Can I borrow your beer bottle for ten seconds?" The guy —one of the older ones- looked at him in confusion and shrugged. Mike tapped the side of the bottle with a dinner fork. It took rather a lot of tapping to get everyone's attention. "Sorry to interrupt you dinner gentlemen, but you all know the kid who has been helping out in the kitchen? His name is Robert Furness and he' missing. Some of you may know about the excitement yesterday afternoon. There was some shooting. No one got hurt, but it was right before the boy went missing. The police think he has been kidnapped. He's a nice kid -about thirteen or fourteen years old. His big sister has been helping out in the laundry room. They both are nice kids, from a nice old-time-Williston family."

He held up the stack of flyers he had gotten from the boy's mother that afternoon. "What we'd like… what his mom and dad would like is for you do, is keep an eye out for him. Like when you spread out across the country-side and stop off for coffee or gas somewhere, ask if anyone has seen a kid riding around with…" Here he stopped. Some of these men undoubtedly knew the Mahon woman who had run the camp up until a couple of weeks ago. She was a suspect and all, but what was the proper role for him in this direction. "Just ask around if anyone has seen a boy who fits this description. Call either the police or…" He glanced at the flier. "I guess you are supposed to call the number at the bottom."

The guys were polite and quiet when he spoke, but seemed mostly disinterested. They went back to their pizza and TV. Mike felt a little stupid –a little too goody-goody. He made another trip to the kitchen and ran into his old roommate Kermit as he was coming back into the dining room with a big bowl of salad and a few bottles of dressing.

"Hey Kermit. Good to see you. You got a minute?"

"Sure."

"You remember I told you about the kids helping out around here? Well, the kid who has been helping me out in the kitchen got kidnapped. They think it might have been the woman who used to manage the place"

"No shit? I think I met his sister. She was doing maid work right?"

"Yep. Same kid. You heard about the shooting? It was the same time the kid turned up missing."

"Heard something. I tend to ignore about seventy five percent of what I hear from the hands. Who got shot?"

"No one got shot. Looks like they were shooting at the lawyer who owns the place, but no one is sure. But the kid was right there and then he wasn't. But I wanted to ask you something."

"OK."

"The family printed up a flier –his description and a picture and all. I handed them out as I was serving dinner and made a little announcement about maybe the guys keeping an eye out for the kid. Truth to tell, I think they kind'a ignored me. I mean they listened and all, but then they went right on eating."

"I know what you mean. You got to understand these guys work pretty hard all damn day. I 'spect some of them have a hard choice to make between eating and hitting the sack. This is kind'a why they's s'posed to be a meth problem, I guess."

"So you figure it's a waste of time?"

Kermit shrugged. "Hell, if you was to get the girl and the boys mama out here –'ticularally if she's even the least little bit hot, and they was to tell their story, well, I bet the guys would pay attention." Kermit laughed at his own joke. Mike wasn't sure just how much of a joke it was.

"You are probably right Kermit. Go eat. It's pizza again. I got a call to make. Oh, and remind me to tell you why I spent the morning in jail."

"What the fuck?"

"Long story. The FBI and police put their heads together and fucked things up. I'll tell you another time. I want to call the kid's parents and see what and what we ought to do about what."

He took another load of pizza to the trailer. He had learned that it was best to dole out the 'za gradually to give the vegetables and beans a chance to do their healthy job. He ducked out again and made a call. "Hello. This is Mike Williams, the cook out at the man camp. Is this Robby's sister? I think we met yesterday."

"Yes Mr. Williams. D'ya want to talk to my mom or dad?"

Polite kid he thought, "Yes please, if one or the other of them is… if they are not busy"

The phone was set down and in a moment another woman's voice: "Good evening Mr. Williams. This is Sherrie." Her voice was utterly flat.

"Hi Sherrie. Sorry to bother you, but I'm not sure what to tell my guys about the flier and who to call and such." Was he being insensitive? "Any word on the lad?"

"No. I'll let you talk to Vern." There was another pause and more introduction.

"Howdy Mr. Williams. How are things out at the camp?"

"Um. well, I handed out a few of the fliers and told the first crowd of guys about Robby and all. I can't say it went over well. And there is some question as to the phone number."

"Oh, that's right. Glad you called. There is a new plan. Don't do anything with the fliers any more. The police think it's apt to get the kidnapper nervous. Be dangerous for Robby."

"Oh. OK. Anything I can do otherwise?"

"Well, ya there is. We think Robby might be held up in a grain bin or silo or something. If you could get your guys to check them out all over the country side?"

"Happy to try, but…" Mike thought about Kermit's suggestion. He decided it was tactless and then decided it all was too important for tact. "Mr. Furness, I'm not proud to say it, but these guys are hard workers, tired and hungry. And horney. No, that's not what I want to say. They are starved for women. And that's not right either." Williams ran out of steam. There was along pause and the kid's dad was silent.

"Look. I was talking to another old hand and he suggested maybe if your wife or daughter were to make the request the men would be more attentive. It was kind of a joke, but damned if I don't think he might have nailed it."

When he finally spoke, his voice was even and deliberate. "I agree. Is there time for them to come out tonight?"

"Well, I suppose so. Maybe half the guys who eat have already eaten, but I still have a lot of food to get out. How far off are you? Tell you what. I can stall on putting out more food and that will slow them down."

"We will be there in fifteen minutes."

Mike remembered Mrs. Furness as an average looking woman of early middle age when he picked up the fliers that afternoon. She had somehow changed. It took him a moment as he watched her speaking to the guys in the dining trailer to realize what had changed. Lipstick maybe. But there was more. He couldn't put his finger on it. Must have been make-up. She also was wearing a tight pair of blue jeans and vee-neck blouse. He hadn't noticed her trim little figure that afternoon either. Strange things women and even more so, men's various perceptions of them. But it was working. The guys were watching and a few asked questions. She finished by repeating her phone number and urging them to call as they checked the various farm structures on their way to and from work. She would be keeping track of what they had checked. It did strike Mike as curious, however, that she urged them not to bother the police with it. "Best to call me directly."

One voice from the back said "Right on." It occurred to him later that at least some of them did not have warm-fuzzy feelings toward the police who frowned on the things the workers enjoyed during their off-hours.

Chapter 65

Darkness finally came and Robby now thought he knew about what time it was. He was still a little fuzzy on what day it was, but knew it was evening. It was somehow now less important than it had been earlier. He moved back and forth between sleep and drowsy day-dreaming. Sleep lead to nightmares and terrified cold awakenings. His favorite thoughts were remembrances of time with his family. There were the family camping trips in Minnesota with his cousins when they fished and paddled around in canoes. They also fell out of canoes. One time they fell out because he and Beth shared a canoe and were fighting about where they were to go. It had seemed terribly important at the time. It wasn't his fault, but now it all seemed silly.

Then there was the time some big kids were picking on Beth when they were walking home from school. He tried to protect her and got his butt kicked, but his dad was proud and it didn't hurt as much as he might have thought it would. Even Beth stuck up for him at home. If only he had not fallen down when he head-butted the big kid and then if he had gotten up off the ground before the other even bigger kid joined in. His mind settled into a satisfying loop of replaying the event –adjusting it here and modifying it here and there with each replay until it was a perfect kung-fu ballet in his mind. He had no idea of how time passed, but it seemed this mental video kept him entertained for hours as he drifted between awareness and not-quite-sleep.

There was another time at lunch when his clowning around made Beth laugh so hard that milk sprayed all over the table. He was able to remember every Christmas, or most of them anyway. He reviewed all the family traditions leading up to the big day: baking, the advent wreath with its candles, decorating the tree before a family dinner starting with herring, then meatballs, and potatoes pancakes. He didn't like herring, but he liked the rest of it. He was so-so on going to church Christmas morning too, but Christmas Day was the best. Maybe even better than the last of school before summer started.

The shivering fits had started at what he guessed was mid-day, but was now pretty much constant. At one point he had gotten up planning to kick the straw into a thicker bed to stay warmer. But when he stood up, he fainted. He had no idea how long he was out but, when he awoke, he was shivering more violently than ever. He was barely able to get his arms and hands to work well enough to scoop the straw into a slightly thicker pile and crawl back into the sleeping bag. He lay with his hands between his legs till they warmed up enough to zip up the sleeping bag. It did little good. The little thing in the back of his throat was bigger than ever and his tongue felt funny. He wasn't hungry anymore, but he was gosh-awful thirsty.

Chapter 66

Kermit had forgotten all about the missing boy till the cold dark early morning. He was one of the first guys at the dining trailer and found the cook chatting with the kid's mother from the previous night. There was also a young woman –about sixteen– standing there and fidgeting. The girl looked familiar. When he left the trailer the previous night, he was in bed and asleep fifteen minutes later. For that matter, he was asleep in a warm bed about twenty minutes before he got to breakfast. Unless the woman slept in the camp, which he doubted, she had had only a short night's sleep. Mike looked up from a pan of scrambled eggs. "Kermit, did you meet Mrs. Furness last night? And this is Beth Furness, the boy's sister. Mrs. Furness, Kermit is a good hand and a good guy to have on our side." As Kermit shook the woman's hand, he saw the exhaustion and fear in her eyes.

"Hi Beth. I think you was hauling sheets and towels out of out of our trailer one afternoon a week or two back, when I was slouching around on the couch." He turned to the girl's mom and smiled. "I don't get days off a lot –so I remember it pretty well. So these farm things, something like the ones just up the road from here?"

"Exactly."

"My company has crews running all over hell and… all over the place."

They sorted out the details of phone calls and reporting in. Just before Kermit left, Sherrie asked him if he had any advice on how best to talk to the men over breakfast. Kermit remembered her shirt unbuttoned just one button lower than might had been what he would expect from a house-frau. He couldn't help himself -he involuntarily glanced at her front. He was embarrassed but Sherrie smiled. "Thank you for reminding me. I got dressed in a hurry this morning." She undid a button and Kermit went off to work. It was still dark but less miserably cold than usual.

When he got to work, the first thing Kermit did was to review the gauges on his workbench. Everything was urgent, but everything was always urgent in the oil patch, and just a couple were desperate. One gauge had passed an over-night pressure test and needed to be delivered to the rig ASAP, but he waited till his boss got in and had time to get himself a cup of coffee. Kermit got one too and sat down in front of the guy's desk. "Morning Bob. Got a minute?"

"What's on your mind?"

"You might have heard about the excitement up yonder at the Bakken Lodge?" His boss nodded.

"Well, it appears there was more to it than just the shooting. A young boy was kidnapped." The company paid the guy a generous housing allowance for an apartment in town rather than a bedroom in a trailer at a man camp. This was because he was an executive and because he had a family, so Kermit played his trump card. "You have kids yourself don't you boss?"

Bob smiled. "Subtle Kermit. Very subtle. Now what can Slumberburton do about it."

It took as only long as it took them to finish their coffee for Bob to spread a big map out over his desk and start working the problem. He told Kermit to deliver the gauge up north and check any farm building he passed on the way back. He started calling all the crew-chiefs in western North Dakota and eastern Montana. He had a single crew in south-east Montana working another formation, the Gammon, and figured what the hell –he'd call them too.

He usually blocked out a little time to talk to all each of the supervisors on all of the department's frack jobs. This morning, however, it took a little longer as he explained the missing kid and the theory as to where he might have been stashed. All of the men were willing to help out.

His third call was to a supervisor working a well about an hour west of Williston. The guy was an old friend who had studied engineering rather then management like he had. Their rapport was based on ribbing each other about one sitting behind a desk all day and the other guy getting dirty all day.

This particular job was a big frack job. It had twelve semi-truck mounted pumps lined up around the well with four more sitting ready if needed. Each flat-bed had a 2200 horse power engine driving a three piston pump to force the sand and water underground at as much as ten thousand pounds per square inch. The well bore went two miles down and a little over a mile horizontally thru the Bakken Formation that was only thirty-five feet thick. The water would open cracks into the shale formation and the sand they pumped down with the water would hold the cracks open to let the oil and gas out. Besides the trucks, there were an even eighteen twenty-thousand gallon portable tanks full of clean water lined up on one side of the mile long road into the well pad and five sand trucks on the other side.

They had spent a long night hooking up high pressure pipes between a manifold running between the truck mounted pumps, a big portable tank, and the well-head itself. Shortly the pumps would be fired up and the pressure would start to build. The pressure on the field engineer and the company man would also start to build as well, but now they were in the middle of the bucket test. Everything else stopped while the chemicals man and blender-tender went around and opening little valves at various points on the pipe-fitter's-nightmare that was a frack job. One held a gallon bucket and the other a stop watch. Nothing happened for about an hour until these two guys agreed everything was flowing at the proper rate and the right pressure. Had the call come from is friend Bob an hour earlier or an hour later, he would have let it ring, or told whomever answered the call in the trailer to take a message

"Is it cold enough for you Tom? Nice and warn here in my office."

"Toasty warn here in the trailer too Bob. You're not getting too many of 'em nasty paper-cuts I hope.?"

"Listen Tom, I have a weird one. Seems a young boy has gotten himself kidnapped and they think he's locked up in a grain silo or some damn thing somewhere out in the country side" Neither man were given to wasting words. It took about a minute for Bob to outline the situation for the on-site guy.

When he hung up, the frack supervisor keyed his headset to the pipe-crew chief. "You guys all buttoned up?" He didn't wait for an answer. "Someone lost his kid. He might be in a grain bin. Have the derrick-hand run up to the cat-walk again and look off in the distance for silos and them squatty grain storage things. You know, like the ones we pass where we turn off the county road and come into the pad."

"Sure thing boss. What about that one out by the road?"

"Send me that green-hat. I'll have him go check."

"We got two green-hats. Which one you want?"

"I'll leave it up to you,"

"That college boy is the more worthlesser of the two. That's the one."
When he keyed off his headset, he noticed it was just beginning to get light in the east.

Chapter 67

When Kevin Amundsen woke up much later than usual the next morning, it occurred to him that the previous few days had been more exhausting than he realized. He felt good this morning anyway. His ankle was stiff, but he went thru his morning routine with the crutches leaning forgotten against the wall by the front door. He called Beulah first thing and told her to open the office at nine —an hour later usual- and hold down the office till further notice. If it was very important, he would take calls on his cell phone. He then called the Furness household. Fortunately Vern answered and they decided he would come by and man the phones as the various men spread out across the country with a new search plan. Vern was less articulate than usual, but Kevin was able to sort out the other man's meaning. It was all about cell phones, maps and a fast lap-top with Google Satellite.

He was at the door of the library when the opened at eight and quickly got every map they would let him have. There were a surprising number of them, but it took the senior librarian to find them. Sherrie opened the door for him when he got to their house and she was –if not pleasant- she was not unpleasant. He figured Vern had done a little ground work on his behalf before he got there. He was surprised to see the crowd of assorted law enforcement people sitting around the big dining room table including the older FBI guy that was in his office the afternoon before. He nodded to them all but was glad to see Vern gesturing to him from the living room. "We've had seven guys from the man camp call in. They are out looking, but there is some confusion as to just where they are, I got six of my guys out too." They sat at the couch in the living room. There was a highway map with little sticky notes spread out on the coffee table. "It's kind of a mess. The phone numbers are all we have written down, but it's a start. Maybe you can call out on your cell phone 'cause we are keeping Sherrie's phone open for incoming calls?"

Kevin nodded expecting Vern to go on, but he just stood there. Clearly the guy was about worn out. "Sure thing Vern. I'll be on it like a duck on a June bug."

Vern seemed to wake up. "Oh. One more thing. The FBI is not in favor of what we are doing. Best that you work here and leave them alone in the dining room." Other than being curious about the young woman in the suit with the lap-top, he had absolutely no interest in any of what was going on in the other room. The less he had to do with them, the less the opportunity for difficult questions about Mel's 'recovery' expert and even more so, what ever Mel's woman had going on out at the man-camp.

Within an hour, Kevin had called all of numbers on the little pink sticky-notes and was putting little ex's on the map to indicate silos and bins that had been checked. He had three other maps spread out on the couch and was surprised to see that he could zoom into Google Satellite far enough to see the actual farm structures. Not as valuable as having eyes in place because he had to zoom to a view that covered about a half mile wide stretch of countryside and there were a lot of half mile stretches of the North Dakota country-side. He was also surprised to find he was pretty good at using maps to tell men where to go and what to do. He idly considered what might have happened if he had gone into the military.

Sherrie seemed relieved to give up her cell phone to him and he fielded more calls from oil crews heading out and looking. Clearly the appeal to the men at the man-camp was working. Poor Vern and his wife were wondering back and forth between the living room, the kitchen, and dining room, more or less aimlessly. Kevin had totaled twenty-seven little exes on his maps and fourteen total searchers when their daughter came down of the hall in PJ's and robe, and went into the kitchen. There was a knock on the door and Beth turned to answer it, but it opened before she got there. It was an old guy carrying a funny looking bag who looked vaguely familiar to Kevin. Beth hugged the old guy, "Hi Grampa."

"Well howdy Bethy. How you holding up kiddo?"

"I'm OK Grampa."

Beth's mom called from the dining room. "We are all sitting around the table Evert. Come on in and I'll introduce you around." Beth went into the kitchen to make herself some breakfast but did so quietly and pulled a stool close to the dining room. Kevin realized she was listening to every thing the assorted suits were saying.

After they went around the table with introductions and the lawyer made a mental note to remember the stern looking young woman was named Lori Green, but otherwise stuck with his maps. The Grandpa spoke first. "I got the money. Come to find they ain't but so many small bills in all of this part of the country and we got near all of them. Now what we doing about finding my grandson?"

Kevin decided the show unfolding in the dining room was worth the risk of the FBI's attention and went to lean against the door where he could watch. The older FBI agent that answered the question. "We will take custody of the money and inventory it."

"Will you now?" The old guy stood up. "You figure to use your gun to get it off me do you sonny?" Vern choked back a laugh. Kevin wondered how long it had been that Vern had been able to laugh even this little bit.

"We just want to record the cereal numbers."

"And how does that get my grandson back sonny?"

The FBI guy just shrugged. Sherrie called out from the kitchen. "Come have some coffee and a little breakfast Evert."

Vern, Sherrie, and Vern's father all went onto the kitchen. The canvas bag full of money went with them. Kevin went back to his maps and Google-Maps website, and Beth shuffled back down the hall.

Chapter 68

The green-hat hated his green hard-hat. All the new hands at Slumberburton – the green hands- had to wear a green hardhats for six months. Some companies made them wear it for a full year, but there was so much work to be done and crews had gotten so specialized that laborers could learn enough in six months not to get themselves killed too terribly often. Nor fuck things up for the other guys too badly. Or the company for that matter. He had been swinging a five pound sledge to tighten up the collars on high pressure unions all damn night and was looking forward to kicking back in the warmth of the crew truck. That was the way of it on a frack crew. Work like a som'na bitch for ten hours and sit around waiting, trying to stay warm -and just maybe catch some sleep- for another ten hours. But you got paid for all 20 hours and over-time for most of it.

But now he was supposed to drive over to that farm house and ask Farmer Who-the-Fuck for permission to look for some missing kid in a silo or some damn thing. Small consolation was getting to drive the crew's pickup. He never got to drive the pick-up, but he was still going to take his own damn time. Maybe the farmer had a fat wife who was baking something wonderful for breakfast and he could get himself invited to sit down and have a bite. Of maybe he had a pretty daughter. Farmers are always supposed to have willing and pretty daughters. He noticed the goofy direction his mind was wandering and figured it was exhaustion. He also resented the supervisor –his boss's boss- telling him not to get too high-faluting with the farmer.

He parked right at the frond door of a small white clapboard farm-house, got out and started up the walk. Then he turned back and threw his hard-hat back in the truck.

When he knocked, he heard a dog barking from inside, but no dogs showed up on his side of the door. It took a minute for a scrawny mean-looking old guy to answer the door. If he had a daughter, she would have to be sixty years old. And if she looked anything like this guy, he would want no part of her at any age. The warm inside air flowed out the door and washed over the green-hat. It carried some smell that might have been food, but if it was food, he wanted no part of that either.

"Good morning sir. I'm work at the rig out there. We have word that a boy has been kidnapped and might'a been stuck in someone's grain bin some where. May I go have a look at your silo's over there?" That sure-as-shit was too high-faluten.

The old guy just stared at him a moment then lifted a half empty cola bottle to his lips and hissed a stream of greenish brown spit into it with practiced accuracy. It was chewing tobacco that the green-hat had been smelling. The old guy seemed to be working up another stream but finally spoke, "Ain't a silo –it's a grain bin. You oil field fuckers are always driving all over the place doing some damn thing or other. Tearing up fields and leaving gates open. I don't pay you no mind no more. Go have a look for your own dang self." He shut the door.

The green-hat got half way down the walk when the door opened again. "Wait whilst I put on my boots and I'll come out wit' you."

They walked across the frozen field in silence till they got to the first of three grain bins. "Ain't but one of them empty. This'n here's and that one at the end's full of silage.' When they got to the second the farmer stopped. "What the Sam hell? That ain't my lock on the hatch door."

The green-hat pounded on corrugated metal of the bin, "Anyone home?" He felt a little silly and figured he had done what the boss told him to do and it was time to head back to the big crew truck and see if he couldn't catch a few winks or at least get something to eat. "Thank you for you help sir. Sorry to bother you." He started back to the pick-up.

He hadn't gone ten feet when the farmer hollered, "Hold on boy. Something ain't right here. I surely didn't put no lock on my own go'damned silage. When did you say the lad got took?"

"Couple of days ago I guess."

"Might'a been yesterday morning. They was a car parked here for a spell. Didn't have no business that I knew, so I figured it was one of 'em God damned oil fuckers doing some'im all geological and I di'nt pay it no mind." The old boy stepped up to the bin and kicked it. The sheet metal rang with a low dull clang.

The green-hat started to ask, "Are there more bins..."

"Shut the fuck up"

The farmer kicked the side of the bin again and lifted the ear flap of his filthy red plaid bomber-cap. He puts his ear against the side of the bin. They both heard it this time, a faint knock against the bin –from the inside. The farmer took a deep breath and yelled, "Cain' you talk boy? Holler out your name." *My God* thought the green-hat. They could hear this old guy at the drill pad over the sound of all the pump motors running at once.

They barely heard a high pitched croak that wasn't quite human, but the knocks started and didn't stop. They were week but urgent. "You got you a bolt cutter on that pussy red pick-up of yours? Go fetch it. And if you ain't, you hurry your ass off to that oil rig over yonder and fetch one back. They's sure to have one."

The green-hat started across the prairie and the farmer let loose again. "Run you stupid shit. The boy's in a bad way." Almost a bachelors in linguistics or not –there was no arguing with an old farmer with lungs like that. He started running. He popped open the cover in the back of the crew truck, climbed up, and started rummaging thru the tools in the back. *Fuck it* –if we are about to save some kids life, he figured let's *get'er done* so he simply tossed everything that wasn't a bolt cutter over the side of the truck bed. Most of it had to do with the truck: tire-tools, extra antifreeze, a socket set, two different shovels, and some shit he had no idea what it was about. He found what he thought might have been a bolt cutter, but it was rusty it was like the ones he saw the drivers using when they cut the big steel bands holding bundles of pipe.

As he was hurrying back to the bin, he heard the old farmer hollering at the corrugated metal. "Hold on boy. We are getting you out'a there." When he held the tool out to him, the old guy snorted. "You dumb fuck. These'n are tin snips. They's for cutting sheet metal, not a lock. I got to do it m'own self if'n I want it done right, don't I. You stay here and talk to the boy. He's a drifting and I think we need to keep him awake." The old guy took off across the prairie with his ear-flaps flapping. He moved at pretty damn spry dog-trot for an old guy,.

Green-hat couldn't think of anything to say to the side of the grain bin so he pulled out his cell phone and called his crew chief. "Hey boss. I think we found the boy. He's not saying much. And he's locked in. The farmer is going for a bigger cutter thing. The one in the truck was too small. You got a bigger one? What do we do when we get him out?"

"Calm down dude. A bigger cutter thing? What the fuck you talking about? Is the kid there or not?"

"We think so. We can't get… *bolt* cutter –that's what it's called. We need a big bolt cutter to cut the lock to get the kid out."

"Sit tight kid. We need to get someone at a higher pay grade involved."

The farmer trotted back a small sledge in one hand and a pry bar in the other. "Stand back." He snapped the lock off with a single accurate swat. He opened the hatch and knelt down. "How you doing kid?" He looked up at the green-hat. "Get on in there boy and help the lad out."

He crawled thru the hatch and it took a minute for his eyes to adjust to the dim light. There were a couple of eyes looking out at him from the folds of a sleeping bag but no movement. He crawled over to the eyes. "Hi kid. Are you ready to go home?" The head with the eyes nodded but the eyes didn't move. "Can't you move?" The head shook. "Sit tight kid." He called out to the old guy. "He can't move. What do I do?"

"Ya dumb shit. Grab aholt of that sleeping beg and drag him over here. We can both of us carry him 'tween us to the house."

They got him out of the bin and into the daylight. He was deathly pale and his eyes were sunken. His tongue was sticking out of his mouth. They left him in the sleeping bag. The green hat lifted him under the arms and the farmer lifted him under the knees. When they were only halfway back to the farmhouse, the younger man wanted to ask to stop and rest, but the old guy kept going so he sucked it up. Once inside, they lay Robby on a ratty old couch. The farmer pulled up a kitchen chair and sat down facing him. "What's your name lad?"

" 'Oobee Furce." Louder. " 'Robee Fursss" He started sobbing, but it was a choked sob.

"Can't talk? That's OK." He turned to the other guy. "Go into the kitchen and fetch a glass of warm water. Not too warm."

It took him a minute to find a clean glass. Any idea of a wife baking something was clearly a stupid dream. The old guy obviously lived alone and never cleaned any thing. He called out from the kitchen, "Shouldn't we call an ambulance or something?"

"Call your boss. "You oil peckerheads are s'posed to be boy scouts. Lets see how all prepared they is." When the green-hat came to the couch with the water the farmer had the boys wrist in his hand. He appeared to have fallen asleep. "His pulse is week and I recon it's slow –for a youngen. When you get someone from your oil rig who knows his ass from a hole in the ground to come over here."

"I already did."

"Good, call 9-1-1. Tell them to get a doctor on the line pronto. We need someone who knows what to do." He gently lifted Robby's chin. "Wake up boy. You want a little drink of water?" Robby opened his eyes and nodded. The farmer held the glass to his lips. "Just a sip. Just wet your whistle."

The green-hat had made some progress on the phone. "They aren't answering 9-1-1. Oh, wait. Hello. 911? We need a doctor." "I don't know the address. We are out in the field somewhere west of Williston."

The farmer stood. "Gim'me that damn phone." He put it to his ear. "We need a doctor on the line. He listened for only a few seconds and erupted "What the fuck do it matter what my name is. We got a boy here in a bad way –froze near to death. We is way out in the country." There was another pause. "My address?" The old boy looked to heaven. "Listen here sweet heart, you gon'na get a doctor on the line or not?" He tossed the phone to the green-hat. "Hang this damn thing up. We ain't got time to fiddle fuck around with 'em peckerheads." He stomped into the kitchen and looked at something on the wall "Call this number." He read a off a number. And came back into the living room. "You dial it up right?"

The green-hat listened for a moment. "It's a doctor's office."

"Gim'me the phone." Iz'is Betty? Howdy Betty. This is Luther. I got to talk to Ben right now. Have us an emergency."

The green-hat sat next to the kid and spooned the warm water into his mouth. The kid was barely awake, but was able to swallow –reflexes maybe. The old farmer went into it with the doctor on the phone. "We have us a kid what's been kidnapped. We found him in my grain bin. 'Pears he has been locked up for at least a day –day and a half. In a crappy sleeping bag, but nothing to eat or drink. His tounge is swole up and he's mostly asleep. Whad do we do?"

The old boy looked closely at Robby.

"Nope, he ain't shivering none." Pause. "That's bad, eh? Better he be shivering?" The old guy stepped up and laid the back of his hand on the boy's cheek. "Ya, his skin is pretty cold. Should we stick him in a hot bath?"

The green hat could hear the doctor shouting thru the phone in the old guys hand. "Don't do that. You'd stop his heart." The doctor's voice went back to a more normal tone.

The old farmer listened a long while. "OK doc. You will sort out the ambulance and all. I'll get back to you when we's on the road." He tossed the phone back to the green-hat.

"Here's the plan. Then we gon'na bundle him as best we can and put him in the pussy red pick-up of your'n and head into Williston. You' gon'na keep spooning warm water into his mouth so long as he don't choke on it.

The green-hat nodded and the old guy went on. "We gon'na keep an eye out for an ambulance coming up the road with sirens and all. When we see it, coming, we's to flash our lights and pull over. They will pull up beside us and take the kid the rest of the way to the hospital. They got ox'gen and such that might be handy. Now get on out there and back that truck up to the porch. And turn the heater up to high."

Robby had swallowed about half a thermos of warm water before they met the ambulance. He was in the emergency room in Williston fifty five minutes after leaving the farm. His heart stopped just as they wheeled him into the emergency room.

Chapter 69

Jeff faced a few interesting challenges: First was to resist calling Janet after their cuddly celibate night together. He had a notion that the proper thing to do was to wail till at least the second day. Or maybe the third. *Weren't no big deal to sleep with a beautiful woman and not have sex with her. He did it all the time.* Or that was the message he was hoping to send anyway.

Worked out that the second challenge helped him resolve the first. He needed to get a mess of mini-dinosaurs for Ricky to North Dakota and it took some time. Even so, he paid a ridiculous price to have ten pounds of live crawdads shipped overnight to his counter at the warehouse at work. They were always getting various parts and materials that UPS or FedEx delivered every day, so it was no big deal to set aside a Styrofoam cooler addressed to him from Louisiana Crawfish Farms. He figured it cost him half a day's pay, but he often watched his roommates peel off a twenty to get a carton or two of Chinese food or some rubber hamburgers delivered. And they did it day after day while he was heating up a can of soup or slicing SPAM for sandwiches, so he figured he was entitled.

The third problem was finding himself some proper andouille sausage like his daddy made. His mamma -God love her- was from down-town New Orleans and a proper city lady who never did understand about real Cajun cooking, so his daddy often took him out to the back porch and taught him how it was done over a portable propane

cooker set up beside a beat-up old picnic table. He had been trying to find real andouille
sausage ever since he got to North Dakota and had no luck what-so-ever. The closest he
could come was spicy Polish sausage from Walmart. Piss-poor substitute, but he didn't
have time to make his own and he was pretty sure Janet would not know the difference.
Ricky dang sure wouldn't ether.

There was also the need to get some corn still on the cob, red 'taters, onions, and
garlic, but Walmart would do well enough in this direction too. Another problem was the
boil. He had some Cajun seasoning on the shelf that he sprinkled on his eggs in the
morning. It was his Daddy's recipe and he made it from scratch, but not near enough for
even a little ten pound boil. It took a mess of ingredients to make a proper boil-powder
and given time, he might could assemble enough to make his daddy proud, but if he was
going to shower after work and get over to Janet's house by dinner time, he didn't have
time to assemble all twenty spices –even if he could find all of them on the shelf at
Walmart. He figured he would make due with a mess of paprika, and whatever else he
could find on the shelf at Walmart. They ought to have, rosemary, oregano, garlic, and
cayenne, and that was the heart of what all went into a proper boil.

He admitted to himself that he was having fun. It would be very nice indeed if
he and Janet were to get it on, but the thought of having fun with Ricky doing the
cooking and eating tiny dinosaurs was appealing. All in all, he imagined a terrific show
all mapped out in his mind. The tricky bit was going to be the call. He needed to get
himself invited to dinner. While he hoped his own sparkling personality would be all it
took, but he was not confident. The other night went well and all, but she was pretty
shook up and had not her usual –no other way to say it- bitchy self. He would use
Ricky's tiny dinosaurs shamelessly, but he wanted it to be a surprise. Worse come to
worse, there was always math they could be dong together, but that seemed to be going
backwards.

About three that afternoon, Janet solved the problem by calling him. "Hi Jeff.
You want to come over tonight for dinner?"

"Hey Janet. "That would be right nice. But tell you what, why don't I fetch us
along some dinner."

She laughed. "Were my weenies and beans not up to your standards?"

"No. That's not it at all, not nary a bit, but I have a surprise for Ricky."

"Is it… what did you say? Tiny dinosaurs?"

"Yep."

"What are you talking about Jeff? You bringing some weird food from the
swamp? Aligators or something?"

"Nope you silly woman. Every'n knows alligators is out of season till come
summer. More'n that, I ain't saying. You just have to wait."

They agreed to his coming by at seven. He would need to leave work a little
early to get all cleaned up, but it had been a quiet day and he had plenty of brownie-
points with his boss.

Chapter 70

Vern's dad give him the bag of money and left. But only after making a point to the FBI that he was NOT giving it to them for inventory or any damn thing, but rather giving it to his son to do with as he thought best. Sherrie noticed a brief look of pride on Vern's face when his dad told the FBI what was what. Then, as the old guy was leaving, he mentioned that it might be nice to see the whole family in church and then out to Sunday supper at the old place. They were by no means a hugging kind of family, but Vern and his dad managed an awkward one before Evert hurried out the door. Sherrie noticed this too and wondered if whatever happened, there might be a reconciliation between her husband and his father.

Shortly after that, Deputy Bohler showed up. Of all the people here, Sherrie thought Sven was the only one that Vern could lean on. He had to be strong for her and Beth. The assorted pecker-heads in the dining room were worthless at anything besides filing reports, and what was worse, treated him like he was a child. But with Sven, she hoped Vern could admit to being frightened and feeling helpless. It was about the time Vern went off to join the navy and far before she met him that Sven had dated Vern's little sister, Veronica. Nothing came of it and however it ended; Sven was a good friend of the family even if they only saw him a couple of time a year.

Then two calls came one after the other. What was it they said? *The worst call a parent would ever get.* Their child was in the emergency room. Vern wasn't sure if things were good or bad. They said his son was in stable condition, but that was all they would tell him. But they knew where he was.

The second call came a moment later as Vern was putting on his coat to rush to the hospital. It came to Kevin on Sherrie's call phone, and it came by a convoluted route. Kevin got the call from a guy somewhere in town. He said he got the call from another guy sitting on a rig out west by the Montana border. This guy, in turn, got the call from one of his workers who either was or wasn't in an ambulance heading into town, but the guy seemed pretty confident it was Robby in the ambulance and their son was on his way to the hospital.

The FBI and Williston Police had lots of questions –most of which seemed to be matters of who, what, and when for their records. Vern was so relieved that he was able to resist the impulse to tell them all to go to hell and get out of his house. Sven took matters in hand and got Vern, Sherrie, and Beth into their coats and out to his cruiser. Beth was crying and wearing her PJ's under her coat. Sherrie was in a daze and Vern took perverse pleasure as Sven blew thru traffic and red-lights with the cruiser's sirens screaming and lights flashing.

Vern had no memory of the family finding its way to the emergency room. What he did remember –and would remember for the rest of his life- was the sight of Robby on some kind of operating bed, under a blanket that seemed to have tubes coming out of it, more tubes going into his arm, and a final tube going to a clear plastic mask over his nose and mouth. A guy in a white coat looked up and made his way around the bed to head them off at the door. "Are you the lad's parents?"

Vern tried to make his away around the guy. Sherrie answered, "Yes we are. How is my son?"

The guy was not to be outflanked. "He's asleep and needs some quiet. Can we talk first? Perhaps out in the hall?"

In retrospect, Vern's memory seemed to continue to be spotty. He remembered 'The boy will be OK' and 'He had a cardiac event on the way in.' and the words 'dehydration' and 'hypothermia' going by several times. He also was aware Sherrie was asking questions –lots of questions- and he was glad to let her do it. When she was ready, she would tell him what he needed to know. For the moment at least, his son was safe and there was nothing further he could do for him. Maybe not out of the woods, but there was nothing his son needed that he could give him. He felt the weight of it all fall from his shoulders. He turned and walked off as Sherrie and the doctor were discussing something about electrolytic balances as they might unfold over the next few days. He found an ugly seat with yellow vinyl cushions in the hall and collapsed.

Chapter 71

She has been driving aimlessly around the north-west corner of the state for an afternoon and a night with the kid in the trunk. She was worried about the kid screaming if she stopped for gas so she gassed up at an unattended station that took credit cards. As it was, the kid was silent. But the feeling that she was pushing her luck grew on her. No way in hell she was going to be able to talk her way out of trouble if they found the kid in the trunk of her car. *Gosh officer, I have no idea how he got there.* This image amused her so much that she laughed hysterically for a mile or so, and giggled for a few miles more.

She made one risky late-night trip thru town and drove by Furness Civil that the kid's dad owned. There was a big ugly Butler Building –like so many others on the outskirts of town. The building sat in the corner of a fenced lot with a lot of expensive looking heavy equipment behind the fence.

She drove back out of town to the west on Highway 2 when she nodded off and found herself bouncing across the prairie for the second time in the last couple of weeks. Damn lucky she has swerved to the right. Even at this hour, there was more than enough traffic –and most of it big trucks, that swerving to the left would have been pretty much all-she-wrote. *All-she-wrote?* Where did that come from? Pretty clearly she needed rest, but first she needed to get rid of the kid.   Would have been easy enough to kill him and leave his body somewhere -anywhere- out in the country side, Or for that matter, leave him alive at the end of some long road to nowhere and be well on her way back home before anyone found the kid or he got himself to help.

There was still the hope that she could get the ransom money and get on with a new life. Nothing left for her in Minnesota –nothing after the bank got thru with her. Damn shame that she had missed when she shot at Amundsen, and another shame that she couldn't take better revenge on him. Kidnapping his friend's kid was probably not the smartest thing she had ever done, but once she was home again –where ever home would come to be- she could carefully think up a better revenge.

The idea of putting him in a grain bin like that little prick the cook had done to her came to her slowly. She had noticed the squat gray corrugated buildings all over the place, but paid them no mind. Like so many people, grocery stores were all she knew about the supply chain that fed her. It would be stupid to put the kid in the same one she had been trapped in, but earlier that day she had gone down a road that lead to a farm and nowhere else. She had to turn around and head back out the way she came in but she was almost sure there some grain bins beside the road. And wasn't there an oil rig just to the south? These things were light up like Christmas trees and could be seen for miles. She was heading that way anyway. Worth a try, but first the thought of murder crossed her mind. There was no sense of concern for the kid, but it would be easy enough to get at least the sleeping bag. Too late to buy one, and she certainly didn't want to be seen anywhere like a well-lighted store. The gas station was risky enough. She turned to the north and drove to the prairie by the Bakken Lodge. She was almost beyond caring, but still she sat in her car for five minutes before she was able to get out of her car and approach the grain-bin where she had spent the four cold miserable days. Crawling in and dragging out the sleeping bag was the hardest thing she had ever done. She nearly panicked and crawled out again so quickly that she tore her new coat.

Luck or an innate sense of direction, finding the deserted farm she picked proved to be easier than she had any right to expect. She found the oil rig, then she found the road, and finally, she found the grain bins. They were a little closer to an old farm house than she would have liked, but in the darkness it looked run down and abandoned so she went on with her plan.

One of three grain bin had a spike thru the hasp but the second one was open. She rummaged around in the glove compartment for an old lock she guessed her daughter used to chain her bike, opened the trunk, poked the kid awake and made him crawl into the grain bin. She was on her way in ten minutes feeling better about things every mile further down the road she drove.

When she got back to the kid's dad's shop, she found the gate opened, but there were no lights in the building. Why someone would bother to put up a fence around a lot full of heavy equipment and then leave the gate open was a mystery for another time. She just managed to squeeze her daughter's Buick behind a dump truck in the far corner against a chain-link fence. The big truck looked like it hadn't been moved for a long time and her car was quite well hidden from the road and most of the yard where other machines were parked –many on flat-bed trailers.

On a whim, she tried the keys the kid gave up. One of them worked on the man-door beside the first of three big overhead doors. She risked turning on the lights and discovered there wasn't much to steal. Tools and heavy equipment. Undoubtedly some of it was expensive, but not the sort of thing you could take to a pawn shop. Three over-head doors and three bays for working on machinery, only one had anything –a yellow front-end loader that looked to her like it was partially disassembled. There was a work bench all along the wall opposite the overhead doors. At the back of the shop there were shelves holding machinery parts and a stationary air-compressor in one corner. Along the front wall -the one toward the street, there was a pair of bathrooms and a single closed door. She made a booby-trap alarm out of buckets by the man-door, and turned off the lights and felt her way to what she thought was the office door.

The door was unlocked and it was an office. Because there was a window facing the road, she didn't risk turning on the light. She had sat behind the desk with her rifle across her lap waited in the darkness till it was light enough to look around the office more carefully. Another surprise: it was neat and had a coordinated décor that contradicted the greasy clutter of the shop. There was also a closet with sliding doors. There were a few thick coats and some padded coveralls hanging at one end and at the other end, the floor was stacked about four feet high with banker boxes each labeled with dates. It was an easy matter to restack them and make herself a comfortable hidey-hole. She had also pulled down the coats and made herself an impromptu mattress and pillow. Before she went to sleep, she turned the thermostat on the wall by the door up to seventy five. The early morning sun shone into the office with an orange glare. She lay on her mattress, slid the doors closed, and laid the rifle across her chest. She felt she had learned a few things about waiting while she was trapped in the grain bin. Here at least she was warm. She was asleep in ten minutes.

Chapter 72

When the finally let them in to see Robby, he was so weak and worn out that he only recognized his mom and started crying. He mumbled something about being ready to testify. Then he fell asleep. The doctor was standing by Vern and whispered something about kids that had been thru the sort of thing Robby had been thru, often reverted to the state where they just wanted their mothers. That seemed to be all there was to it. The doctor touched Vern's arm and gestured to the hallway. "I know this is difficult, but there is nothing you can do for your son now. There will come a time – perhaps shortly or perhaps in a week or two, when he will need his dad. He will need to know that he was –he was a man about it all. Sounds silly, but right now he needs to be a little kid."

Vern thought he understood. "What about his heart?"

The doctor shrugged. "He is young, and may make a complete recovery, but he will be week for a while. He will not be the same kid he was before. He may never be. You must –you MUST be patient. The damage to his heart is in some ways not as critical as the damage to his mind and his perception of the world."

Vern and Sherrie had friends who sent their kids to therapy and psychologists and both thought it was damn foolishness, but for his kid, he would have to rethink things. "Do we need a shrink?"

"Perhaps too soon to tell, but maybe. I have the impression yours is not the sort of family that holds with such things?"

Vern didn't know quite what to say. Finally he shook his head.

The doctor nodded. "I think I understand and I pretty much agree. Psychologists and crazy over-protective mothers have messed up more kids than all the bad teachers and video games and all the other shit kids get into -all put together. But I can recommend a good man in this direction. What ever you do though, don't let the boy think he is… don't let him think he is um… well… crazy. A always remember he has been thru something that you and I can not entirely understand. Were you in the military?"

Vern understand where he was going. "Ya, the navy, but I was never saw combat."

The doctor nodded. "Call me if you need me. I'll be watching Robby carefully and keep you posted." He walked off and Vern went back into Robby's room. Sherrie was sitting by the boy's bed. She glanced at him and almost smiled. She looked very tired, but happy.

"Honey. I hate being here. Nothing I can do. Do you mind?"

"No Vern. I understand. I'll be here when Robby wakes up. Go do what you have to do. Please."

Can I get you anything before I go?"

She shook here head and turned back to Robby.

Vern found Sven –God love him- waiting just down the hall. "It's over Sven. Thank…." Vern stopped. "Words are kind'a pitifull aren't they? But all I can say is thanks."

"Glad to help out Vern. And them's not just words."

"Oh! I need a ride back home. Can you help me out one last time.? We can get it from here."

Vern had no memory of leaving the hospital or going home. Nor had he any memory of driving to his shop. Later he would wonder if it was possible to drive safely while in a trance. When he opened the man door by the first overhead door there was a hell of a racket. Some empty five gallon had been stacked just inside the door for some reason. Dumb. He would have to have that talk to his guys about housekeeping once again. When he went thru the door to his office, he turned to the thermostat on the wall to turn it up out of habit. It was already set at seventy five. One more thing to mention to his guys –forgetting to turn down the thermostat when no one was there. For that matter, why had someone even been *in* his office?

He went to his desk and just sat. He had no idea what to do, but this was where he needed to be. He glanced at his Day-Timer for some notion of what to do. There were two days of tasks that were now over-due but none of them seemed worth the effort. He leaned back in his chair and noticed the closet door was open. Had it been open when he came in? For that matter, when he came in, had there been the muzzle of a rifle pointing at him? Or why was there an ugly woman sitting in his closet on a pile of banker's boxes holding that rifle?

Well, this is all very curious and he giggled on the verge of hysteria. He collected himself and addressed the woman in his closet. "You must be Sara Mahon?"

"Yes. You have the money?" Her voice was completely flat and a little drool slid down from the corner of her mouth. Was she crazy or had she just awaken?

The money? Did he really leave a quarter million dollars sitting on the kitchen counter when they left for the hospital. Or did he bring it with him and leave it somewhere at the hospital? He had no idea. "Um, no. We raised it, but I don't have it with me."

"If you want to see your son alive, you had best get it. Once I have it and I'm on my way, I'll tell you where to find him."

He almost told her that Robby was safe in the hospital, but while one part of his exhausted brain tried to make sense of where she was coming from, another part made him keep his mouth shut. "You want me to go get it and bring it back here?"

"Where is it?"

"It's at home."

"Get you wife or someone to bring it here."

He almost said *She's with Robby in the hospital* but caught himself. Vern tried to see the woman from a Christian place, but all he could see was Robby in a hospital bed with tubes. His brain was not working right. "May I call my wife?"

"Ya. Don't be cute or the kid dies. You only get him back when I'm on the road. That fucker Amundsen took everything I own -I got nothing to loose. Any cops and he dies."

Vern nodded and turned to land-line on the far corner of his desk. The little automatic seemed to appear in his hand without his having had anything to do with it. He brought it across the top of his desk and pointed it at the woman. Was there was a button somewhere that needed pushing to turn off the safety? For the moment, he only planned to point it at her. He wasn't sure what he planned to do beyond that. Then he saw his son crying for his mother with tubes and the gun jumped. There must have been a loud bang, but he didn't hear it. Nor did he hear the crack of her rifle but the lamp beside him on his desk exploded.

There was the sound of a small wet animal crying in the closet. It didn't so much stop as run down like a tire leaking out the last of its air. It seemed to take a long time and Vern watched with mild interest.

When there were no more sounds coming from the closet, he put down the gun and called his friend Sven's private cell number. "Hi buddy, I lied about not needing your help anymore. Can you come by my shop? I have a little problem I need your help with. Sorry to take up so much of your time lately, but you have been a life saver."

"You sounding a lot better Vern. News about Robby?"

"Nope, nothing new from there, but something has come up here in the shop. You far off?"

"I can be there in ten minutes."

"Thanks. I'll leave the man-door open for you." He looked down at his Day-Timer he had tried to make sense of earlier. For the first time in since Robby had been taken, he felt in charge of things. He felt there were things to do -things that he was well capable of doing. There was the matter of the dead woman in his closet, but he was pretty sure the police would sort that out as only the police could. Heavens knew, they had been worthless thus far. Then there was the matter of the questions the police would inevitably ask. This was what Sven was for. Was it murder or was it self defense. Sven would tell him what to say and how to say it. Then there was the matter of the money. That was a little embarrassing to have mislaid a bag of his dad's money. Wouldn't the old man have a fit? There was the time when he was a kid and left a toolbox out in the field when he had finished fixing a tractor. The tool box cost a lot less that a quarter of a million dollars. He giggled at the picture of his dad stomping and swearing about a missing bag of money. Vern glanced at the dead woman in his closet and wondered if he was going insane to be giggling ten feet from someone he had just killed. He would have to think about it later. Then there was the matter of his customers, contracts with due-dates, and his men still out in the field. He called Sherrie's cell phone and Kevin answered. "Just making sure you called off the search, Kevin ." I may need a spot of your help in an hour or two."

"Robby, is OK isn't he?

"Looks like he may be but the doctors are hedging."

"This is what doctors do Vern. They never say anything for sure. Everything will be all right."

"Hope so. But why I called, is I just killed Sara Mahon."

There was a long pause. "I thought you said you just killed the Mahon woman."

"Yep. That's what I said. Deputy Bohler is on his way. I suspect I will be arrested. Oh, by the way. Is the bag of money there? We kind'a took off for the hospital and left it somewhere."

"Don't say anything to anyone till I get there. And the FBI has the money and still doing their inventory."

"Well. That should make them happy -forms to fill out and all. Otherwise, sit tight Kevin. I'll call you when the police are done with me. Do you suppose a quarter million will be enough for my bail?

Chapter 73

Ricky was delighted with the tiny dinosaurs. His mom, not so much. She turned out to be squeamish about tossing living things into boiling water. Ricky picked up on his mom's concerns and decided he would keep them all as pets. When Jeff explained that they lived in water, Ricky wanted to put them all in the bathtub. Janet faced with the possibility of a bath tub full of tiny dinosaurs, decided that maybe boiling them was a good option after all. Then Ricky decided he wanted to keep just a few of them in a bowl.

Things were not going quite the way Jeff planned, but they were having fun. Or he and Ricky were anyway. He noticed that Janet was not sure quite what to do. Clearly a bathtub full of crawdads was too much, but a bowl of just a few? Jeff took Ricky onto his lap. "Hold on there slugger. We have to be smart about this. 'Em tiny dinosaurs is what we call 'mud-bugs' down in Louisiana. They's just that, bugs, Big bugs, but they's still bugs. Good eating too. Now if you were to put then a bowl, what would you feed them?"

"I don't know. Weenies?"

"Nope. That won't serve -not weenies -not nary a bit. 'Em mud-bugs eat other even li'ler bugs in the pond where they live. We got no ponds around here –least wise none what ain't froze solid. Best thing is to cook 'em up along with some other good food and have us a nice meal. You recon you could help me cook up a nice meal for your mama?"

That did the trick for Ricky. Janet, however, made it a point to need to go out to her car for something when the water came up to a boil and the crawdads were about to go in.

After Jeff taught both of them how to pop the tails off the mud-bugs and suck out the meat, the meal was a success. They got thru the entire ten pounds, but Jeff ate more than his share. The only left-overs were potatoes, and some corn.

Jeff spent the night again. It was wonderful.